# RADICAL FEMININITY

MANCHESTER
UNIVERSITY PRESS

# Radical femininity

## Women's self-representation in the public sphere

EDITED BY EILEEN JANES YEO

MANCHESTER UNIVERSITY PRESS
Manchester and New York

distributed exclusively in the USA by St. Martin's Press

*Published by* Manchester University Press
Oxford Road, Manchester M13 9NR, UK
*and* Room 400, 175 Fifth Avenue, New York,
NY 10010, USA

*Distributed exclusively in the USA by*
St. Martin's Press, Inc., 175 Fifth Avenue, New York, NY 10010, USA

*Distributed exclusively in Canada by*
UBC Press, University of British Columbia, 6344 Memorial Road,
Vancouver, BC, Canada V6T 1Z2

*British Library Cataloguing-in-Publication Data*
A catalogue record for this book is available from the British Library

*Library of Congress Cataloging-in-Publication Data*
Radical femininity : women's self-representation in the public sphere
    / edited by Eileen Janes Yeo.
      p.   cm.
    Includes bibliographical references and index.
    ISBN 0-7190-5243-2 (cloth). – ISBN 0-7190-5244-0 (pbk.)
    1. Women in public life – Great Britain – History.   2. Women in public life –
Great Britain–Language.   3. Women radicals – Great Britain – History.   4.
Women radicals – Great Britain – Language.   5. Women social reformers –
Great Britain – History.   6. Women social reformers – Great Britain –
Language.   7. Femininity – Great Britain – History. – I. Yeo, Eileen.
HQ1391. G7R33 – 1998
305.42'0941 – dc21

ISBN   0 7190 5243 2 *hardback*
       0 7190 5244 0 *paperback*

First published 1998

05  04  03  02  01  00  99  98      10 9 8 7 6 5 4 3 2 1

Typeset by Action Typesetting Limited, Gloucester
Printed in Great Britain by Bell & Bain Ltd, Glasgow

# CONTENTS

# NOTES ON CONTRIBUTORS

**Michelle de Larrabeiti**, after finishing a history degree at the University of Sussex, returned to her previous work in the media where she has been the assistant producer on many television programmes including the transmission of the concert welcoming Nelson Mandela on his first trip to Britain after being freed from prison. She recently gained an M.A. in scriptwriting and is weaving together her historical and media expertise.

**Sophie Hamilton** studied history at the University of Sussex and has since then been working both as a film and factual researcher for television. She has worked on a wide range of documentaries including 'An Almost Complete Guide to the Twentieth Century', 'Scott of the Arms Antics' – an award-winning Channel 4 Special on the Scott Report, 'The Terror and the Truth' – a three-part series for the BBC looking at human rights abuses and their legacy and 'A Woman's Fight to Choose', a documentary marking the thirtieth anniversary of the 1967 Abortion Bill.

**Gerry Holloway** is Lecturer in Women's Studies in the Centre for Continuing Education at the University of Sussex. Her Sussex Ph.D. thesis (1995) explored 'A Common Cause? Class Dynamics in the Industrial Women's Movement, 1888–1918'. She has contributed chapters to *Engaging with Difference. The Other in Adult Education* (1995), *Class Matters* (1997) and *Mary Wollstonecraft and 200 Years of Feminisms* (1997). She is on the Steering Committee of the Women's History Network, both nationally and in the Southern Region.

**Sandra Stanley Holton** took an honours degree in history in the School of English and American Studies at the University of Sussex and went on to complete a Ph.D. at the University of Stirling. She is presently an ARC Australian Research Fellow in the History Department of the University of Adelaide, South Australia. She has published two books on the women's suffrage movement in Britain: *Feminism and Democracy* (1986) and *Suffrage Days* (1996), as well as a number of articles. Presently she is writing a biography of Alice Clark, industrialist, suffragist and pioneer historian of women's work.

**Helen Rogers** lectures in cultural history in the Department of Literature, Life and Thought, Liverpool John Moores University. After studying history at the University of Sussex, she completed her doctorate 'Poetesses and Politicians: Gender, Knowledge and Power in Radical Culture, 1830–1870' at the University of York in 1994 and is working on a book on the same topic.

**Gillian Scott** teaches in the School of Historical and Critical Studies at the University of Brighton and previously did educational work in the co-operative movement. She first became involved with the women's movement as a student in the 1970s, and it was as a result of that activity that she began to investigate the relationship between feminism and working-class women historically. She studied history as an undergraduate and as a Ph.D. student at Sussex. She has published several articles on the Women's Co-operative Guild and a book entitled *Feminism and the Politics of Working Women* (1998).

**Alison Twells** teaches history at the University of Nottingham. She has also developed resources for the secondary education history curriculum on South Yorkshire and colonialism in the eighteenth and nineteenth centuries. She read history at Sussex and has recently completed a Ph.D. at the University of York. She is author of '"Happy English Children": Class, Ethnicity and the Making of Missionary Women, 1800–40', *Women's Studies International Forum* (1998) and of a chapter on '"A Christian and Civilised Land": The British Middle Class and the Civilising Mission in the 1820s and 1830s', in Alan Kidd and David Nicholl (eds), *Gender, Culture and Identity: The British Middle Classes, 1780–1940* (1998).

**Eileen Janes Yeo** teaches history at the University of Sussex and has supervised much undergraduate and postgraduate work on women and social action. She has recently written *The Contest for Social Science. Relations and Representations of Gender and Class* (1996) and edited *Mary Wollstonecraft and 200 Years of Feminisms* (1997). With Barbara Einhorn, she edited *Women and Market Societies. Crisis and Opportunity* (1995), written by scholars from Sussex and East Asia and presented at the Fourth World Conference on Women.

## PREFACE

This book is written by women who developed their historical work at the University of Sussex, either in the Chartism History Special Subject, in postgraduate research, in colleagual relations, in the Women's Studies Research Seminar or in the 'Gender and History' group organised by graduate students. Issues concerning women and social action have been an enduring focus of concern at Sussex with the accent on women's discourses and identities in historical contexts of power relations.

The contributors wish to thank the librarians and archivists who welcomed them to the various collections cited in the book. As editor, I am grateful to Michelle de Larrabeiti, Gerry Holloway, Gill Scott and Helen Rogers for reading and commenting on the Introduction. I also wish to thank the University of Melbourne for giving me the time, as an Arts Faculty Visiting Scholar in the History Department, to complete my work on the volume.

Trying to find an illustration for the cover turned out to be another interesting way of exploring issues of self-representation. With the exception of a few radical images of men and women campaigning together, for example at Peterloo, I could find little visual material from the nineteenth century which portrayed publicly active women in a positive way, and even fewer of such images produced by women themselves. This absence seemed to say again how treacherous was public visibility, although women were gaining entry to the public sphere by means of their written words.

The suffrage movements of the first decade of the twentieth century deliberately set out to change this, both by utilising public demonstrations, which had been well tried in earlier male radical movements, and by encouraging the formation of artists' suffrage workshops which supplied some of the banners and placards for the processions. As the organisers intended, these occasions were widely photographed by friendly as well as by hostile eyes and the Fawcett Collection at London Guildhall University has a rich collection of the results.

EJY

# Some paradoxes of empowerment

EILEEN JANES YEO

Public space has been dangerous territory for women. In nineteenth-century Britain, while a public man was a citizen, a 'public woman' meant a prostitute.[1] This book explores how women from different social groups challenged such assumptions, created empowering identities and represented themselves in public movements between 1790 and 1914. By way of introduction, I will consider how contested was the whole process of women attempting self-representation in the public sphere. It might be visualised as taking place in a field of cultural force where groups with unequal power pulled femininity in different directions all at the same time and made the situation constantly unstable. First, I will explore how powerful voices from religion, science and the state produced stronger prescriptions about the gendering of public and private spheres for a variety of reasons including their fear of women's activity as part of wider social 'disorder'. Then I will explore how women mobilised themselves by creating identities largely within and against the dominant discourses of their time. Finally I will explore the contradictions that riddled some of women's most ingenious use of intellectual, rhetorical and psychological resources, contradictions which could, as much as any hostility from outside, undermine the effectiveness of their activism.

## Enclosing the public sphere against disorderly outsiders

Recently, stimulated by the work of Jürgen Habermas, much scholarly attention has focused on the emergence of a middle-class public sphere of literary culture and political association, first in eighteenth-century Britain and later elsewhere in Europe.[2] The new public sphere has been described with positive words like polite,

tasteful, rational, enlightened and open to access by negotiation.
But feminist historians and others have begun to show that it was
also restrictive and gendered in eighteenth-century Britain, exclud-
ing the common people at the same time as refusing women
citizenship 'in the republic of taste' as well as in the political
nation. If women were assigned an important role in 'the empire of
feeling', which gave them a place in religion (increasingly seen as
an affair of the emotions), reason was elevated to the position of
overall master in order to put the 'vir back into virtue'.[3] Looking at
France, Joan Landes has made the most careful study so far of the
gendering of a public sphere, showing the process whereby the
salon culture of the Old Regime gave way to a brief moment of
public activism for a wider social spectrum of women during the
Revolution, which was then closed by a hardening bourgeois
culture which made the public into an exclusively masculine
sphere.[4]

The French Revolution had enormous impact in Britain. It
previewed class and gender reversals so threatening, that the
ruling and the middling classes, whatever their quarrels with each
other, closed ranks to launch a cultural counter-revolution to put
the 'lower' world back in place. As political repression deepened,
from 1795 onwards, even the Jacobin and feminist fringe of bourgeois activists scurried for safer ideological cover. One exception,
Mary Wollstonecraft, who had been lionised in the blissful early
days of the revolution, was now smeared as a sexual and political
transgressor, despite arguing for women's responsible maternal
citizenship. Prime Minister Horace Walpole called her a 'Hyena in
Petticoats'; while the Evangelical Hannah More dismissed her
work, without reading it, as 'A Vindication of Adultery'.[5] Gender
relations were an important focus of counter-revolutionary
concern and militant religion one of the most important makers of
meanings about proper femininity. The Evangelical party in the
Church of England, once a fanatical rump but now the moral
vanguard of the ruling classes, insisted on the separate natures of
men and women and their consequently distinctive roles in separate social spheres. Men were physically and intellectually robust
and more suited to the abrasive public sphere of business and politics; women, although more delicate, had spiritual power which
could best be concentrated and exercised in the private sphere of
the home.[6]

The domestic ideology was put into action by a burgeoning number of philanthropic agencies from 1790 onwards, often driven by Evangelical energy, like the Society for Bettering the Condition of the Poor.[7] Alison Twells's account of the work of Hannah Kilham in chapter 1 vividly illustrates how the public activity of women was strategic in creating domesticated femininity. Once widowed, Kilham became incorrigible in spreading the domestic gospel, first as a visitor for the Bettering Society in the slums of Sheffield, then in 1822 as a member of the British and Irish Ladies' Society for Improving the Condition and Promoting the Industry and Welfare of the Female Peasantry in Ireland and finally as a missionary in West Africa.

Religious teaching about femininity exerted such power not least because it became an integral part of the identity especially (but not exclusively) of the rising middle classes who made their religious family life a key factor in their claim to moral authority. Central here was the married mother presiding over the private sphere of home as a redemptive guardian of the spiritual condition of her whole family for now and all eternity, in contrast to the vanity and frivolity of the unreconstructed upper classes or the ignorance and vice of lower-class women. Davidoff and Hall have shown how this religious teaching interacted with changes in property patterns and the organisation of economic life increasingly to remove women from an active role in the family enterprise, and largely to exclude them from the growing civic sphere of voluntary association.[8]

These views of proper femininity were promulgated more aggressively during the turbulent years between 1830 and 1850 when working-class agitation seemed irrepressible. As Michelle de Larrabeiti notes in chapter 4, the Revd Francis Close read the theological riot act to women Chartists who demonstrated in his church in 1839. He damned the women who crossed the line between the private circle of home and the world of public agitation with all the denigrating images he could summon: they were unwomanly, unEnglish and indeed unhuman like their demonic French sisters 'who glutted themselves with blood; and danced like maniacs amidst the most fearful scenes of the Reign of Terror!'. He fumed that, 'so destitute are they of all sense of female decorum, of female modesty and diffidence, that they become themselves political agitators – female dictators – female mobs – female Chartists!'.[9]

The religious barrage was reinforced by an onslaught from the state trying to direct gender practices along the same lines, even where this meant crossing swords with self-interested employers. Sophie Hamilton, in chapter 3, shows how key state investigations of the 1830s and 1840s constructed true womanhood as married and domestic and gave these views teeth by writing them into regulative legislation which punished illegitimacy, limited women's working hours in factories and expelled women from the mines altogether – whether or not the women wanted these changes. Hamilton argues that the Commissions on the Poor Law (1834), on the Employment of Children in Factories (1833) and on Children's Employment in the Mines (1842) all depicted women either as sexually vulnerable or voracious, and therefore in need of protection or regulation. The final Poor Law *Report* portrayed single mothers as temptresses who seduced men in order to become pregnant and live off the child allowance provided by the father or the parish. Giving mothers the responsibility of supporting their bastards would force women to abandon their sexual promiscuity and, at the same time, reduce state expenditure – a coupling of aims which has persisted to this day!

Ideals of domesticity were taken up by unexpected allies who had different intentions from either evangelical Christians or state authorities. However much husbands really knew that their family survival depended upon the ability of their wives to bring some kind of income into the household or procure goods and services by means of barter, trade union men publicly negotiated for a family wage to support a domesticated wife and children assumed to be dependants. Most women philanthropists, working in trade unions or other areas of social work, as Holloway shows in chapter 7, largely supported a vision of working-class femininity being based at home, with work for wages especially outside the home being tolerable only as a necessary evil.

If religious authority had demonised political agitation and state authority had sexualised public work, science (both natural and social), especially from the mid-nineteenth century onwards tried to biologise 'normality' and 'deviance'. While medical science and public health had made earlier prescriptions about remedying the disorder of women, the developing medical profession from the 1860s 'discovered' a vast number of female illnesses, which only they were competent to treat, most of which were connected with dysfunction of the reproductive system. The best-known example is hysteria which from antiquity meant a disorder of the womb (*hysteria*). The mid-nineteenth-century version spread like a contagion among affluent women and was often treated by the 'rest cure' which forced the loud-mouthed, badly behaved patient into total passivity. In this climate, women activists, often called the 'shrieking sisterhood', were sometimes diagnosed not only as surplus women (because they had not married) but as hysterical dried up spinsters whose wombs had shrivelled from disuse.[10]

Evolutionary biology, even in its more benign form, which rejected competitive struggle and saw development achieved through co-operation and sacrifice, tended to regard women largely as the great mothers of the process whether in human or insect life. Eugenics, the science of race improvement, which permeated virtually every social and political discourse from the 1880s onwards, saw women mainly as mothers or, to use a more radical formulation: citizens engaged in race production.[11] The deeply felt sense of national crisis in Britain at the turn of the twentieth century was articulated in eugenic terms, especially once the Boer War revealed the unfitness of army recruits and the Inter-Departmental Committee on Physical Deterioration (1904) set the terms for discussing the state of the nation and laid much of the responsibility for poor health on the already burdened backs of working-class mothers.[12] Now the issue of mothers raising a good quantity and quality of children was an issue of greatest national importance: it would seal the fate of the economy and even of the empire (chapter 7).

With such a proliferation of discourses about femininity as domestic married motherhood, coming even from the mouths of friends and indeed partners, the way into the public sphere might seem increasingly blocked. Certainly the revolutionary panache of a Mary Wollstonecraft or an Eliza Sharples (chapter 2) was already giving way in the Chartist movement to more cautious self-presentation hedged round with apology (chapter 4). The next moment of throwing caution to the winds was arguably when the militant suffragettes exhausted their constitutional strategy and turned to violence. They changed direction partly as a deliberate tactic to create fear by living up to hostile representations of them as uncontrolled hysterics, although their self-image was more that of Jeanne d'Arcs, heroic soldier-martyrs in a holy war (chapter 6).[13] They were the minority. How then did most publicly active women create identities for themselves which enabled them to remain respectable in their own eyes and yet to break new ground into public movements and utterance?

## Within and against the dominant discourses

Such women who wished to communicate with and persuade often doubtful and hostile groups would not, on the whole, invent brand new identities for themselves. In fact few historical men and women, no matter how daring, have ever created immaculately new revolutionary identities. Karl Marx called attention to the paradox of how revolutionaries take on identities from the past to dignify their cause, adopting 'names, battle cries and costumes in order to present the new scene of world history in this time-honoured disguise and this borrowed language'.[14] Sandra Holton in chapter 6 shows precisely how the early suffrage campaigners wrote themselves into the history of the constitution as ancient British freewomen. But it is not only discourses from the past which are utilised.

One of the fascinating and recurrent patterns in this book is how women subverted the dominant ideas and most resonant rhetorics and representations of their day, including those of recent origin, and changed them in the process. As de Larrabeiti argues in chapter 4, even the most seemingly unpromising languages are contestable, in the sense that old meanings of important concepts and representations can be challenged and new meanings created. The Marxist philosopher of language, V. N. Volosinov argued as long ago as 1929 that it is precisely the capacity of any powerful sign to carry different meanings, which makes for its 'vitality and dynamism and the capacity for further development'.[15] Here I will explore how women created their public identities by contesting ideas and languages of religion, of constitutionalism and slavery, of family and domesticity, and, finally, of citizenship and productive work.

Throughout the period covered by this book, religion remained one of the most powerful custodians of understandings of femininity. Evangelical Christians made Eve the terrible template of womanhood. The Revd Close, in his sermon, argued that God had punished women three-fold for Eve's sin of tempting Adam in the

Garden of Eden, first, by 'the very constitution of their bodies', giving them 'nerves' and 'feelings' which could experience pain more acutely than men's, second, by making childbirth painful and third, by giving husbands rule over them. God then redeemed the situation by making Mary the mother of Jesus, as a result of which women could return to their paradisical level, but only if they kept to their proper sphere:

> the centre of all your virtues, and the fountain of all your influence in society, *is your home* – your own fire-side – it is amongst your children, it is in the bosom of your family, and in that little circle of friends with whom you are more immediately connected, there your legitimate influence must be exercised; there you are born to shine.[16]

To counter this theology the most radical women, like Eliza Sharples, discussed in chapter 2, or the Owenite socialist women of the 1830s and 1840s, reinterpreted and reclaimed Eve. For Sharples, as Helen Rogers shows, Eve was 'the personification of wisdom, of liberty, of resistance to tyranny; the mother of human knowledge; the proper help meet for man'. In the Garden of Eden, when the 'tyrant God, Necessity' refused to let man eat from the tree of knowledge, Eve intervened and offered the fruit to her husband. Not only did her 'glorious fall' mark the beginnings of human development but she represented a rationality which also included knowledge gained through the very emotions and body which Close had declared a curse. Sharples called her paper *The Isis*, after the powerful Egyptian goddess who, like Eve, combined powerful knowledge with fertility.[17] More conventional activists concentrated less on Eve and more on feminising Protestant divinity in order to dignify the so-called feminine elements of humanity and the value of real women. I show in chapter 5 how mid-nineteenth-century Protestant activists from the middle class and gentry borrowed from Catholic tradition and rehabilitated the Virgin Mary and female Catholic saints, like Catherine of Siena, portraying her as called to a life of public activism by God.

The evangelical idea of women's moral influence and her more intense religiosity was obviously available for extension beyond the magic circle of the home into the public sphere. Hannah Kilham, discussed in chapter 1, lived out new possibilities for missionary work in the domestic slums and then in the outreaches of the empire. Middle-class women especially mobilised the idea of themselves as a moral vanguard to justify their entry into their first public campaign, against colonial slavery, and continued to assert this identity right through the century into the suffrage agitation. In the 1820s and 1830s, as Clare Midgley has shown, they brushed aside interdictions against their involvement in politics saying that the slavery issue was, in the words of Sheffield campaigners, 'not exclusively a political but, pre-eminently a *moral* question, on which the humble-minded reader of the Bible, which enriches his cottage shelf, is immeasurably a better politician than the states-man versed in the intrigues of Cabinets'.[18] Indeed they argued their stronger adherence to Christian principle than the more expe-dient men, an argument which sometimes turned on its tail as when Quaker women from the 1870s to the end of the century, claimed that their moral courage entitled them not to an equally authoritative role in secular politics but in their own Church.[19]

Women activists continually tried to address issues about reli-gious authority on earth as well as in heaven. Several of the women had difficulty staying within institutional Churches and experi-enced serial conversions on their way out: having converted to Methodism, Hannah Kilham rejected even her late husband's 'Tom Paine' Methodism for Quakerism which gave authority to the inner light in the human heart which came directly from God; Sharples also converted from Methodism to freethought. Mid-century femi-nists who stayed within denominations, like fervent Anglican Josephine Butler, none the less scraped away the historical encrus-tations of the patriarchal church (including St Paul) and appealed to Jesus and his vision of non-gendered human value ('there is neither male nor female, neither plebeian nor noble but all are equal before me'). She argued that the religious authority rested with those men and women prophets throughout history who resonated with Christ's message of human liberation.

Male radicals, like the Chartists, often used Christianity to justify their political actions. As chapter 4 indicates, their womenfolk also joined in, quoting from the Scriptures to spur on their men: 'tis better to die by the sword than by famine'.[20] However, the most prominent language of legitimation (which often overlapped with Christianity) between 1760 and 1860 was constitutionalism.[21] The appeal to 'the rights of man', which Wollstonecraft insisted should include women too, became less common after the severe counter-revolutionary repression of the Napoleonic war period. Instead, both British radicals and conservatives vied for control over a language of constitutionality which shaded into a language of patriotism[22] and contained images of slavery providing very powerful representations of oppression.

Central to the constitutional outlook were ideas that the ancient Constitution guaranteed liberty to freeborn Britons who were the People, the source of all legitimate power whether in politics or religion: *vox populi, vox dei*. Their political forms were dubbed with the adjective 'public' as in public meeting or demonstration. Obviously who was included in and who excluded out of this central category was highly contentious, and American revolutionaries, eighteenth-century middling-class parliamentary reformers, Church and King mobs, and Chartist men, all of whom used the language to dignify themselves, had very different ideas of who belonged in the People. Leaving that aside for the moment, constitutionalism not only conferred political rights and powers but also a right to rebellion. Oppressive power came from tyrants who turned Britons into slaves. Slaves had a right of resistance to regain their liberty.

Radical women like Sharples, as her description of Eve in Eden showed, deployed this rhetoric freely (chapter 2): women Chartists considered themselves as much a part of the People as their menfolk, even if they were not claiming the vote. Thus Mary Ann Moore of Perth addressed her female audience as 'respected and honoured patriots; unflinching advocates of the people' (chapter 4). Some of the more radical of the bourgeois abolitionists like Elizabeth Heyrick also drew upon this rhetoric in the first half of the century,[23] and Josephine Butler made startling use of it in the 'great crusade' against the Contagious Diseases Acts which empowered police in military towns to order suspected prostitutes to undergo medical examination for venereal disease. Her book, *The Constitution Violated*, even insisted that prostitutes were being denied rights guaranteed to all freeborn Britons by Magna Carta, like trial by jury for a crime in law (chapter 5).

The propertied women's suffrage campaigns from the mid-century onwards also mined this rich rhetorical vein, as Sandra Holton shows in chapter 6, not only arguing for a restitution to British freewomen of their ancient constitutional rights but also by making use of the public cultural forms which had been created by men in their earlier campaigns for reform. Their presentation of petitions to parliament and their holding of public meetings were early examples, later augmented in the first decade of the twentieth century, with huge public demonstrations and even a series of Women's Parliaments resembling the Chartist People's Parliament. Sometimes the suffrage campaigners were treated as violently as their Chartist precursors, who during the height of their agitation, had been seen as the mob rather than the People.

Emmeline Pankhurst gave a revealing account of what happened when her daughter Christabel and Annie Kenney tried to follow consitutional etiquette at their first public meeting, a political meeting with the Liberal candidate Winston Churchill present:

> They sat quietly through the meeting, at the close of which questions were invited. Several questions were asked by men and were courteously answered. Then Annie Kenney arose and asked: 'If the Liberal party is returned to power, will they take steps to give votes for women?' At the same time Christabel held aloft the little banner that every one in the hall might understand the nature of the question. Sir Edward Grey returned no answer to Annie's question, and the men sitting near her forced her rudely into her seat while a steward of the meeting pressed his hat over her face. A babel of shouts, cries and catcalls sounded from all over the hall.[24]

This episode took place in 1905, and the response to women moving into public constitutional forms was first to ignore them, then to try to make them invisible (with hats over faces), next to drown out their speech and finally to bundle them out of the hall (supposedly six stewards 'escorted' Christabel alone) and shortly thereafter to arrest them for obstruction and assault!

The language of slavery and the right to resistance, which was also part of the constitutional idiom, was continuously used and remade by activist women. This was a very complex and powerful language. Besides being a common representation for eighteenth-century male radicals or American colonists who considered themselves politically oppressed, women writers also used a language of slavery to invoke gender oppression. Moira Ferguson has noted how 'conservative and radical women alike railed against marriage, love and education as forms of slavery perpetrated upon women by men and by the conventions of society at large',[25] a usage culminating in Wollstonecraft's *A Vindication of the*

*Rights of Woman* which invoked slavery as a structuring metaphor. The rhetoric of slavery also contained a much older religious layer. In the Judaeo-Christian tradition, the story of Moses leading the chosen people out of bondage in Egypt was the model liberation saga, in which women (Pharaoh's daughter, Moses's sister Miriam, for example) had played a significant part.[26]

In the 1790s the language of slavery took on another layer of meaning as a result of abolitionist activity and then the successful slave revolt in 1791 in the French colony of San Domingo which became independent Haiti.[27] During the economic depression that followed the French wars, a class dimension was added to enslavement, as British workers began to call themselves white slaves in analogy to black slaves. This usage then dominated the Ten Hours Movement of the 1830s and 1840s, after Richard Oastler published his famous letter on 'Yorkshire Slavery' (1830) and attacked millowners in leading abolitionist William Wilberforce's own parliamentary constituency who treated their workers with less concern than slave owners in the West Indies.[28]

Working-class activist women from the beginning to the end of the century could mobilise all these political, religious, race, class and gender meanings at the same time, and keep adding to them. From the time that the Females of Royston carried a banner to the Peterloo massacre of 1819 which read 'let us die like men, and not be sold like slaves', right through to Ada Nield Chew's assertions (in chapter 7) that married working women suffered a two-fold bondage (babies and domestic toil) and that it was impossible 'to breed a free people from slave mothers'. Chew also claimed that women had a 'right to rebellion' and to fight for social support systems which would free them to become human. Women from the more propertied classes tended to emphasise the gender aspects of the rhetoric, particularly when talking about the legal position of married women as *femmes couvertes*. Yet their most dramatic invocation of images of slavery depicted the treatment of less powerful women like colonial slaves and prostitutes, and not least the family disruption and sexual abuse they endured, perhaps partly a displaced way of talking about experiences which affected other classes as well but which respectable women could not openly express.

Of all the 'mind forg'd manacles' holding women in the private sphere, the most difficult to crack would ostensibly be the family discourse because it most explicitly secured their domestic place. Thus one of the most interesting developments is how women stretched various family roles precisely to ratify their public activism. In chapter 4, de Larrabeiti shows how the Chartist women in their heavily invigilated public addresses, watched both by men of another class and their own, presented themselves as militant family members, as concerned wives, mothers and sisters suffering severe family disruption as a result of the abuse of political, economic and religious power. These women Chartists maintained that they had to agitate in order to help create a durable framework for proper family life. In the words of the Newcastle Female Political Union:

> We have been told that the province of woman is her home, and the field of politics should be left to men; this we deny; the nature of things render it impossible … Is it not true that the interests of our fathers, husbands and brothers, ought to be ours? If they are oppressed and impoverished, do we not share those evils with them? … We have read the records of the past, and our hearts have responded to the historian's praise of those women, who struggled against tyranny and urged their countrymen to be free or die.[29]

This militant family stance drew upon and developed earlier traditions where women had featured in public activity, for example, as family consumers in eighteenth-century food riots over fair prices right into Chartist exclusive dealing tactics which urged purchase only from shopkeepers sympathetic to the cause. Women marched behind the banners they had so painstakingly embroidered, most recently in two campaigns which highlighted family issues, the movements against the New Poor Law (which separated families in the workhouse) and in favour of a ten-hour working day.

Some feminist historians have rapped Chartist women on the knuckles for not being as vocal about patriarchy as their Owenite sisters, but de Larrabeiti argues that their stance was not in any simple way conservative. Not only did they energise themselves for public activity and publicly upbraid men who chose (rather than were forced) to abandon a protective role, but they actually shifted Chartist ideology to take into account the importance of family both in political analysis and action. By contrast, the more women put themselves beyond the rhetorical pale, so to speak, the less they communicated persuasively. As Rogers indicates in

chapter 2, Sharples's proclamation of her 'moral marriage' to
Richard Carlile after his 'moral divorce' from his first wife Jane,
lost her support among plebeian women as well as men and undermined her call for sisterhood.

The Owenites themselves had to tread very carefully on the issue
of divorce when they found that many women preferred the
protective conventions of marriage to what they feared as a possible Casanova's charter. Given the onslaught from capitalist
industry and the central state on cherished family forms at the
time, the Chartist women were reluctant to focus on the power
dynamics of their families. Later, at the turn of the twentieth
century, when motherhood was unanimously being celebrated, the
Women's Co-operative Guild not only exposed the gap between
the eugenic idealisation and their own often harrowing experience
of pregnancy and childbirth; they also 'lifted the curtain' on the
private sphere, exposing the domestic abuse which sometimes was
the reality of the family romance. Moreover, as Scott shows, they
were willing to take the consequences for insisting on a gender
politics and brave the withdrawal of financial support by the men's
movement which protested that issues like divorce had no place in
co-operation (chapter 8)!

Women activists from other social classes tended to mobilise
languages of motherhood and sisterhood to structure their identities as public activists in politics and/or social work in relation to
less well-off women. I show in chapter 5 how one attraction of the
Catholic tradition was its icons, like the Virgin Mother, and institutions, like the Sisters of Charity, which proved particularly helpful
to single women who wanted dignified public work and yet would
not vacate the resonant categories of familial femininity: they
utilised the resources from Catholicism to create versions of motherhood and sisterhood which fitted the childless single woman.
Gerry Holloway, in chapter 7, also points to the ways in which a
rhetoric of motherhood could be used as a way of bridging class
difference. Another direction for reworking family discourse,
marking out some of the more radical women of the various movements from their more cautious sisters whether in Chartism,
socialism or the campaign against the Contagious Diseases Acts,
was their willingness to expand the concept of the family beyond
the nuclear patriarchal family and to find key relational roles for
women within the universal family of humankind.

If languages endure and make for very tangled rhetorical thickets, none the less in the experience of struggle they also change, and to use Raymond Williams's helpful categories, become emergent, dominant or residual.[30] By the late nineteenth century, women were still remaking family discourse but in a changed context. The 1867 parliamentary reform agitation, although it did not deliver any votes for women, none the less gave the vote to a small section of working-class men and again demonstrated the constitution's elasticity under pressure. At the same time, 'the People' became increasingly equated with the more negative category of the masses (paradoxically seen as both apathetic and violent) while those entitled to political rights and powers were now more regularly called the 'citizens'.[31] The mid-century feminist movement, led by women from the middle class and gentry, and associated with the Langham Place cultural centre, had articulated ambitions for a dignified working life and proper education to prepare for it.[32] But women wanting to enter the citizenry and the world of work at the turn of the twentieth century had to contend with very strong eugenic pressures, as Holloway shows in chapter 7, assigning women the role of mothers of the race. Different groups of women created different versions of a mother-worker-citizen role for themselves in the public sphere.

Scott shows in chapter 8 how women of the Co-operative Guild not only mobilised their actual experience of maternity to demand social reforms which would bring them into congruity with dominant ideologies of motherhood, but ingeniously tried to find a place within the resonant representations used by the men of their own class. They made sure that men were given as central a role in the marital family discourse as women and then extended the idea of family into every area of public life with a secure place for women in 'the larger family of the store, the municipality and the State'. The most positive self-representation of working-class men, for the whole of the century, had been that of the productive and useful classes whose active labour created all valuable, in the sense of needed, goods and services. The Women's Guild, like other sections of what Holloway calls the Industrial Women's Movement, were well aware of the devaluation of women's work, performed by what they called women workers (paid) and working women (unpaid).[33] The Women's Guild tried to dignify women's work by presenting both kinds as useful (but exploited) contributions to the life of the nation: homes were 'workshops of many trades, where overtime abounds, and where an eight hours' day would be a very welcome reform'. The concept of citizenship offered a capacious container for the development of women as fully human beings: as General Secretary Margaret Llewelyn Davies insisted, 'citizenship is above sex, party, class and sect ... A citizen is a human being, belonging to a community, with rights and duties arising out of a common life'. Not only were women a hitherto untapped source of strength in 'national life', but they had every right to 'organise and educate themselves and undertake public works and responsibilities' (chapter 8).

In their carefully scripted public demonstrations starting in 1908, middle- and upper-class activists also exhibited the useful contribution of working women to the nation. Especially in the processions organised by the National Union of Women's Suffrage Societies, the contingents of occupations or professions tried to manifest this importance, with the nurses (the consummate social mothers) always getting the most applause, and with the attractive women graduates a living repudiation of the idea that educated women channelled their vital energy to the brain and became ugly hags.[34] Like women of all classes, they turned motherhood into an argument for citizenship: if men's claim to citizenship on the basis of their humanity rather than property rested on their willingness to die for their country, then women made an equally important contribution by creating the lives that might be sacrificed. Childbearing, declared gynaecologist and member of the Fabian Women's Group, Dr Ethel Vaughan-Sawyer, 'is the supreme service, which she alone can render to the State of which she is a member, and is on a par with the primary duty of the adult male to defend his country against invasion'.[35] Motherhood could be stretched in many directions to allow for women's public participation: political rights were necessary so that women could safeguard and support the role of mothers, and even so that women could aspire to become human, in Ada Nield Chew's words, 'and act to end the starvation of the minds and bodies of themselves and their children'.

### Unequal sisters – unequal genders

However ingeniously women remade dominant discourses so as to empower public femininity, they were sometimes insensitive to the

way in which their very formulations were undercut by, and indeed
even helped to sharpen, social differences among women. By taking
the chance to focus upon these contradictions, I do not mean to
devalue the women's efforts but rather to increase awareness of the
pitfalls which surround any attempt to create the collective identities which are a necessary feature of social struggle. Contradictions
riddled every area of discourse so far presented. In the area of religion, Hannah Kilham's insistence on spiritual equality sat uneasily
with her belief in social, ethnic, racial and national subordinations.
She found even the most democratic schism of the time, the
Kilhamite or New Connexion Methodists, too constraining. Yet her
philanthropy operated a clear order of merit, with the British
middle-class home at the top of the ladder; she wished to educate
women up to the next rung – and change working-class slum
dwellings in Sheffield into homes, Irish cabins into dwellings, West
African huts into cabins. For Kilham, there was a corresponding
ladder of womanhood which graduated, in ascending order, from
African 'females', to Irish 'women' to British 'ladies'. Given that she
was active at what Twells calls 'a formative moment in the construction of British class and national identities', her effort helped to
create ethnicity, class and race not as relations of cultural diversity
but as relations of cultural hierarchy. Holton explores how, later in
the century, suffrage histories 'scientifically' arranged women of
different racial and ethnic groups into hierarchies of evolutionary
development culminating with the British freewoman at the apex.

Again within family discourse, women from middle-class and
gentry backgrounds could unwittingly use languages of motherhood and sisterhood as instruments of power, and end up
constraining the possibilities of other women. Kilham stood in a
long tradition of women who preached a redemptive gospel of
domesticity for others, but were anything but domesticated themselves; once widowed, Kilham moved off from Sheffield to do
missionary work in Ireland and then in West Africa. Single or
indeed married women, acting as social mothers, extended public
space for themselves but arguably at the same time could help to
narrow the cultural space of the recipients of their care. Mary
MacArthur and Margaret MacDonald, in Holloway's chapter,
could favour domesticity as the ideal for working-class women
while being freed up by affluence and servants from their own
maternal and domestic duties. Elsewhere, I have explored how

motherhood and sisterhood can have many contradictory facets
and contain quite pronounced authority relationships, particularly
when disciplining and even protective motherhood is deemed
necessary for dealing with unruly or defenceless 'daughters', for
example the prostitutes on whose behalf Butler appealed 'as a
mother to mothers. Listen to me while I plead for the children'.[36]

Another relation of unequal power can result when some sisters
see themselves as bigger, better educated, more leisured and therefore feel they must think, speak and act on behalf of their little
sisters constructed as suffering, weak, victims unable now, or
perhaps ever, to take action on their own behalf. This version of
sisterhood was conspicuous not only in some areas of the
Industrial Women's Movement but in relations between British
women activists and native women in the empire. Thus Mrs Bayle
Bernard urged British women to

> throw their hearts and souls into the [educational] work, and
> determine never to rest until they have raised their Eastern sisters
> to their own level; and then may the women of India at last attain
> a position honourable to themselves and to England, instead of, as
> is now so generally the case, filling one which can only be contem-
> plated with feelings of shame and sorrow.[37]

These subordinating uses of family discourse preclude a politics of
self-representation for all women.

In the abolitionist movement a contorted version of representation sometimes occurred where British activists established their
right to a public presence by stressing the plight of disrupted slave
families, but put their own feelings and words into the mouths of
the slaves in order, more persuasively, to plead the cause of emancipation.[38] At the same time, the only known instance of
self-representation by a British West Indian slave, Mary Prince's
autobiography, was expurgated by her editor, and some of the very
qualities which gave Prince the courage to seek independence,
were classed among her faults: 'a somewhat violent and hasty
temper, and a considerable share of natural pride and self-impor-
tance'. Midgley suggests that, as a result, 'black agency in
undermining slavery is devalued, and under the auspices of the
Anti-Slavery Society, freedom is granted as the gift of white philanthropists who leave class relations undisturbed'.[39]

The issue of denying other women the opportunity for self-representation continually recurs. Holloway shows how, at the turn of the twentieth century, it transmuted into a kind of social scientific ventriloquism: for all of the excellent fact-ferreting done by the professional investigators of the Women's Industrial Council, Holloway argues that they never really asked what their working-class informants thought or wanted. The Women's Co-operative Guild was very sensitive to this kind of inadvertent concealment and developed a politics and investigative practice of self-representation, as Scott shows. The same issue is still with us today and has resurfaced recently in feminist sociology.[40]

Pointing to another key area of dissonance, the overwhelming late nineteenth-century chorus of *viva mama* sometimes clashed with assertions of shared human nature between men and women and common human rights. I do not want to get bogged down in unhelpful assumptions of a polarity between equality and difference; as Joan Scott has argued, both offer viable strategies for women's movements and which combination will yield most results will depend on the historical moment within which struggles have to take place.[41] But how to equilibrate the two has been a matter for complicated experiment from Wollstonecraft at the beginning of the Western feminist tradition, to Sharples in the heroic days of plebeian radicalism, to Harriet Taylor Mill on the more egalitarian edge of mid-century feminism, to the Women's Co-operative Guild and Fabian Women's Group at different ends of the social spectrum and continuing right into the present. Certainly at the end of the nineteenth century such was the cult of motherhood, that it would have been difficult for women to create public identities and strategies totally outside it. Moreover, as chapter 5 suggests, motherhood might have been drawing power from ancient wells far deeper than the nuclear family, by harnessing the psychic energy of feminine archetypes, just as some radical feminist groups and as feminist theologians try to do today with their resurrection of the great mother goddesses.

None the less, it is important to keep monitoring just where cosmic theories of 'difference' and of the complementarity of masculine and feminine principles translate into social life as subordination or stunted growth for the feminine element. Going back to Volosinov, the most dynamic representations are so vibrant because they pull in several directions at once; they never simply flatten into a unilinear movement. So as women pull representations of femininity and motherhood in one way, often other groups pull them back at the same time, and vice versa. In the very cultural moment when Ruskin was citing complementarity as the reason for containing women in the private sphere, many women reformers were arguing the need for a sexual 'communion of labour' to complete social progress in every area of public life (chapter 5). None the less women tended to accept caring roles within the public sphere and auxiliary and helpmeet status in their co-operation with men. Moreover, assigning all the nurturing emotionality of the feminine principle to the female sex alone inhibits the human development of women and men alike. Although Josephine Butler tried to argue that even fathers could be mothers (chapter 5), the shock effect of applying the word 'mother' to a man exposes the constraining limits of the language, and the need for other terms like parenting to convey ambisexual nurturance becomes more clear.

But parenting is no simple answer either because family discourse has remained problematic and contested right up to the present day. What constitutes a proper family compared with an illegitimate one has been continuously at issue. Chapter 3 identifies a key moment when unmarried motherhood was pronounced deviant by the New Poor Law of 1834 as conventional cultural patterns were swamped by new ideological currents from Church and state. Lone mothers are still treated as social scapegoats, and now seen as the fecund source of pregnant teenage girls and adolescent warrior males. During the whole of the twentieth century, after the chronology covered by the chapters here, nuclear marital family ideology has been continually reinvoked, especially after the world wars which gave women the chance to live out expanded and even reversed gender roles. Motherhood was still at the centre of family discourse, although upgraded into scientific domestic management after the First World War or modernity's maternal consumerism after the Second World War and extended with permission for part-time paid employment around the margins.[42] The political parties have also contributed to this hegemonic idea, with the Labour Party's unwillingness to engage with a controversial feminist agenda even contributing to the upset of the unique balance that the Women's Co-operative Guild had achieved between gender and class politics (chapter 8).

Whatever its insensitivity to class and race, the 'Four Demands'

of the second wave Women's Liberation Movement in Britain tried
to base entitlement to human development both on sexual difference, insisting on twenty-four-hour nurseries and contraception
and abortion on demand, as well as on equality in educational and
employment opportunities.[43] None the less feminists still live out
motherhood in a society built around domestic ideology, with few
social supports for other roles unless they can be privately
afforded, in a national situation where women are increasingly
more able to find 'flexible' (exploitative) employment than men.
An international dimension has added to the chorus of concern
over multiple burdens as all the benefits accorded to the worker-
mother in the former communist countries of East Central Europe
(and in China) are being dismantled and women find themselves
especially poorly placed in market competition as well as being
inhibited from taking public action by the association of politics
with the old detested Stalinist regimes.[44] The problems which faced
the women who appear in this book representing themselves and
trying to shape their own lives, although perhaps not precisely as
they might wish, are still with us today. How, in an intractable
social context is it possible to struggle towards fuller development
as beings who are, at one and the same time, woman and human?

## Notes

1 See *Oxford English Dictionary*, and see also J. Landes, *Women and the Public
  Sphere in the Age of the French Revolution* (Ithaca, Cornell University Press,
  1988), pp. 2–3; L. Colley, *Britons. Forging the Nation 1707–1837* (London,
  Vintage, [1992] 1996), pp. 260–1.
2 J. Habermas, *The Structural Transformation of the Public Sphere: An Inquiry into
  a Category of Bourgeois Society*, trans. T. Burger and F. Lawrence (Cambridge,
  Mass., Harvard University Press, 1989). For Britain, John Brewer's work
  has been key, starting with N. McKendrick, J. Brewer and J. H. Plumb,
  *The Birth of a Consumer Society: The Commercialization of Eighteenth-Century
  England* (London, Europa, 1982). Voluminous writing on France includes
  K. Michael Baker, 'Defining the Public Sphere in Eighteenth-Century
  France: Variations on a Theme by Habermas', in C. Calhoun (ed.), *Habermas
  and the Public Sphere* (Cambridge, MIT Press, 1992); see note 3 below.
3 For these developing conventions and Mary Wollstonecraft's challenge
  within and against them, see E. J. Yeo (ed.), *Mary Wollstonecraft and 200
  Years of Feminisms* (London, Rivers Oram, 1997), chs by Barbara Taylor,
  Joan Landes and Kate Soper.
4 Landes, *Women and the Public Sphere*; also J. W. Scott, *Only Paradoxes to
  Offer: French Feminists and the Rights of Man* (Cambridge, Mass., Harvard
  University Press, 1996).

5  B. Taylor, *Eve and the New Jerusalem. Socialism and Feminism in the Nineteenth Century* (London, Virago, 1983), pp. 14–18.

6  For the revolutionary panic and its gender dimensions see my *The Contest for Social Science: Relations and Representations of Gender and Class* (London, Rivers Oram, 1996), pp. 3–9 and C. Hall, 'The Early Formation of the Victorian Domestic Ideology', in her *White, Male and Middle Class* (Cambridge, Polity, 1992).

7  For women's role see Yeo, *Contest for Social Science*, pp. 10–15; F. R. Prochaska, 'Women in English Philanthropy, 1790–1830', *International Review of Social History*, 19 (1974), pp. 428–31.

8  L. Davidoff and C. Hall, *Family Fortunes: Men and Women of the English Middle Class, 1780–1850* (London, Hutchinson, 1987); C. Hall, 'Gender Divisions and Class Formation in the Birmingham Middle Class, 1780–1850', in her *White, Male and Middle Class*, pp. 101–3; D. Wahrman, *Imagining the Middle Class: The Political Representation of Class in Britain, c. 1780–1840* (Cambridge, Cambridge University Press, 1995), pp. 400–7. A. Vickery, 'Golden Age to Separate Spheres? A Review of the Categories and Chronology of English Women's History', *Historical Journal*, 36:2 (1993) and J. Liddington, *Female Fortune: Land, Gender and Authority* (London, Rivers Oram, 1998) have called attention to publicly powerful women especially from the gentry, but the growing prescriptive consensus, what Raymond Williams called 'the social character', was that women's proper place was in the private sphere.

9  Revd F. Close, *A Sermon Addressed to the Female Chartists of Cheltenham ... 25 Aug. 1839* (London, Hamilton, Adams, 1839), pp. 16 and 13 which also talks of 'dissipation' in the 'upper ranks' and vice in the 'humbler class of life'.

10  There is much good writing on medicine, starting with B. Ehrenreich and D. English, *For their own Good: 150 Years of the Experts' Advice to Women* (Garden City, New York, Anchor, 1979), ch. 4, and including E. Showalter, *Women, Madness and English Culture, 1830–1980* (London, Virago, 1987) and more recently, J. Ussher, *Women's Madness: Misogyny or Mental Illness?* (New York and London, Harvester Wheatsheaf, 1991), chs 4, 5. A. Owen, *The Darkened Room: Women, Power and Spiritualism in Late Victorian England* (London, Virago, 1989), chs 2, 5 and 6 shows how women turned their supposed passivity into a source of power and medical skill. See L. Tickner, *The Spectacle of Women. Imagery of the Suffrage Campaign 1907–14* (London, Chatto and Windus, 1987), pp. 192–205 for hostile representations of suffragists as hysterics.

11  Yeo, *Contest for Social Science*, pp. 193–4, 196–7, p. 337, n. 4; also C. Eagle Russett, *Sexual Science: The Victorian Construction of Womanhood* (Cambridge, Mass., Harvard University Press, 1989), pp. 40–2, 93, 149.

12  See A. Davin's classic 'Imperialism and Motherhood', *History Workshop*, 5 (Spring 1978).

13  Also Tickner, *Spectacle of Women*, pp. 208–11: see Dr Sir A. E. Wright's notorious letter on 'Militant Hysteria' to *The Times*, 28 March 1912.

14  K. Marx, 'The Eighteenth Brumaire of Louis Bonaparte', in Marx and Engels, *Selected Works* (Moscow, Foreign Languages Publishing House, [1869] 1962), vol. l, p. 247.

**15** V. N. Volosinov, *Marxism and the Philosophy of Language*, trans. L. Matejka and I. Titunik (Cambridge, Mass., Harvard University Press, [1929] 1986), p. 23.

**16** Close, *Sermon*, pp. 14–15, 3–5, 8.

**17** Isis was the great mother goddess from whom the creation and most of the gods came; she tricked Ra the sun god into sharing his powerful knowledge.

**18** Quoted in C. Midgley, *Women Against Slavery: The British Campaigns, 1780–1870* (London, Routledge, 1992), p. 110. L. Shimmin, *Women and Leadership in Nineteenth-Century England* (London, Macmillan, 1992), chs 4 and 11, discusses women in the temperance movement where their role as a moral vanguard was also mobilised for public action.

**19** S. Stanley Holton and M. Allen, 'Offices and Services: Women's Pursuit of Sexual Equality Within the Society of Friends, 1873–1907', *Quaker Studies*, 2 (1997), p. 22. Shimmin, *Women and Leadership*, chs 1 and 2, tracks the shrinking role of women preachers within Methodism; ch. 7 considers mid-nineteenth-century revivalism.

**20** See E. Yeo, 'Christianity and Chartist Struggle, 1838–42', *Past and Present*, 91 (1981).

**21** The large literature on this includes E. P. Thompson, *The Making of the English Working Class* (Harmondsworth, Pelican, 1968), ch. 4; G. Stedman Jones, 'Rethinking Chartism', in his *Languages of Class. Studies in English Working-Class History, 1832–1982* (Cambridge, Cambridge University Press, 1983); J. Epstein, *Radical Expression: Political Language, Ritual and Symbol in England, 1790–1850* (New York, Oxford University Press, 1994), ch. 1.

**22** See H. Cunningham, 'The Language of Patriotism, 1750–1914', *History Workshop*, 12 (Autumn 1981); L. Colley, 'Whose Nation? Class and National Consciousness in Britain 1750–1820', *Past and Present*, 113 (1986).

**23** Midgley, *Women Against Slavery*, p. 113.

**24** See E. Pankhurst, *My Own Story* (London, Eveleigh Nash, 1914), pp. 46–8. I am developing these themes in my book-in-progress on 'Class, Gender and the Public Sphere'. For problems of earlier platform women, see F. P. Cobbe, 'Social Science Congresses and Women's Part in Them', *Macmillan's Magazine*, 5 (Dec. 1861), pp. 92–3 and Shimmin, *Women and Leadership*, ch. 9 for temperance, chs 12 and 13 for the Tory Primrose League and the Women's Liberal Federation (1880s ff.) which wanted to restrict women to a door-to-door canvassing role. For women beginning to hold local office on School Boards and Poor Law Guardians, see P. Hollis, *Women Elect: Women in English Local Government 1865–1914* (Oxford, Clarendon Press, 1987).

**25** M. Ferguson, 'Mary Wollstonecraft and the Problematic of Slavery', in Yeo, *Mary Wollstonecraft*, p. 90; C. Plasa and B. Ring (eds), *The Discourse of Slavery. Aphra Behn to Toni Morrison* (London, Routledge, 1994).

**26** For the importance of the Moses story, see my 'Chartist Religious Belief and the Theology of Liberation', in J. Obelkevich *et al.* (eds), *Disciplines of Faith* (London, Routledge and Kegan Paul, 1987); D. Valenze shows how the doctrine of Mothers in Israel legitimated public preaching in her *Prophetic Sons and Daughters: Female Preaching and Popular Religion in the*

*Industrial Revolution* (Guildford, Princeton University Press, 1985), pp. 35–7; the same doctrine, called 'nursing mothers to the Christian Church', was used by temperance activist C. Lucas Balfour, *The Women of Scripture*, 2nd edn (London, Houlston and Stoneman, 1850), pp. 358–9.

27 Ferguson, 'Wollstonecraft and the Problematic of Slavery', p. 94.

28 *Leeds Mercury*, 16 Oct. 1830.

29 'Address of the Female Political Union of Newcastle', *Northern Star*, 9 Feb. 1839, closely echoed by the Birmingham Female Political Union, *The Charter*, 10 Nov. 1839.

30 R. Williams, *Marxism and Literature* (London, Oxford University Press, 1977), ch. 7.

31 I discuss this changing rhetoric in 'Language and Contestation: The Case of "the People", 1832 to the Present', in J. Belchem and N. Kirk (eds), *Languages of Labour* (Aldershot, Scolar, 1997), pp. 51–2.

32 Their ambitions and activities are discussed in P. Levine, *Victorian Feminism, 1850–1900* (Tallahassee, Florida State University Press, 1987).

33 B. Hutchins uses these terms in *Women in Modern Industry* (Wakefield, EP Reprint, [1915] 1978), pp. 195–6.

34 Tickner, *Spectacle of Women*, p. 89.

35 Fabian Women's Group, *A Summary of Eight Papers and Discussion upon the Disabilities of Mothers as Workers* (London, Fabian Women's Group, 1910), p. 8. See S. Stanley Holton, *Suffrage Days: Stories from the Women's Suffrage Movement* (London, Routledge, 1996), pp. 80–1 for earlier similar views.

36 J. Butler, *A Letter to the Mothers of England: Commended also to the Attention of Fathers, Ministers of Religion and Legislators* [1881], Josephine Butler Society Collection, Fawcett Library, London Guildhall University. See also my *Contest for Social Science*, pp. 141–6 and my 'Gender and Class: Women's Languages of Power', *Labour History Review*, 60:3 (1995), pp. 15–22.

37 Mrs Bernard quoted in V. Ware, *Beyond the Pale: White Women, Racism and History* (London, Verso, 1992), p. 130, but see p. 121 for Keshub Chunder Sen using the same language in England to recruit governesses.

38 See p. 112, and also *An Appeal to the Christian Women of Sheffield from the Association for the Universal Abolition of Slavery* (Sheffield, 1827), pp. 11–12, John Rylands University Library of Manchester.

39 Midgley, *Women Against Slavery*, pp. 90, 87–91. See also M. Ferguson (ed.), *The History of Mary Prince, a West Indian Slave, Related by Herself* (London, Pandora, [1831] 1987).

40 See M. Maynard, 'Methods, Practice and Epistemology: The Debate about Feminism and Research', in M. Maynard and J. Purvis (eds), *Researching Women's Lives from a Feminist Perspective* (London, Taylor and Francis, 1994).

41 J. Scott, 'Deconstructing Equality-Versus-Difference: Or, the Uses of Post-Structuralist Theory for Feminism', *Feminist Studies*, 14:1 (1988).

42 I shall be exploring these themes in my forthcoming *Meanings of Motherhood in Europe and America, 1750 to the Present*. For post-war motherhood, S. Rowbotham, *A Century of Women: The History of Women in Britain and the United States* (London, Viking, 1997), pp. 136–9, 161, 164–5; E. Wilson, *Only Half-Way to Paradise: Women in Post-War Britain* (London, Tavistock, 1980), pp. 36–40, 58–9; J. Lewis, *Women in Britain since 1945* (London, Blackwell, 1992), pp. 76–7.

**43** For the demands, see M. Wandor (ed.), *The Body Politic: Writings from the Women's Liberation Movement in Britain, 1969–72* (London, Stage 1, 1972), p. 2.

**44** See B. Einhorn, *Cinderella Goes to Market: Citizenship, Gender and Women's Movements in East Central Europe* (London, Verso, 1993); also B. Einhorn and E. J. Yeo (eds), *Women and Market Societies: Crisis and Opportunity* (Aldershot, Edward Elgar, 1995), especially intro., chs 9, 15.

# 1

# 'Let us begin well at home': class, ethnicity and Christian motherhood in the writing of Hannah Kilham, 1774–1832

## ALISON TWELLS

> On the wall of my sitting room is a coloured copy of what we call the missionary map, drawn by my Daughter from your *Register*, and describing the dreary extent of Paganism beyond every other description of ... religion. My hope is that *Christianity* itself – not the mere outward theory, but the living, the regenerating, *Principle of Christianity* is fast advancing in the world ...[1]

In the above letter, written in 1816 to Edward Bickersteth, Assistant Secretary of the Church Missionary Society, Hannah Kilham enquired as to the suitability of her booklets, *Scripture Selections* and the recently published *Family Maxims*, for missionary education overseas. Although written with the religious instruction of British working-class women and girls in mind, Kilham, a Quaker philanthropist and educationalist from Sheffield, shared with the Church Missionary Society its commitment to spreading 'real religion' throughout the world and was increasingly concerned to find ways of becoming involved in such work. During 1822–23 she travelled to Ireland as a member of the British and Irish Ladies' Society, an organisation established for the relief of Irish people suffering the effects of famine. Later in 1823, she made the first of three visits to West Africa, where she was involved in the establishment of a system of education which would enable Christian instruction in both English and West African languages.

The image of Kilham and her stepdaughter surveying the progress of Christianity from their sitting room is very pertinent for this essay, pointing to a relationship between women's domestic space and the world beyond. Kilham's journeys were intensely problematic for a single woman. As her journal reveals, she was required to negotiate contemporary notions of femininity which, emphasising women's natural affinity with the domestic sphere, had constructed 'the public' as dangerous for the respectable woman. West Africa in particular, as the home of slavery, polygamy and heathenism, had long been associated with danger in the Christian mind.[2] Kilham's success at pushing the boundaries of acceptable female activity has been celebrated by various biographers and writers. Sarah Biller, Kilham's stepdaughter and editor of her *Memoirs* in the 1830s, represented her as a pioneering woman, breaking the confines of feminine domesticity to carve a useful role for women as educators and missionaries.[3] This reading of Kilham as a radical woman was endorsed by Clara Lucas Balfour, writing in 1854, who praised her emphasis on women's suitability for philanthropic and missionary work.[4] Other writers have celebrated Kilham's achievements in the field of linguistics and her success in challenging outmoded conventions of English femininity and attitudes to African education.[5]

My interest here is in Kilham as a Christian missionary and the implications of the notion of 'woman's mission' for middle-class women's identity. Kilham saw philanthropy and education as central to women's sphere of influence. Discussing her desire in the early 1830s for more women to become involved in missionary work, she wrote that she thought 'the idea of its being a political subject has been one great preventative. Mercy and good-will are subjects for women to plead everywhere'. While identifying politics as a masculine activity, Kilham represented mercy and goodwill as feminine qualities, to be expressed in missionary philanthropy. As Davidoff and Hall have argued, women were able to exploit contradictions within evangelical theology which represented them as simultaneously spiritually equal and socially subordinate. Emphasising their roles as moral guardians, they were able to assume responsibility for the religious and moral education of not only children and servants in their own household but, through charitable and religious work, of the poor in their neighbourhoods. Blurring the boundaries between the 'separate spheres' of male and female activities, philanthropic women negotiated with middle-class men in the reconstruction of gender roles and identities, thus carving an extended role for themselves as public women.[7]

The extension of middle-class women's sphere in the early nineteenth century was not, however, an unproblematic process. As suggested by Hannah More's maxim, 'Charity is the calling of a lady' and 'the care of the poor ... her profession',[8] representations of middle-class women as 'carriers of civilisation' involved a wider power dynamic. Carving a role for themselves as educators and missionaries involved the construction of other social groups as morally degenerate and less civilised, and in need of their reforming care. In their philanthropic and educational work, women such as Hannah Kilham drew on a range of languages which differentiated themselves from those on the receiving end of their mission. Such a process was central not only to the empowerment of white, middle-class women, but was a crucial component of the languages of class and colonialism through which the emerging middle class asserted its difference from and superiority over the working class in Britain and colonised peoples overseas.

This essay is primarily concerned with the exploration of issues of empowerment and subordination in the writing of Hannah Kilham. I begin by focusing on her inter-denominational moves between the Wesleyan Methodists, the Methodist New Connexion and the Society of Friends between 1794 and 1803, exploring the significance of evangelical belief and practice, particularly the traditions of spiritual equality and the inner light, for women's empowerment. Second, I discuss Kilham's philanthropic and missionary work with poor women in Sheffield, Ireland and West Africa between 1803 and 1832.

It is my argument that notions of domesticity and femininity were central to the tension in missionary practice between the evangelical emphasis on spiritual equality, which enabled women to become active as lay people and preachers, and a wider Christian imperialist impulse which involved the subordination of other social groups. In focusing on their missionary work on domestic reform, a practice described by Eileen Yeo as 'order[ing] the poor and their dwellings into families and homes',[9] middle-class women were able both to reinforce and to subvert the dominant discourse of domestic femininity, with the effect of distancing themselves from the women on the receiving end of their mission. Hannah Kilham, writing at a formative moment in the construction of British class and national identities, can be seen to be making an intervention in the process through which new meanings of gender, class, 'race' and ethnicity were produced and disseminated, contributing to the construction of a new world view which placed the British middle class – and British womanhood – at its centre.

## Hannah Kilham's 'religion of the heart'

Hannah Kilham, or Spurr as she was then, experienced her conversion to Methodism in December 1794, at the height of the revival which had been sweeping through the manufacturing towns of the north of England since 1793.[10] Although she had been brought up in the Church of England, Kilham had begun attending Methodist services on her return to Sheffield in 1790 from Chesterfield, where she had attended boarding school following the deaths of her parents. Living with her elder sister, Hannah became increasingly critical of the fashion- and status-conscious circles of the emerging middle classes in which the family increasingly moved, and found the seriousness of Methodist culture appealing.[11] For her, conversion, the experience of 'pouring out her full heart before God' was intensely joyful, involving not only a personal transformation but participation in the band-meeting and wider aspects of Methodist communal life.[12]

While the Methodist community evidently fulfilled many of her needs for both communal and spiritual fulfilment, Kilham was to leave the Society in 1797 to join the New Connexion, one of the major secessions from the Methodist Society and which centred on Sheffield and Leeds. Led by Alexander Kilham, members of the new faction had dissented on issues of democracy and organisation and were known as the 'Tom Paine Methodists' because of their connections with radical political activity.[13] Hannah Kilham attended one of Alexander's services in Sheffield in August 1797 and, following a short period of indecision, decided that her sympathies lay with the Kilhamites. She joined the Society, and married Alexander Kilham in 1798. The couple moved to Nottingham, where Hannah threw herself into a new life as the wife of a prominent and persecuted religious leader.[14]

Hannah Kilham's decision to join the New Connexion and her later move between 1801 and 1803, whereby she became a member of the Society of Friends, can be interpreted as motivated by her personal suffering. Mora Dickson has argued that Hannah identified with Alexander Kilham, seeing in his suffering and his rebellion both a validation of her own feelings and a means of escape from the confinement she was experiencing. Her decision to join them, Dickson argues, was motivated by an 'inward rebellion', stemming from 'the nature of her own temperament and upbringing, and the frustration of thwarted intelligence' rather than a pursuit of the radical, democratic ideals, the 'stirring in the nation', which was dividing the Methodist Connexion.[15] 'Who are these poor Kilhamites', she wrote, 'so despised by some and pitied by others?'[16]

Similarly, Kilham's initial acquaintance with the Society of Friends had emerged out of personal turmoil. After only eight months of marriage, Hannah had been widowed, left with a step-daughter to care for and pregnant with another child. While visiting her in-laws at Epworth at midsummer 1800, she had been overcome with painful memories of her husband and attended the Epworth Meeting in the hope of finding some consolation. Within months she had decided to leave the Methodists and two years later, shortly after the death from smallpox of her two-year-old daughter, Mary, she applied to join the Quaker meeting at Balby, near Doncaster. Her religious feeling, therefore, can be located in a tradition of female identification with the suffering of Christ;[17] a response to her needs for community, companionship and reassurance at times of great uncertainty and personal loss, and which addressed profound and very private sorrows. 'Oh!, that whatever is of myself may be destroyed', she wrote after Mary's death, 'and let my dispositions, my pursuits and even my sorrows, be cast behind, and let God live in me'.[18]

While it is important not to lose a sense of the personal and spiritual motivations for religious belonging, there are other levels at which Hannah Kilham's shifts between denominations can be interpreted. Making a religious commitment involved not only the potential isolation of putting oneself outside of mainstream society, but also inclusion in a community in which women were accorded considerable worth and personal autonomy. As Davidoff and Hall have shown, alongside the insistence on women's social subordination was a commitment to spiritual equality which enabled the extension of their roles as wives and mothers, to become involved in charitable work, teaching and, in many cases, preaching.[19] This included not only women who *were* wives and mothers, but single women and widows, who were accorded an active role in the community through the notion of social motherhood.[20] Indeed, in her writing Kilham does not explicitly acknowledge the contested nature of women's public role. Operating within the Quaker tradition in which all believers, receiving God's message in their own hearts, were accorded the power to speak, preach and, indeed, to protest, Kilham, her inner light representing a direct connection with God, assumes her right to exempt herself from the need to negotiate nineteenth-century notions of feminine propriety.[21]

The centrality of the notion of spiritual equality, of the belief that truth resides in her own heart, is evident from the beginning of Hannah Kilham's religious 'career'. Her discussion of the secession of the New Connexion in 1797 focused on her belief that the dissenters (just as she) should be allowed to follow their own hearts. She wrote:

> I have this day a great spirit of enquiry. I want to see things as they are. I want to be informed, when good men disagree in their judgement, how we may know who is in the right. It appears to me that the original justice of a cause cannot depend on the multitude of its adherents, nor on the stability of those who profess themselves followers. Truth comes from God ... Truth depends not on any man's receiving or rejecting it. If Mr Kilham's friends have truth on their side, they will prosper though all men forsake them. With these views I went this evening to their chapel.[22]

While never empathising explicitly with the radicalism of the 'Tom Paine Methodists' Hannah, resisting the pressure placed upon her not to attend Alexander Kilham's service, expressed sympathy with their anti-authoritarian and democratic beliefs.

Such faith in her right to follow her own heart is also in evidence in her differences with the New Connexion, articulated initially in terms of conflict with her husband. In 1797, for example, their correspondence reveals an exchange concerning the training of teachers at the newly established New Connexion Sunday school. After a number of confrontations Hannah, herself a teacher at the school, stood firm: 'You may think me obstinate and foolish', she wrote,

> but I am not yet satisfied respecting the regulations about the teachers for our new Sunday School ... As yet there is no barrier fixed to prevent the most improper persons from engaging as teachers; – no attention is taken either of their abilities or their piety.[23]

Her worry that some of the teachers may be 'the most improper persons', merely conforming outwardly while their 'hearts are yet carnal', was not shared by her husband; for Alexander, the fact of their involvement in the New Connexion was enough to qualify them for the task of teaching. Representing herself as an instrument of God's will, Hannah Kilham is willing to defer to no one but Him.

At the heart of the dispute between Hannah and her husband was her concern that the Methodist Church was not sufficiently attentive to the quality of religious feeling and understanding among its flock. Her emphasis on feelings was to become an increasingly prominent theme in her writing and central to her decision to leave the New Connexion in 1801. Preparing her letter of dissent to Hockley Chapel, Nottingham, Kilham expressed her dissatisfaction with the 'inconsistencies' in Methodist worship. 'I now became painfully sensible', she wrote,

> of a want of spirituality, and indeed of truth, in much of the worship in which I had been accustomed to join. I was pained excessively to observe that the preaching of some seemed only calculated to please, without reaching the heart, or leading to a true reformation in the life; and, in general, I felt persuaded that the custom of filling up a certain time in outward worship, – preaching, singing, and prayer, – was contrary to the real nature of sincerity, of true worship, and of effectual teaching.[24]

Far from being a betrayal of her husband, she represented her decision to leave the New Connexion as proof that she had profited from his insistence on the rightfulness of adhering to one's own conscience. 'I cannot abide in a way of worship', she wrote, 'which I believe to be in some things inconsistent with the will of God'.[25]

This concern with Methodism's focus on the outward forms of worship was a common feature of criticism by the Old Dissent. For Kilham, true faith increasingly came to mean an inward transformation, a change of heart alongside religious practice. The belief behind her husband's exhortation, in response to her depression some years earlier, to 'live by our faith and not by our feelings (as the weather ... may alter our feelings, but God is unchangeable', was as unacceptable to Hannah in 1801 as it had been then.[26] The Methodist ministry, with its concerns about numbers of conversions and ritualised worship, was experienced by her as obstructing the process of feeling. In emphasising the 'inner light' the Society of Friends gave expression to her belief that God was about more than just the Scriptures: 'Is it right', she asked rhetorically, 'to estimate the state of anyone by the loudness with which he says Amen?'. 'There could be no true ministry', she asserted, 'but that which is the effect of the power of Christ in the heart.'[27]

Alongside the image of a grieving and unhappy Hannah Kilham is another, much more powerful (and predominant) image of a woman absolutely assured in her possession of spiritual equality, of her right to stand up to any authority in the process of being true to herself and to God.[28] However, while the notion of spiritual equality, expressed in a language of separate spheres and woman's mission, was central to Hannah Kilham's personal religious identity and active religious life, her relationship to the concept was rather more problematic. Alongside her insistence on following her own feelings is a tendency to query the validity or sincerity of those of others. Despite her later reflections on the importance of the concept of spiritual equality in influencing her decision to join the Methodists,[29] implicit in her decision to leave the New Connexion is the assumption that while all are capable of salvation, it takes more than just the conversion experience to bring about true piety; many people – heathens and Christians alike – still needed to be educated into the values of 'real' religion, to enable them to be truly receptive to God's truth.

### Woman's mission and domestic reform

The missionary impulse was central to the evangelical revival of the late eighteenth century. Alongside the expansion of the Sunday school movement and the emergence of organisations for the improvement of the poor, such as the Society for Bettering the Condition of the Poor and the monitorial system of education in Britain, the 1790s also saw the formation of the national bodies for missions overseas: the Baptist, London and Church Missionary Societies, formed between 1792 and 1799.[30] There was a considerable overlap of personnel in the founders and supporters of the domestic and overseas missions, many of whom were members of the new middle classes. Such societies shared a common origin, moreover, in the desire to marshal the forces of order which characterised the tumultuous decade that followed the French Revolution. Their supporters interpreted the condition of the people on the receiving end of their missionary enterprise in terms of a broad cultural deficit and sought to inculcate religion, morality and habits of frugality, temperance and industry as part of a far-reaching process of domestic and social reform.

## Sheffield's 'haunts of squalor'

In her various roles as layperson, Methodist minister's wife and Quaker preacher, Hannah Kilham was involved in many of the new educational and philanthropic initiatives to emerge in Sheffield in the early years of the nineteenth century. Her involvement in religious education had begun with assisting at the New Connexion Sunday school in Sheffield from 1797 and, after her marriage, at a day school in Nottingham. After the death of her husband in 1798, she was required to take paid employment in order to keep herself, her stepdaughter and her daughter, and in 1802 she returned to Sheffield to teach in a friend's school before opening her own day and boarding school for daughters of well-to-do Quakers. Kilham became a founder member in 1803 of the Sheffield Society for Bettering the Condition of the Poor, and over the next few years became active in the Society for Superseding the Necessity for Climbing Boys (formed in 1807), Sheffield Bible Association and the Society for Visiting and Relieving Aged Females (1810) and the Girls' Lancasterian School (1813).[31] In 1813 she began writing texts intended for the religious instruction of the poor in their homes and at school, publishing *Scripture Selections* in 1813 and *Family Maxims* two years later.[32]

The Sheffield Society for Bettering the Condition of the Poor sought to promote 'the welfare and comfort of the poor, by the encouragement of industry, economy and order' in their domestic lives.[33] To this end, it formed a committee of lady visitors who, dividing the town into manageable districts, attended to poor women in their homes and those in the workhouse and debtor's prison on a weekly or fortnightly basis.

Shaped by evangelical political economy, the Society was principally concerned with what its members understood as the cycle of poverty: with the effects of human weakness and immorality in the exacerbation of poverty, and with the debilitating impact of poverty in preventing the possibility of, or desire for, improvement.[34] The ladies saw their role in promoting independence, 'inducing and seconding the exertions of the poor in their own behalf'.[35] Although provisions such as clothing, bedding, whitewashing material and, at times of particular hardship, food, were all distributed, the aim of the Society was to impart moral instruction rather than material assistance and 'gratuitous relief'. The ladies were to 'remind' the poor of the virtues of 'cleanliness, order, the care of their families and of the disadvantages of running into debt, or dealing with pawnbrokers ...'.[36] They also operated a Thrift Club, encouraging poor women to deposit small instalments of money. In the hope of encouraging responsibility for finances, each depositor was provided with a book for their accounts, and although they could withdraw their money each month, they were encouraged not to do so, but to save in order to purchase goods such as the rugs and blankets which were subsidised by the Society.[37] Such endeavours within the home were to be supported from other vital 'sites' of reform within the community. In her *Report* of 1812 Hannah Kilham emphasised the role of the Society in introducing the poor to the Bible Society, General Infirmary, Lancasterian School and other such institutions which were forming a new network of public missionary bodies.[38]

In their interventions in the domestic affairs of working-class women, the apparent affinity between middle-class women and domestic order and respectability was underlined. At the same time, middle-class ladies were enabled to go into hitherto forbidden territories in the urban environment. Hannah Kilham saw the practice of visiting and distributing tracts as 'an excellent means of ... bringing the general state of poor families into view', exposing the miseries of the poor and thereby beginning the process of remedying social ills.[39] As she wrote of Sheffield in 1818: 'I will not despair of my native town being yet brought fully into view of its benevolent inhabitants, both male and female, and the residents of every street and lane and court made known to disinterested committees of both sexes.'[40] Her use of optical imagery is interesting: only through seeing, exposing and knowing could the houses of the poor be improved.

The acquisition of knowledge about the domestic situations of the poor had its class dimension. Kilham wrote:

> The first step towards bettering the condition of the poor is to know what that state really is, and this by persons who have judgement and feeling to improve their condition, and have the power to be instruments to its improvement. The state of the poor will be best known by seeing them in their own houses, and hearing from themselves the affecting detail of their sufferings and privations.[41]

The process of 'hearing from themselves', allowing the poor a degree of self-representation, is in tension with the educative, leading role accorded to middle-class visitors; it is the ladies who have both the necessary 'judgement and feeling' with which to see and properly interpret, and the moral authority to introduce 'order and harmony into dwellings':[42]

> Oh! that we might, by affectionate conversations with them, and by lending them books in which are examples of piety, and the counsels of the pious, be happily instrumental in leading them to a State, in which the prospect of a happy futurity, and the consciousness of heavenly favour, could make even the wilderness to bloom and become beautiful, and the lowliest habitations to be cheered and enlivened by the beams of an unfading sun.[43]

Despite the criticism she incurred, Hannah Kilham enlisted girls from her school on her visiting 'errands'. In her autobiography, Mary Howitt recalled one of a number of occasions when, as a twelve-year-old pupil at this 'Friend's School of high repute', she waited in a 'desolate' area of 'broken-up ground and half-built ruinous houses' while her teacher visited a 'haunt of squalor'.[44]

Although domestic reform was to be delivered through the medium of lady visitors, working-class women were not seen as passive receptacles in the process. Hannah Kilham envisaged the home as active and productive, seeing 'useful and sufficiently productive employment, especially for single females' as 'the first step to civilization'.[45] This emphasis on domesticity and independence was reflected in Kilham's *Family Maxims*, a small book consisting of a number of short tracts devoted to themes such as 'self-discipline', 'honesty', 'forbearance', 'watchfulness', 'neglect' and 'happiness' and which were designed to be displayed in the homes of the poor. Exhortations to hard work and respectability – such as: 'Retire early to rest, and be "early to rise". Industry promotes health, order and happiness'; 'Use every endeavour to make home a scene of happiness and satisfaction, that all may return to it with willingness and pleasure'; and 'Wholesome food, decent clothing, and a decent dwelling are all to be desired if we value health and comfort; but these may all be spoiled and lost by idleness and neglect' – were intended to awaken religious feeling and serve as reminders to the poor that they were responsible for their own well-being and improvement.[46]

Ireland's 'wretched cabins'

These same concerns characterised Kilham's work in Ireland, where she travelled in 1822–23 as a member of the British and Irish Ladies' Society, the women's section of the London Committee which comprised a number of high-standing gentlemen who were organising relief in response to distress in Ireland. As its full title suggests, the *British and Irish Ladies' Society for improving the condition and promoting the industry and welfare of the female peasantry in Ireland* was particularly concerned with the domestic reform of Irish women. Adopting the system employed by Bettering Societies in England, the Society aimed

> to visit the dwellings of the poor, to obtain a knowledge of their situation, under certain heads. To aid the sick by the loan of linen, obtaining medical advice, etc. To encourage industry, and attention to domestic duty; to encourage parents to send their children to school; to assist the poor in any other way that their circumstances may appear to require.[47]

The 'other ways' included distributing spinning wheels, nets for fishery, flax, wool and flannel to women and children; establishing shops and a Repository in London for which women would produce their goods and then buy them back at a subsidised rate; supplying lime to enable women to whitewash their homes; and 'supplying means for distributing presents among such as may distinguish themselves by clean, orderly and decent appearance of their children'.[48] Women were to be sent from England to work alongside the ladies of the Ascendancy in this process.

In providing 'useful employment' for women, the Society aimed not only to procure Ireland's material improvement but also to stimulate 'a moral reaction', a general desire for improvement among the people. Drawing on evangelical notions of the home as the site of (im)morality, the Society looked to the 'wretched cabin' as the locus of Ireland's ills: the 'apathy and listlessness', 'despondency, dependence and idleness' which were believed to characterise the 'indolent' Irish peasant could all be 'traced back to the miserable habits in the midst of which he is born and bred'.[49] Even drunkenness, Hannah Kilham confirmed, was the product of domestic failure, the result of 'their wretched condition at home'.[50] Supplying Irish women with the means to improve their livelihood would both enable them to produce clothing and articles 'requisite for their health and comfort' and inculcate a spirit of industry and moral independency.[51]

This was to be a *domestic* revolution in Ireland. 'By the influence of the Ladies over the female peasantry in their respective districts', stated the *First Report*,

> they hope that not only ideas of comfort and cleanliness, hitherto little known, may be introduced, and industry excited by the prospect of a due remuneration; but that likewise benefits of a higher nature may be conferred, by the improvement of moral principle and the repression of mean, degrading and vicious habits; and though the reformation may be gradual, the immediate change not strikingly apparent, yet every real advancement in the moral feeling, on the part of the future mothers of the families of Ireland, is calculated to have the most extensive and desirable effects on the habits of the rising generation.[52]

Contesting the increasingly popular belief among the English that Irish people were naturally 'lazy, bigoted and ungrateful', the British and Irish Ladies' Society claimed that through the inculcation of values of 'virtue and piety' and 'habits of industry, cleanliness and an attention to domestic duty', Ireland could be transformed.[53]

Such ideas are central to Kilham's *Thoughts for the House*, written in 1824.[54] The *Thoughts* consist of four sheets, each illustrated and decorated with a fancy border and intended, as *Family Maxims*, to be displayed in the homes of the poor. The illustrations depict peasant families engaged in useful employment, such as spinning, knitting, and bonnet- and basket-making, in clean, sparse and well-aired homes. Focusing on themes such as 'industry', 'discipline', 'debt' and 'honesty', the *Thoughts* exhort women to send their children to school and to concentrate on making a good home. 'It is by doing useful things', urges one, 'a little and a little, that a man will in time make a barren spot beautiful, and a woman make her house tidy, clean, snug and pleasant.' 'When the mother of a family is conscientious, kind, cheerful, neat, orderly, and diligent', proclaimed another, 'she will be doing good to the whole house – every day'. Such sentiments were echoed in the reports of the British and Irish Ladies' Society: 'Whatever tends to create industry and civilization among the females', declared the *First Report*, 'will be found to influence the whole family.'[55]

Ireland's 'future mothers' were to receive further training in domestic skills and 'moral feeling' in newly established schools. In 1827, the British and Irish Ladies' Society set up a Model Infant School in Longford, with the intention that its focus on the education of peasant children in domestic and manual skills and, in true Lancasterian fashion, training of young women teachers, should be replicated elsewhere. As outlined in *An Address to the School Mistress of the Longford Infant School*, both sexes were to learn skills in knitting, plaiting and basket-making; the boys were also to garden, while girls hemmed and sewed and stayed behind after lessons to clean up.[56] This focus on practical skills was to be supplemented by shorter periods devoted to religious education, play and instruction in reading and writing. Among the texts the children were to be taught from were Hannah Kilham's *Scripture Selections* and *First Principles of the Christian Religion*.[57] It was, however, considered inappropriate to place too great an emphasis on intellectual knowledge: 'The Committee', stated the author of the *Report*, 'think it more likely to be hurtful than useful to children who are to labour for their bread.'[58] As skilled and virtuous labourers and domestic workers, Ireland's children were to be instruments of national regeneration.

The *Reports* of the British and Irish Ladies' Society abound with 'success stories', joyful accounts of the 'wretched and disconsolate' becoming 'cheerful smiling faces'; women who had become more clean and self-respecting; who would now willingly walk miles to each other's houses in order to spin; women whose motivation enabled them to work all night long.[59] 'A spirit of industry has been excited', proclaimed a contribution from Waterford, 'and the generality of our poor women seem as if awakening from a long dream of depression, indolence and wretchedness.'[60] An account from Carlow emphasised the impact of employment:

> Visitors appointed from time to time to inspect their cabins uniformly reported that they were filthy, where the inmates were idle, but clean and comfortable where they were employed; so true is it, that cleanliness and industry go hand in hand.[61]

Hannah Kilham endorsed such accounts. 'I am informed that in the city of Cork', she wrote in her journal, 'there is already an evident effect from the visits of the ladies, in the poor being stimulated to cleanliness.'[62] 'It was cheering', she wrote following a day's visiting with the Countess of Clare, 'to see the industry, cleanliness and comfort that could be found in a cabin ...'[63]

The relationship between the missionary and recipient is, however, much more complex than the above interpretation allows. As is illustrated by the following story, the women on the receiving end of the ladies' mission often used their charity to quite different ends. In a typical and enthusiastic account of the personal transformation of a woman whose cabin, on their initial visit, was 'dyed with smoke, and hung with spider's webs ... [and] the colour of the floor had evidently not been seen for a long time past', two visitors from Limerick discussed her response to their offers of assistance. Their suggestion that they could provide the necessary lime for whitewashing was received 'languidly', the woman occupant stating that she would prefer to be given the price of the lime, with which she would buy potatoes. However, when the ladies offered to lend her a spinning wheel, 'her countenance brightened up in a moment, and she earnestly replied "Ah! If you'll lend me a wheel, *and let me spin*, I'll whitewash and do anything you please!"'. She promptly applied to the Board of Health for white-washing materials, expressing her desire that her home should be clean before they called again.[64] This is suggestive of a more complex system of exchange. While some aspects of the middle-class civilising mission were seen as beneficial to them, Irish women did not accept the ladies' interpretation of their lives. For them, a spinning wheel meant employment, money, food, a degree of independence, and not moral regeneration.

Such apparent 'improvement' nevertheless delighted the ladies who, it seems, were also feeling the benefit of their engagement in visiting work. Writing from Dublin, Hannah Kilham emphasised the positive effect on the 'young ladies of Portarlington', hitherto 'accustomed only to the ample abodes of their relatives and friends', who were shocked to discover people living 'in a state so wretched – worse fed and lodged than their own dogs and horses'.[65] Such discoveries supported her critique of the indulgent and idle lives of the ladies of the aristocracy and middle classes.

Kilham's emphasis on the importance of women's roles as visitors can be seen as a way of legitimising women's involvement in such activities. The work of the British and Irish Ladies' Society in Ireland began with visiting dwellings, collecting information concerning family size, the details of women's (un)employment and children's schooling. Writing from Limerick in January 1823, again drawing on optical imagery, Kilham emphasised the need, having seen, to act:

> It is impossible to convey by any description the just idea of the wretchedness that exists among the people in the old parts of this city. It can only be known by going into their dwellings, and seeing it with our own eyes; and having seen and felt with the sufferers, I could not, without violating the claims of humanity, and the sacred sense of individual duty, forbear attempting in some degree to convey the feeling.[66]

Feeling from the heart thus justified women's extended sphere of missionary activity.

'Seeing', however, always occurred through the eyes of the ladies who, in Ireland, were not merely of another class but, in the case of Kilham and others, were English and Protestant. The ladies saw Ireland's 'dwellings' as characterised by a particular wretchedness, a depravity of a scale unknown in England. Contrasted with English 'civilised life', they were taken as indicators of a lower level of civilisation. 'I do not conceive it possible', Kilham wrote in her journal,

> for any language or picture of destitution to have conveyed to any mind the impressions received from the *actual sight* of the peasantry, as they at present exist. The wretched cabin built by the hard-strained efforts of extreme poverty, is destitute of almost everything that could mark any attainment of civilized life.[67]

The attempt to impose domestic femininity shaped by Protestant evangelicalism has, in the context of the colonial relationship, another dimension. The image of the Irish as indolent, passive, undomesticated and lazy can been seen as intimately connected to their being both Catholic and colonised.[68] Likewise, the qualities of moral independency, industry and virtue are central not only to Protestant Britain, but to its identity as coloniser.

### West African 'huts' and 'hovels'

During the early 1820s, Hannah Kilham was preoccupied with persuading the Friends to allow her to travel to West Africa. In this she was confronted with two considerable obstacles. First, the Quakers were traditionally hostile to missionary work. For them, the emphasis on the written text of the Bible was at odds with the notions of the inner light and the divine ministry, which were believed to give all peoples access to God without the interventions of a missionary intermediary. Kilham addressed this issue in her *Address to Friends, on a Proposal made by a Member of our Society to Instruct some African Negroes,* put to the Committee for African Instruction in February 1820. Offering the assurance that she accepted the 'sound and charitable principle ... that the heathen to whom the outer knowledge of the gospel has not reached, do not necessarily perish for the want of it', she argued that the slave trade had itself produced obstacles, a 'mental darkness', which prevented Africans from seeing their inner light.[69]

Second, although women's role both in the domestic mission and as supporters of the local auxiliary branches of the overseas societies was well established by the 1820s, it continued to be much more difficult for women to be directly involved in missions overseas. While the practice of employing missionary couples instead of single men was gradually gaining favour during this period, prompted not only by the perceived value of women's skills in the domestic education of other women but, as suggested by numerous articles in the *Missionary Register*, a need to check the sexual behaviour of male missionaries, the African mission field continued to be deemed an unsuitable place for a single white woman.[70] During 1821 the Friends decided to support William Singleton, a Quaker schoolteacher from Sheffield, in his plans to travel to the Gambia, and Hannah Kilham focused her attentions on the Christian education of two West African men, Sandanee and Mahmadee, whom she had met in London and who were teaching her the languages of Wolof and Mandingo. It was not until Singleton's return with assurances that permission had been granted by West African leaders that Kilham received the support to form her own missionary party.[71]

On her arrival in the Gambia in December 1823, domestic education remained at the top of Kilham's agenda for reform. While she confessed in a number of places in her journal that she did not know as much as she would have liked to about domestic situations in West Africa – 'as they were out at the door, there was little occasion to enter the huts, but I went in one or two'[72] – she was much encouraged by the successes of the missionary wives in teaching African girls to be 'clever cooks, house-maids and laundresses'.[73] Kilham saw the employment of African servants in missionary homes as a particularly valuable way of exerting influence and, while leading to a few anxious comparisons with the skills of British servants, she believed that the experience of working in a lady's house might in time lead the 'African FEMALE to regard with desire and admiration' the 'decency, quietness, cleanliness' and 'domestic order' of Christian family life.[74] An interesting choice of language, the use of the word 'female' is suggestive of African women's position in her hierarchy of ladies, women and females.

The main strategy for 'improvement' in West Africa was through the education of children and young men and women. Kilham insisted that the 'British' (monitorial) system of reading, writing and learning from the Scriptures should be accompanied by practical skills for 'useful employment'. On their arrival in Bathurst, Kilham and her companion Ann Thompson, a Quaker from Cooladine, Ireland, established schools for 'King's Boys' and girls, children 'liberated' from slave traders still operating on the West African coast, while Richard Smith and John Thompson, the men in their party, began agricultural work with African males. 'The girls', she wrote, 'should be taught from books the theory of domestic business, and in turns the practice of it. The boys should be taught agriculture and mechanics.'[75] Although the school was intended for girls only, some young married women also attended, only to be sent away again because of their having small children with them. Unable to ignore such an opportunity, however, Hannah Kilham supplied them all with 'presents' of work-bags, such that they might 'manage their needlework at home'.[76] During her subsequent trips to Sierra Leone in 1827–28 and 1830–32 Kilham co-operated with Wesleyan and Anglican missionaries in the establishment of a system of schooling, opening her own school for girls in the 'free village' of Charlotte in 1830.

Of fundamental importance in shaping missionary work in West Africa was the issue of language difference. Hannah Kilham was critical of current educational practice in West Africa whereby children were presented with English texts without any translation, and argued that learning a few 'leading words' in their own language was the first step to understanding the Scriptures. Her language books, *First Lessons in Jaloof* (1820) and *African Lessons* (1823), compiled as a result of her work with Sandanee and

Mahmadee, reflected her emphasis on mother-tongue teaching. Written in three parts, *African Lessons* consists of vocabulary – of objects, food, parts of the body, etc., finishing with 'heaven' and, in capitals, 'ALLA, The Supreme being, God' – in both English and a phonetic translation in Wolof.[77] The second section, entitled 'family advices', is a repeat of many of the tracts included in *Family Maxims*, published for use by the poor in Britain five years earlier, illustrating the centrality of domestic ideology both to her interpretation of the Scriptures and to her vision of what Africa might become. This, as the third section, questions-and-answers on the Scriptures very similar in format to *Scripture Selections*, indicates her belief that such 'truths' had universal meaning.

Hannah Kilham's vision was that the process of Christianisation begun by the British should be taken over by Africans themselves. Educated at mission schools, they would 'promote by friendly Christian communication, the instruction, the civilisation, and the evangelising of the people of this continent'.[78] Crucially, however, this would initially require British supervision. It was well known, Kilham maintained in her *Report* of 1828, that schools employing unsupervised Africans were of notoriously low quality, and while it was her desire that her own school at Charlotte should, on her departure, be left 'under coloured teachers, who could permanently take the charge', she felt it necessary to arrange for frequent visits by 'a small committee from Free Town, leaving the way for a European, should one be disposed to take the charge'. Indeed, following her death in 1832, various girls' schools in Sierra Leone's 'free villages' were sponsored by the Peckham Ladies' Anti-Slavery Association.[79]

Kilham drew on a language of family to articulate the relationship between Great Britain and West Africa. Acknowledging that Sierra Leone was not exhibiting 'all those encouraging marks of advancement, either in civil or religious knowledge, which have been anxiously desired', she argued that both African nations and their people were 'in a state of infancy',[80] children in need of care, guidance and control. Writing on her return from Sierra Leone in 1828, she proclaimed:

> Our great duty towards Africa is to strengthen the hands of the people *to promote each other's good* ... It is the Africans themselves that must be the travellers and instructors of Africa. Let Europeans

aid them with Christian kindness, as senior brothers would the younger and feebler members of their father's family.[81]

Interestingly, while Kilham here draws on images of masculinity, of brothers and fathers, it was women who were envisaged to have a crucial role in this supervisory process. Indeed, British women had much at stake in the debate concerning Africa's capacity for improvement: to argue that Africa was at an early stage in its development and required European assistance and guidance provided a possible opening for their involvement in missionary activity, which would not be required were Africa to be left alone.

For Kilham, women and domestic reform were central to successful missionary practice. Her assessment of the prevalence of sickness and disorder in Sierra Leone was informed by a belief in the importance of domestic management. 'This lack', she wrote,

> arose from the state of a comparatively new settlement, where in many families there is no female superintendent, no good cook or house-servant, nor anyone to take a general oversight of domestic concerns, so that health is badly supported, and the sick generally neglected as to diet and judicious, attentive nursing.[82]

When in 1830 she made an unsuccessful attempt to revive her earlier plan to bring students to England to be educated and to assist in the process of transcribing West African languages, her initial proposal for twenty-four 'well-chosen' young men who were to be housed near London under the supervision of a master, housekeeper and servant, was revised a few months later to involve 12–13-year-old girls. Under her care, they would be taught reading, writing, scripture and domestic skills and so 'contribute to the advancement of the Female character on the coast of Africa'.[83] In her vision for Africa, Kilham constructed a kind of global monitorial system, with Britain – and British womanhood – placed at its command.

Domestic reform – the creation of 'homes' for all – was thus represented as crucial to global improvement. There is in Kilham's writing a constant cross-referencing between domestic situations in England, Ireland and West Africa. In the Gambia in 1824, she compared African 'huts', 'so close, and dirty and comfortless – so unlike what we could desire to see as human habitations',[84] with 'cabins' in Ireland, concluding that 'degraded as are the poor peasantry of Ireland, they are in some respects much better prepared for improvement than the Jolas are'.[85] 'I long to see the people here put in the way of forming better dwellings', Kilham wrote, '... many of the *poorer* Irish cabins I have seen are like little palaces in comparison with some of these African huts.'[86] This description of Irish homes has little bearing on her experience of them; rather it serves to emphasise Africa's uncivilised state. Notions of home and domesticity thus became a means of establishing a hierarchy of civilisation; while the British middle class lived in 'homes', the Irish lived in 'dwellings' and 'cabins', the Africans in 'dwellings' and 'huts'. Through the notion of the overseas domestic mission, women could construct for themselves a kind of maternal supervisory role in Africa, their ability to transform 'huts' into 'homes' represented as crucial to the evangelising of the 'dark continent'.

## Conclusion

Denise Riley has argued that middle-class women's representation of missionary work as both public and feminine both enabled and was facilitated by the increased association of the category 'woman' with the newly constructed concept of 'the social' in the early nineteenth century. 'This new production of "the social"', writes Riley, 'offered a magnificent occasion for the rehabilitation of "women". In its very founding conceptions, it was feminised.' Such an association, however, required the designation of certain social groups as in need of such rehabilitation. As Riley continues, 'in its detail, it provided the chances for some women to enter upon the work of restoring other, more damaged, women to a newly conceived sphere of grace'.[87] Adapting resources drawn from Christianity, occupying the space afforded women as writers and educators and making use of the growing emphasis on domesticity, the legitimation of the public presence of the white, middle-class woman also rested upon the differentiation of herself from those on the receiving end of her Christian mission.

Hannah Kilham's representations of missionary 'others' are riddled with contradictions. The British working class occupies a complex position in her writing, providing hope and consolation when the 'darkness and sinfulness of many parts of the world' was too depressing, while appearing at other times to be even more impervious to Christian influence. 'There is much to do in England', she lamented in 1826,

> Let friends in London consider what is due at our hands in the
> diffusion of Christian truth at home and abroad; for surely
> throughout the world we should include our own country as well
> as those more distant. Many sit in heathen darkness even here.[88]

Such misery and absence of religion within Britain and Ireland, 'a
disgrace to a civilised country', led her momentarily to question
the meaning of Britain's claims to civilisation: *'Should* such misery
exist in a country called Christian?', she asked in a letter to her
friend Mary Thompson in 1818.[89]

Kilham's representation of Africa is similarly inconsistent.
Despite her concern that missionaries should 'begin well at home'
before branching out to the heathen overseas, there is a sense in
which Africa offered Kilham a particular excitement which was
more able to sustain her, to ward off feelings of depression at lack
of progress back in England. As Catherine Hall has written, 'the
encounter with the heathen "other"' can be seen as remedying such
anxiety, giving an 'intensity, laced with ambivalence, to the work,
which may have been hard to maintain' (in Britain).[90] Africa, moreover, represented the possibility of creating a new, ordered world,
the 'free villages', organised around the mission school, becoming
centres for the diffusion of Christianity within the continent.[91]

In Hannah Kilham's dream it was white middle-class women
who were to inculcate such order. Through the domestic reform of
the working class at home and the creation of 'homes' in distant
places such women, as missionary wives and also single women
and widows, were to be accorded an active, authoritative and
public role. Describing her attachment to Africa in 1827, Kilham
wrote:

> Much as there is to interest me in England, my heart is strongly
> attached to Africa. Reason may plead that the same objects might
> be pursued here with far less risk of life, but a bond more power-
> ful than mere human reason seems to bind me to labour for a
> season with and among that people.[92]

Echoing her discussions of the nature of her religious commitment,
Kilham affirmed the superiority of the feeling heart over reason.
Experiencing her calling in her heart, she was empowered by the
doctrine of the inner light to transgress the boundaries of both the
female province and established Quaker practice. The newly
conceived 'woman's mission' upon which she embarked drew upon

notions of sympathy, moral influence and domestic reform to construct British working-class, Catholic Irish and West African women as different from herself, and in need of her civilising care. Hannah Kilham's excitement at West Africa's potential for the fulfilment of missionary aspirations can be read as a comment on the wider significance of missions for British middle-class women. As she wrote in *The Claims*: 'What a field does Sierra Leone present!'[93]

## Notes

1 H. Kilham to E. Bickersteth, 6 Jan. 1816, quoted in M. Dickson, *The Powerful Bond* (London, Dennis Dobson, 1980).

2 See P. Curtin, *The Image of Africa: British Ideas and Action, 1780–1850* (London, Macmillan, 1965).

3 See S. Biller (ed.), *Memoir of the Late Hannah Kilham* (London, Darton and Harvey, 1837), p. 3. Sarah Biller, also a Quaker, had travelled to St Petersburg in 1819 where she became involved in the development of Lancasterian schools and later managed a hospital built by Nicholas I. See R. C. Scott, *Quakers in Russia* (London, Michael Joseph, 1964), pp. 92–4.

4 C. Lucas Balfour, *A Sketch of the Life of Hannah Kilham* (London, W. and F. G. Cash, 1854), p. 43.

5 Ormerod Greenwood, writing in 1962, included a footnote to remind his readers both of 'the antipathy there was at that time to the education of *English* girls, and how much still remains to be accomplished for *African* girls'. See O. Greenwood, 'Hannah Kilham's Plan', *The Sierra Leone Bulletin of Religion*, 4:1 (1962), p. 71. Other writers have emphasised Kilham's achievements in the field of linguistics, describing her work as 'a worthy effort in an untracked field', 'rendering important services to the cause of philological science'. See P. E. H. Hair, in Greenwood, 'Hannah Kilham's Plan', p. 73; A. Werner, 'English Contributions to the Study of African Languages', *Journal of the African Society*, 29:117 (Oct. 1930), p. 78. Kilham's most recent biographer, Mora Dickson, represents her as 'a lone voice', challenging unenlightened attitudes both to women in England and to African education. See Dickson, *Powerful Bond*.

6 Biller, *Memoir of Kilham*, p. 458.

7 L. Davidoff and C. Hall, *Family Fortunes: Men and Women of the English Middle Class* (London, Hutchinson, 1987), pp. 114–18.

8 Quoted in E. Yeo, *The Contest for Social Science: Relations and Representations of Gender and Class* (London, Rivers Oram, 1996), p. 9.

9 *Ibid.*, p. 9.

10 Sheffield was an important centre in this revival. Following the pattern already established in other circuits on the West Riding, Methodist 'enthusiasm' had begun in Sheffield in March 1794, reaching its peak in the summer of that year, and sustained well into 1796. See E. R. Wickham, *Church and People in an Industrial City* (London, Lutterworth Press, 1957); J. Baxter, 'The Great Yorkshire Revival 1792–1796: A Study of Mass Revival Among the Methodists', in M. Hill (ed.), *A Sociological Yearbook of Religion* (London, SCM Press, 1974), pp. 46–76.

**11** See Dickson, *Powerful Bond*, p. 37. Hannah Kilham first attended Methodist services as a child when her mother had taken her to Wesley's morning sermons. Although Mr and Mrs Spurr were both Episcopalian, Hannah's mother seems to have had dissenting sympathies.

**12** Biller, *Memoir of Kilham*, p. 4. For women and Methodist communities, see A. Clark, *The Struggle for the Breeches: Gender and the Making of the British Working Class* (London, University of California Press, 1995), pp. 92–118 and D. M. Valenze, *Prophetic Sons and Daughters: Female Preaching and Popular Religion in Industrial England* (Princeton, Princeton University Press, 1985).

**13** After Wesley's death in 1791 his authority was passed on to a Committee, the Legal Hundred. Many within the Connexion were not content with this concentration of power and, increasingly influenced by democratic political theory, pressed for greater popular involvement in the government of the Connexion. From around 1795, the Conference began a clampdown on dissenters. Alexander Kilham, who had been an itinerant preacher since 1785, was tried and expelled in 1796. In 1797 he and his supporters formed the New Connexion. See B. Semmel, *The Methodist Revolution* (London, Heinemann, 1974), pp. 113–24.

**14** Her marriage to Kilham plunged Hannah into a hectic and stressful life. During his frequent absences, on missionary tours of the country, Hannah kept their home together, taught at the Sunday school and took over responsibility for his young daughter from his first marriage, Sarah.

**15** Dickson, *Powerful Bond*, p. 43.

**16** *Ibid.*, p. 20.

**17** J. Rendall, *The Origins of Modern Feminism: Women in Britain, France and the United States, 1780–1860* (Basingstoke, Macmillan, 1985), p. 77.

**18** Quoted in Balfour, *Life of Hannah Kilham*, p. 20.

**19** This was especially the case for Quaker women. See S. Wright, *Friends in York. The Dynamics of Quaker Revival* (Keele, Keele University Press, 1995), chs 3, 4 and 5. For the continuance of gender divisions within the Society of Friends, see Davidoff and Hall, *Family Fortunes*, pp. 139–40. For Primitive Methodist women preachers, see Valenze, *Prophetic Sons and Daughters*.

**20** Eileen Yeo uses the concept of 'social motherhood' to discuss the protective and punitive practices involved in middle-class women's social work with working-class women in the mid-nineteenth to early twentieth centuries. See E. Janes Yeo, 'Social Motherhood and the Sexual Communion of Labour in British Social Science, 1850–1950', in *Women's History Review*, 1:1 (1992), pp. 63–87, especially pp. 75–82.

**21** For a discussion of the positive impact of Quaker belief and practice on women from the seventeenth century, see P. Mack, 'Gender and Spirituality in Early English Quakerism', in E. Potts-Brown and S. Mosher Stuard (eds), *Witnesses for Change: Quaker Women over Three Centuries* (London, Rutgers University Press, 1989); E. Isichei, *Victorian Quakers* (London, Oxford University Press, 1970) and Wright, *Friends in York*.

**22** Biller, *Memoir of Kilham*, pp. 25–6.

**23** H. Spurr to A. Kilham, Dec. 1797, letter in *ibid.*, pp. 25–6.

**24** Biller, *Memoir of Kilham*, p. 69.

**25** *Ibid.*, p. 84.

26 A. Kilham to H. Spurr, Nov. 1797, letter in *ibid.*, p. 30.
27 Biller, *Memoir of Kilham*, pp. 77–8.
28 Clara Lucas Balfour represents Kilham as operating within a Christian tradition of self-sacrifice and martyrdom. She is, to Balfour, 'a lonely woman, without wealth, station or family influence … a lovely instance of what piety, devotedness and self-renunciation can effect'. While this was one tradition on offer to women in the early nineteenth century, it does not seem to me to accurately represent Kilham. See Balfour, *Life of Hannah Kilham*, p. 8.
29 Biller, *Memoir of Kilham*, p. 40.
30 See E. Stock, *The History of the Church Missionary Society*, vol. 1 (London, CMS, 1899); R. Lovett, *The History of the London Missionary Society 1795–1895*, vol. 1 (London, Henry Frowde, 1899). For Methodism see R. Davies and G. Rupp, *A History of the Methodist Church in Great Britain* (London, Epworth Press, 1983).
31 As Frank Prochaska has demonstrated, women gave considerable support both to overseas societies and to those organisations in Britain which were specifically concerned with the religious, domestic and moral reform of other women, with pregnancies, children's welfare and education and with the education of female servants and the support of elderly widows. See F. Prochaska, *Women and Philanthropy in Nineteenth Century England* (Oxford, Clarendon Press, 1980).
32 H. Kilham, *Scripture Selections* (Sheffield, W. Todd, 1813); *Family Maxims* (Sheffield, Bentham and Ray, [1815] 1818).
33 H. Kilham, *Extract from an Account of the Sheffield Society for Bettering the Condition of the Poor* (Sheffield, James Montgomery, 1812).
34 For evangelical political economy, see: B. Hilton, *The Age of Atonement: The Influence of Evangelicalism on Social and Economic Thought, 1795–1865* (Oxford, Clarendon Press, 1988); M. Dean, *The Constitution of Poverty: Toward a Genealogy of Liberal Governance* (London, Routledge, 1991). For the role of the Bettering Society in social science and scientific philanthropy, see E. Yeo, *Contest for Social Science*, pp. 4–15.
35 Kilham, *Extract*, p. 204.
36 *Ibid.*, p. 210.
37 See *Reports of the Sheffield Society for Bettering the Condition of the Poor* (Sheffield, James Montgomery, 1812, 1813, 1814, 1815, 1816).
38 Kilham, *Extract*, p. 210.
39 Biller, *Memoir of Kilham*, p. 317.
40 H. Kilham to Ann Thompson, 1818, quoted in Balfour, *Life of Hannah Kilham*, p. 21.
41 Biller, *Memoir of Kilham*, p. 114.
42 *Ibid.*, p. 294.
43 *Ibid.*, p. 116.
44 M. Howitt (ed.), *Mary Howitt, An Autobiography*, vol. 1 (London, William Isbister, 1889), p. 86.
45 Biller, *Memoir of Kilham*, p. 294.
46 Kilham, *Family Maxims*.
47 Biller, *Memoir of Kilham*, p. 143.
48 British and Irish Ladies' Society, *First Report* (1823), p. 8.

**49** *Ibid.*, p. 37.

**50** Biller, *Memoir of Kilham*, p. 145.

**51** British and Irish Ladies' Society, *First Report*, p. 26.

**52** *Ibid.*, pp. 39–40.

**53** Biller, *Memoir of Kilham*, p. 147. For English representations of the Irish, see D. Cairns and S. Richards, *Writing Ireland: Colonialism, Nationalism and Culture* (Manchester, Manchester University Press, 1989).

**54** H. Kilham, 'Thoughts for the House', reprinted in the British and Irish Ladies' Society, *Fourth Report* (1826).

**55** British and Irish Ladies' Society, *First Report*, p. 26.

**56** British and Irish Ladies' Society, *Fifth Report* (1827), appendix.

**57** It is interesting to note that Kilham considered these so easily transferable to Ireland, despite differences in language and religion.

**58** British and Irish Ladies' Society, *Fifth Report*, p. 53.

**59** British and Irish Ladies' Society, *Second Report* (1824), p. 28.

**60** *Ibid.*

**61** British and Irish Ladies' Society, *Fifth Report*, p. 5.

**62** Biller, *Memoir of Kilham*, p. 148.

**63** *Ibid.*, p. 150.

**64** British and Irish Ladies' Society, *First Report*, p. 48.

**65** Biller, *Memoir of Kilham*, pp. 153–4.

**66** *Ibid.*, p. 149.

**67** *Ibid.*, p. 163.

**68** See Cairns and Richards, *Writing Ireland*.

**69** H. Kilham, *Address to Friends, on a Proposal made by a Member of our Society to Instruct some African Negroes, with a view to the future translation of the Scriptures, or some portions of them, in the languages of Africa* (London, Committee for African Instruction, 1820).

**70** As Patricia Grimshaw has shown, marriage to a missionary (often hastily arranged days before sailing) was a woman's passport to becoming a missionary herself, and was an option actively sought by many. See P. Grimshaw, *Paths of Duty: American Missionary Wives in Nineteenth-Century Hawaii* (Honolulu, University of Hawaii Press, 1989).

**71** See *Report of the Committee managing a Fund Raised by some Friends, for the purpose of promoting African Instruction: with an account of a visit to the Gambia and Sierra Leone* (London, Darton and Harvey, 1822).

**72** Biller, *Memoir of Kilham*, p. 190; see also p. 417.

**73** *Missionary Register*, July 1824, p. 299.

**74** *Ibid.*, Sept. 1824, pp. 394–5.

**75** *Ibid.*, June 1824, p. 224.

**76** *Ibid.*, July 1824, p. 299.

**77** It is important to note that this area of Africa was part of a sophisticated Muslim empire. Kilham, however, represents Islam in the same terms as she does 'heathenism'; belief in 'Alla' is to be carefully negotiated and ultimately replaced, just as is 'heathen' idolatry.

**78** Biller, *Memoir of Kilham*, p. 215.

**79** H. Kilham, 'Report on a Recent Visit to Sierra Leone, to the Committee for African Instruction, and other Friends concerned in promoting its object', in *Missionary Register*, June 1828, pp. 280–6; Biller, *Memoir of Kilham*, p. 467.

For discussion of the Peckham Ladies, see Clare Midgley, *Women Against Slavery: The British Campaigns* (London, Routledge, 1993), p. 186.

80 Biller, *Memoir of Kilham*, p. 330.
81 H. Kilham, *The Claims of West Africa to Christian Instruction through the Native Languages* (London, Darton and Harvey, 1830), p. 3.
82 Biller, *Memoir of Kilham*, p. 217.
83 H. Kilham to Commitee of Friends on Anti-Slavery Concerns, 12 Apr. 1830; H. Kilham to John Capper, Anti-Slavery Committee, 2 Sept. 1830, in Friends' Library, Friends House, London.
84 Biller, *Memoir of Kilham*, p. 240.
85 *Ibid.*, p. 190.
86 *Ibid.*, p. 183.
87 D. Riley, *Am I that Name? Feminism and the Category of 'Women' in History* (Basingstoke, Macmillan, 1988), p. 48.
88 Biller, *Memoir of Kilham*, pp. 294–5.
89 H. Kilham to M. Thompson, 1818, Friends' Library.
90 C. Hall, *White, Male and Middle Class* (Oxford, Polity Press, 1992), p. 219.
91 Discussing the 'free villages' in the Caribbean in the 1830s, Catherine Hall has argued that they represented ideal societies, 'a dream of a more ordered England': see *ibid.*, p. 243.
92 Biller, *Memoir of Kilham*, pp. 316–17.
93 Kilham, *Claims of West Africa*, p. 7.

# 'The prayer, the passion and the reason' of Eliza Sharples: freethought, women's rights and republicanism, 1832–52

## HELEN ROGERS

Much of our understanding of women's participation in early nineteenth-century radical politics has been derived from the formal addresses composed by female societies that were occasionally printed in the reform press. Few women held prominent positions within political organisations from which they could make public statements about their own opinions and experiences. Even fewer left personal accounts of their involvement in radical politics. Eliza Sharples, who came briefly to prominence in the freethought metropolitan circles of the early 1830s, provides one notable exception. Sharples flamboyantly placed her own experience and that of women at the centre of her unique vision of radical Christianity.

The category of 'experience' has been subjected to much critical analysis in recent studies of nineteenth-century popular radicalism, particularly in view of the 'linguistic turn' and post-structuralist theories of epistemology. Rather than language revealing or concealing a pre-existing reality, or experience, it is argued that all social identities are discursively constructed. Radical rhetoric offered particular ways of ordering a sense of experience.[1] Eliza Sharples attested, likewise, to the power of words to construct knowledge, yet she also believed that political discourses had neglected hitherto the experience and knowledge of women and she set about devising a politics that would speak directly to women. Her own speeches and writings and those of her husband Richard Carlile and her daughter Theophilia Campbell Carlile help us to reconstruct a very personal and particular engagement with radical culture, as well as shedding light on the conditions of and obstacles to women's public politics from the Reform Act of 1832 to Sharples' death in 1852. These sources indicate that political subjectivities were forged out of a number of often contradictory experiences and knowledge and were not developed simply from the formal practices and discourses of radical politics. Sharples' story, and indeed her preoccupation with her own story, alert us to the process by which knowledge, and in particular political knowledge, is both made and unmade.

In the autumn-winter of 1831–32 Eliza Sharples, the 28-year-old daughter of a prosperous counterpane manufacturer from Bolton, underwent a religious conversion from Wesleyan Methodism to freethought and political radicalism. As the new year began, which was to see the passing of the Reform Act, Sharples arrived in London to preach her own mission and launched a campaign to secure the release from gaol of two notorious infidel lecturers. These were the Revd Robert Taylor, imprisoned for blasphemous libel and Richard Carlile, one of the leaders of the 'battle of the press' in the 1820s, sentenced on charges of sedition. Within weeks Sharples had formed a 'moral marriage' with Carlile, and as part of their philosophical and political alliance, became the leading lecturer at his Rotunda theatre. Between February and December 1832 she attained fleeting notoriety as a freethought lecturer and as 'Editress' of her own weekly periodical *The Isis*, the first radical journal published by a woman. Sharples' lectures and journalism promoted the Reform Bill; denounced the Church–state monopoly; delivered her gospel of rational Christianity; and claimed a new role for women in religion and politics.[2]

As 'The Lady of the Rotunda' Eliza Sharples preached to the diverse mix of metropolitan 'infidels', deists, sceptics and atheists, who rejected orthodox readings of Christianity, particularly those of the Established Church. Her audience included a few wealthy benefactors, plebeian radicals, Owenites and co-operators and a number of women. In her first lecture Sharples addressed her male and female listeners separately. To the men she offered herself as a leader: 'Sirs, I shall seek to gather power round me in this establishment; and which of you will not accept me for your general, your leader, your guide?' Her use of the military metaphor is startling here, for women in the early reform movements more often styled themselves as auxiliaries who would inspire and succour their menfolk, rather than as political actors in their own right. While claiming that women had a part to play in the reform movements, Sharples signalled a further challenge to her female audience. Men tyrannised over women, just as bad government tyrannised over its citizens and therefore the struggle for reform demanded the emancipation of women: 'Will you advance, and seek that equality in human society which nature has qualified us for, but which tyranny, the tyranny of our lords and masters, hath suppressed?'[3]

In May 1834 Sharples edited *The Isis* as a folio volume, dedicating the collection 'To the Young Women of England for Generations to come, or until superstition is extinct'. Believing that 'human society' would not improve 'until women participate in an equality of knowledge', she promoted herself as an example to women, urging: 'that, after enquiry, you will participate in publicity; and that by publicity, you may establish equality with men, is both the prayer, the passion, and the reason of THE EDITRESS'.[4] There were few precedents for female public speaking in 1832 and even fewer women who had the audacity to put themselves forward as a leader of men, so theatricality was an important component of Sharples' daring appearance on the public stage.[5] She adopted a number of personae which captured the different aspects of her public duties and her political theology. 'The Editress' underscored the novelty of her task as female editor; 'The Lady of the Rotunda' her respectability as a lecturer. Standing on a floor of white thorn and laurel, dressed in, according to a police informer, a 'showy dress', Sharples spoke as 'Isis', the Egyptian goddess of fertility and wisdom, and as 'Eve', offering through both roles the fruits of her philosophy and her power of prophecy.[6] As 'Liberty' she identified herself with the republican tradition and presented herself as a political leader, while as 'Hypatia', a Greek philosopher raped and murdered by the Romans, Sharples highlighted the personal sacrifice demanded by her mission.

This chapter explores the ways in which Sharples endeavoured to create a politics and theology that combined the pursuit of reason and desire. She attempted to produce new forms of knowledge that would disrupt the Cartesian dualities of mind and body, reason and emotion. Along with some of the other women encountered in this volume Sharples mixed the rhetoric and practice of revivalism with political activism to produce a radical interpretation of 'woman's mission'. Yet Sharples' aspirations to become a leader of men and an example to women were frustrated by her personal connection with Carlile and the resistance of male radicals to claims for female autonomy, while her self-presentation as a 'novelty among women' undermined her call for sisterhood. Her lack of success in mobilising female followers suggests the problems as well as the advantages of making personal experience the basis of political practice and the difficulties faced by women attempting to appropriate the language of political reform in the 1830s and 1840s.

### Eve: conversion and gospel

Sharples' republicanism and freethought were both a subversion and extension of her evangelical upbringing and indeed she articulated her initiation to radical reform as a religious conversion. Confessing to have been 'a slave to Methodism' she explained and legitimised her public prominence by repeated references to her stifling evangelical upbringing. Just as Josephine Butler would be propelled into rescue work by the death of her child, Sharples' religious crisis and political conversion were precipitated by the death of a loving father. Yet she had long been tormented by religious doubts: 'From the first periods of thought in my youth ... I ... felt such difficulties in the abstruseness or absurdity of religious language, that I had the same horror of falling into infidelity as of falling into hell; and often has my prayer been made to the Lord, that he would preserve me from the proneness of my own doubtful thoughts, and snatch me as a brand from the fire.'[7] The failure of prayer to revive her ailing father made Sharples 'almost callous of the idea of a divine Providence'. In her despair she discovered copies of Carlile's journal *The Republican* which he had published mostly from gaol between 1819 and 1825. Paradoxically for a freethinker pledged to combat superstition, she dramatised her political conversion by testifying that *The Republican* revealed 'the ignorance and the errors of my past life told to me as by some magician'.[8] While rejecting the deist and atheist positions outlined in *The Republican*, Sharples was attracted by the journal's emphasis on reason and enquiry which enabled her to make a virtue of religious doubt. Rather than being a failing, doubt provided the spur to knowledge that for Sharples was to be the core element of her rational Christianity.

From its inception the Sharples–Carlile union was conducted as a public and political romance. Carlile heard of Sharples' intended campaign from his newsagent in Bolton who advised him that a

Miss Sharples 'will call and explain her views to you ... they are in the missionary line, and her *debut* will *create* a sensation, as she is a really beautiful girl'.[9] Imprisoned for allegedly inciting agricultural labourers to revolt during the 'Swing Riots' of 1830, Carlile feared losing his influence amongst reformers. In the 1820s he had devised a 'volunteer system' where reformers pledged their individual defiance of press restrictions. His radicalism took an extremely individualistic form and he viewed all 'union' as a form of monopoly and exclusive interest. Consequently he was hostile to the new political unions which in many places had strong associations with the growing trade union and co-operative movements. His opposition to collective principles distanced him from the plebeian radicals who in the 1820s had formed the main constituency of his support.[10]

Carlile's growing political isolation was accompanied by his estrangement from his first wife Jane. In the 1820s Jane had defended her husband's campaign for press freedom, although at her trial for seditious libel in 1821 she pleaded that she had acted out of 'conjugal duty' to her husband and not in her own right. Despite her plea she was convicted and served two years in Dorchester Gaol.[11] After his so-called 'moral divorce' Carlile could no longer rely on such 'conjugal duty' or the support of his first family. The prospect of an attractive girl with missionary ambitions and pledged to his cause must have had much appeal. Such a girl might also pull the crowds like the celebrated freethought lecturer Frances Wright and keep Carlile in the public gaze.[12] He responded immediately to Sharples' invitation pledging as a 'bachelor': 'My unabating zeal to encourage any lady that shall aim at the character of Hypatia and Frances Wright shall wait on every effort made. Such a lady shall be my daughter, my sister, my friend, my companion, my wife, my sweetheart, my everything.'[13]

Sharples and Carlile defended their union as one based on the authority of reason rather than law. Carlile declared: 'Our marriage has been a deliberately reasoned one ... founded not only on personal affection, but a mutual respect for talent, and a passionate love, that arises first and chief above all other considerations from the same principles.'[14] Sharples and Carlile frequently advocated their rational marriage as a blueprint for a new model of marriage, but how far did their 'philosophical partnership' constitute an equal partnership in practice? Fourteen years her senior, Sharples revered Carlile's age and political and intellectual authority.

Positioning herself as his 'disciple', she requested that Carlile become her 'INSTRUCTOR'.[15] Sharples performed the expected duties of a political prisoner's wife, visiting the gaol daily to bring food, discussing business and her forthcoming lectures and consummating the marriage.

The intellectual division of labour in the relationship is unclear. Their daughter believed that 'Carlile outlined all her lectures for her, for it would have been impossible for an inexperienced country girl with the ordinarily narrow education of her time and class to have been able to have pleased a metropolitan audience of reading and thinking men and women.'[16] Carlile certainly directed Sharples' political education and career and participated in the preparation of her discourses. Eliza wrote to him in gaol, 'I want my lecture for this evening to study. When may I expect the one for Sunday?'[17] That Sharples lectured only occasionally after 1832, and often in her husband's place, might suggest that she provided a mouthpiece for Carlile's views. However, Sharples' co-authorship of the lectures is suggested by the closer attention to questions of sexual politics and women's role in radical reform in *The Isis* than in Carlile's other works. Joint authorship is also indicated by Sharples' frequent references to her life history. She was responsible for editing and publishing *The Isis* and brought her own political theology to its pages. *The Isis* is perhaps best seen as the product of an unequal collaboration.

Although Carlile made a significant contribution to *The Isis*, Sharples had in fact initiated their partnership and arrived in London with her own agenda, including the conversion of the two 'infidels' – Taylor and Carlile – to her version of Christianity. In May 1832, Isis proclaimed the success of her 'short ministry' with the 'CONVERSION OF RICHARD CARLILE TO THE CHRISTIAN FAITH, AFTER FOURTEEN YEARS OF OBSTINATE INFIDELITY'. Carlile confessed that having thought for a year that the Scriptures might bear a 'rational interpretation' he had finally been convinced by the Editress's 'First Discourse on the Bible'.[18] With Taylor, Carlile had advocated an allegorical reading of all religions and in 1829 stated that the Christian religion was in no 'way beneficial to mankind; but that it is nothing more than an emanation from the ancient pagan religion'.[19] Sharples offered Carlile a rational interpretation of religion by reconstructing the meaning of Christian practice and aligning it to a radical political practice. Rather than

being a form of idolatry and superstition, true Christianity should
be practised through the pursuit of knowledge. Just as Sharples was
initiated into radical politics through her reading of Carlile's
*Republican*, so Carlile's conversion to Christianity was conducted
through her religious crisis and rebirth.

Sharples' lectures were delivered to a critical audience. Where
many infidels drew on historical forms of biblical criticism or materialist doctrines which questioned the necessity of a Creator,
Sharples argued that the Bible's truth lay in its moral allegory. She
may have been influenced here by the German theologians of the
eighteenth and early nineteenth centuries who argued for the
mystical significance rather than the literal truth of the Bible.[20]
According to Sharples the characters in the Bible represented 'the
personification of principle' rather than real, historical figures.
However, the political struggle narrated in the gospel was not
restricted to a particular historical time and place, but was an
ongoing drama: 'The Gospel, in politics, is essentially a piece of
republicanism; the young Reason, the hero of the Gospel drama,
will not acknowledge the divine right, or any right of kings ...
Young Reason has ever and everywhere been a Radical
Reformer.'[21] Since Jesus was merely a representation of 'Young
Reason', woman as well as man could embody reason and become
a poet, scholar, philosopher or politician.

Sharples' interpretation of the Scriptures as the struggle of
reason against superstition extended previous rationalist criticisms
by analysing the gendered construction of reason in religious texts.
Her argument began with a discussion of the gendered and historically specific language of the Bible. While contemporary reformers
spoke of knowledge and reason in the neuter gender, the ancient
writers, she argued, especially the Hebrews, had 'personified' these
'principles' as masculine or feminine. They had represented in
human form 'all the principles of nature, or every perceptible
quality, so as seldom or never to use the neuter gender'.[22] For
Sharples, the allegorical language of the Bible was ideological and
therefore had to be decoded for a nineteenth-century congregation.
Like recent feminists who trace the gendered etymology of words
and attempt to devise a non-sexist language, Sharples provided a
glossary explaining the universal human characteristics embodied
by biblical men and women.[23]

Deborah Valenze has suggested that sectarian female preachers who were contemporaries of Sharples often invoked the ideal of the 'mother in Israel' to legitimise an extra-familial leadership role for women. They looked especially to four Old Testament mothers, Sarah, Rebecca, Rachel and Leah, who had held equality with chieftain husbands, as 'public counsellors, nurturing protectors, and inspired speakers'.[24] Although Sharples offered rereadings of the Old Testament she did not invoke these female images, nor the Virgin Mary, or Mary Magdalen. Instead, like many early women's rights advocates, she turned to Genesis and the myth of the Fall.[25] Sharples' reconceptualisation of knowledge and femininity were rooted in her renunciation of the doctrine of original sin and celebration of Eve as the bearer of wisdom. She contested the belief that 'woman brought sin into the world and corrupted man, and with her husband, her children and descendants' arguing that the only possible sin was that 'which is opposed to the welfare of human society'. Good and evil were relative concepts. 'Positive evils' included want of food, cold and sickness; 'relative evils' superstition, poverty and tyranny.[26] Rather than the bearer of original sin, Sharples characterised Eve as 'the personification of wisdom, of liberty, of resistance to tyranny; the mother of human knowledge; the proper help meet for man'.[27]

The deity, for Sharples, was an ambivalent figure, embodying good and evil, for while God gave life, he also denied knowledge. As we have seen, Christ, as radical reformer, was in rebellion against the old, tyrannical God. Christ's rebellion, however, was preceded by that of Eve. The story of the Garden of Eden was an 'allegory of liberty and necessity'. When the 'tyrant God, Necessity' refused to allow 'the subject man' to eat from the tree of knowledge Eve, or Liberty, stepped in to offer the fruit to her husband. Sharples rejoiced, 'Do you not, with one voice exclaim, well done woman! LIBERTY FOR EVER! ... If that was a fall, sirs, it was a glorious fall, and such a fall as is now wanted ... '[28] By taking the fruit of knowledge, Eve had created human society, for her expulsion with Adam from the Garden of Eden marked the beginnings of human progress. This interpretation of the Fall was probably known and developed by later Owenite infidels, like Eliza Macauley who also lectured on original sin in the summer of 1832, and Margaret Chappelsmith and Emma Martin who took up similar themes in the 1830s and 1840s.[29] The fusion of the biblical Eve with the republican Liberty provided all these women with a powerful model of female agency.

While Sharples drew from the biblical repertoire and rhetoric of contemporary evangelical and popular millenarian sects, her gospel challenged these groups, particularly over the issues of education and the role of women: 'the most active sin of the present day, is that of the evangelicals in religion ... who thrust their madness upon us in a way that is offensive and requires some resistance'.[30] Of critical importance was women's right to speak with reason and in public. Like other female rationalists Sharples censured the treatment of women in England by comparing the position of women in different historical societies:

> We have been worse conditioned than Asiatic slaves; for, with the name of liberty, we have been the slave of silly etiquette and custom. St. Paul forbade women to speak in churches, and they, who have made St. Paul an authority, have worn long hair and caps, and hats and veils, and have held their tongues in churches, until their whole power of speech has been concentrated for domestic scolding. Suppressed speech gathers into a storm; but freedom of discussion is the most wholesome exercise in which we can be engaged. It is not the mind only, but the body, that becomes expanded, and ripens into the health of full growth. It would be medicine for nearly all the ills that effect the forlorn condition of elderly maiden ladies.[31]

The connections Sharples made between mental activity and bodily health echoed female rationalists like Mary Wollstonecraft and Mary Hays who ascribed female moral and corporal frailty to inadequate education. Sharples departed from this earlier tradition, however, by seeking to reorder the relationship between mind and body, rather than subordinating sensation to reason.

Sharples' attempts to unite reason and sensation were central to her understanding of 'experience'. She defined herself as a theist, observing the motions of the stars, sun and moon and attributing 'everything to God as the first cause, and universal creator'. However, 'God' was also 'incomprehensible' and 'unknowable'. If, however, the Scriptures offered a moral allegory rather than the literal truth, Sharples had to address the question of how Christians were to choose between competing interpretations. Since people had no experience of God, she suggested, they could only examine 'the use of the word [God] in society'. This problem led Sharples to an essentially materialist position and she appealed to a Baconian conception of experience as a way of testing the 'word': *'every word should relate to something known, and no ideas be encouraged but such as are pictures of real things'*.[32] The emphasis on experience was potentially liberating for women like Sharples whose perception of experience did not appear to be validated by dominant forms of knowledge. Religious belief in particular had to be authenticated by personal experience: 'My profession is that of an enquirer, a thinker, a reasoner, a speaker according to no other gospel than my own thoughts. I speak as the *spirit* within me dictates, – that is, according to the impulsations of the body. I take up no man's doctrine, unless I can make it my own, by understanding it, after referring for comparisons to things in existence.'[33] The ultimate authority for Sharples was her own thought, which was the product of the critical interrogation of the 'spirit' with the 'impulsations of the body'. Sharples' validation of female sensation may have been encouraged by Carlile, the first popular propagator of birth control, whose pamphlet *Every Woman's Book, or What is Love?* in 1826 argued that human desire was natural and healthy and called for women's 'right to make advances in all the affairs of genuine love'. Perhaps Sharples had been struck by the book's original cover which displayed a naked Adam and Eve![34] In validating the connection between thought and sensation Sharples stands apart from earlier and contemporary feminists who tended to discuss marriage reform in terms of the rational ordering of human relationships, rather than the liberation of sexuality.[35]

Sharples' commitment to the personal relevancy of 'the gospel' had important implications for her own political identity, and for her understanding of a specifically female knowledge and experience. Sharples frequently referred to her Wesleyan upbringing, religious crisis and disownment by her family to emphasise the sacrifices she had made on behalf of her mission, the power of her gospel, and to provide evidence of religious intolerance, even citing her history in a petition to the King for Taylor's release.[36] She was keen, likewise, for other women to value their own judgement. In her dedication 'To The Young Women of England' in 1834 the Editress warned her female readers: 'Books will aid you, but you must not make an authority of books, or of what is written, – you must try the scripture by the things referred to, and thus prove all things, and hold fast that which is good.'[37] She offered the volume 'as a specimen of labour' that would contribute to 'the slow progress of mental improvement'. She alluded to needlework,

conventionally seen as 'fit work for women' to convey the effort
and labour involved in the production of knowledge. Knowledge
was a process of enquiry rather than an object to be acquired:

> I must tell you, for you should be told it, that to get knowledge
> you must labour. There is a labour of the mind or of the brain, as
> well as of the hands, and as you cannot make the needle do its
> office without the motion of the fingers, so cannot knowledge be
> obtained without the motion of the brain. It will not come by
> prayer, when a superstitious use is made of the word; but it is the
> prayer of thought, the asking, seeking, and knocking, accompa-
> nied with all the means of knowledge-getting, that can alone
> procure it. It steals imperceptibly on the mind as it is toiled for; it
> comes sweetly, as it is strenuously, and even with pain, sought.

While Sharples stressed the idea of knowledge as a form of labour,
she seems to have been indifferent to the realities of women's paid
and even domestic work. It is significant that her allusion to
needlework in this passage was made at the same time that many
tailors were seeking to exclude women from the tailoring trade.
Although the tailors' exclusive practices were challenged in the
early 1830s by a number of female Owenites and trade unionists,
Sharples did not address the question of women's right to labour
and preferred to work with women in the political and freethought
societies rather than in the co-operative and trade union movements.[38]

### Liberty: women and republicanism

Sharples worked closely with the Female Society, otherwise known
as the Friends of the Oppressed, which was established in July 1832
as an auxiliary to the leading union for male suffrage, the National
Union of Working Classes (NUWC), an organisation which
brought together political reformers and trade unionists. The
Friends campaigned primarily for the unstamped press which led
the attack on 'the taxes on knowledge'. The Society aided 'the
wives and children of those persons who suffer in the people's
cause' and spent much time fund-raising for causes like the
Dorchester Labourers transported in 1834 for administering illegal
oaths at trade union meetings.[39] The Society formalised the
participation of women who already attended meetings and
demonstrations as the wives of members of the NUWC.[40] Many of

the officers of the Society were the wives or daughters of prominent male radicals, and the membership seems to have been drawn from the artisan and small business classes that formed the main constituency of metropolitan radicalism.[41]

As suggested by their title, the Friends of the Oppressed saw themselves as auxiliaries to 'the people's cause' that was largely defined and led by men. The Friends and other female reformers who wrote in the pages of the unstamped press identified themselves primarily as part of 'the People'.[42] Since the reform movements of the 1810s and 1820s radical women tended to position themselves as the 'helpmeets' to the politically excluded men of the producing classes, rather than as producers in their own right. They contrasted their gendered experience of class, as the relatives of artisans, mechanics and small business men, with that of aristocratic and wealthy ladies. They appropriated the republican and patriotic symbolism of the French Revolution, identifying themselves as part of the 'industrious classes' and the *patrie*.[43] At the NUWC procession commemorating the 1830 French Revolution, the 'associated ladies' from the Friends of the Oppressed wore 'muslin aprons with tri-coloured borders' and presented Henry Hetherington, the editor of *The Poor Man's Guardian* with 'an elegant tri-coloured silk cap'. Seeking to extend their self-representation as patriotic women, Eliza Sharples told the assembled crowd that these 'Englishwomen, and the greater number wives and mothers' intended 'to be generally active as politicians'.[44] The daughter of an affluent manufacturer, Eliza Sharples rarely talked of women as part of the 'industrious classes'. In place of a 'language of class' she appealed to the ideal of sisterhood.[45] Speaking for the Friends she expanded the Society's role: 'Ours is in reality an improved association of sisters of charity; for there is more charity in seeking to remove a political disease from millions, than in attending the sick beds of suffering individuals.' However, the new 'sisters of charity' would diagnose as well as relieve the ills of society: 'To get knowledge, to disseminate it, and to protect all those who may engage in that business, is our immediate purpose; its overthrow of all that is wrong, our final purpose.'[46]

We have already seen how Sharples defined woman, as the bearer of knowledge and liberty, as 'the proper help meet for man'. Her conception of woman's political and marital role as 'help meet' departed from that of the female republicans in that she saw the family as a major site of male tyranny. This tyranny could only be overthrown by women claiming political and civil equality in marriage. Just before the passing of the Reform Bill she recommended to the political unions a pamphlet called *The New Charter* which advocated the enfranchisement of women.[47] Sharples' objection to the exclusive representation of men was related to her antipathy to all forms of monopoly which, she believed, were necessarily tyrannical. Women's oppression at the hands of oppressive husbands was comparable to that of the working classes by exclusive government. Therefore she appropriated the strategies of the reform movements to the cause of women's emancipation. Women had an 'excellent means of resistance' by refusing to associate with men who did not acknowledge their equality: 'They may deal with men, as Volney has represented the working classes, in his "New Age" dealing with the kings, the priests, and the lords. *Stand apart and live alone. Keep your liberty to yourselves; but keep away from us who are not to share it. If we cannot be your rational companions, we will not be your slaves.'* Conventional marriages were doubly oppressive for they legitimated the law of the priesthood as well as male tyranny, providing the priesthood with an income and function in civil society: 'The despotism of religious, perpetual, undivorceable marriage, right or wrong, sadly deteriorates the female character; and that very state on which women most pride themselves, is the state that tends wholly to their degradation. They truly hug their chains.' To act as a 'proper help meet', woman had to free herself first from man. For Sharples, the 'moral marriage', based on true intellectual and political equality, and 'unbounded' by law, was the tool that would break women's chains: 'Happiness or separation, liberty and mutual independency, must be the foundation of all true dignity of mind.' However, the 'moral marriage' could only be founded on men's respect for women's reason: 'Men should always stand in the character of suitors, for the company and equality of women.'[48]

Women's quest for liberation would be conceived therefore through the re-education of men and women and realised within the moral marriage. Sharples' view of social transformation was ultimately based on individual reformation and she was sceptical of more collective forms of social change such as those imagined by the Owenites. Sharples' extreme form of individualism seems to have impaired her vision of the remodelled family, as illustrated in her lecture 'Liberty and Necessity' which addressed contemporary debates about necessitarianism. The lecture examined the relationship between liberty, or individual will and reason, and necessity, by which Sharples meant material circumstances, social organisation, or God. While admitting her inability to explain 'how man can be at the same time both the creature and the creator of circumstances', Sharples argued that the Owenite doctrine that *'man's character is formed for him not by him'* was overstated. Instead, she claimed there was a dialectical relationship between liberty and necessity: 'Liberty, then, is a relative principle; so also is *necessity*, and neither of the words can be made rationally the foundation of a system and a sect. They run one into the other, and no line can be drawn at which the one begins and the other ends.' Although liberty and necessity were mutually dependent principles, Sharples was deeply suspicious of the threats posed by social systems to individual freedom and therefore advocated that necessity should always be tempered by liberty: 'one should not be positive as a Libertarian, nor the other as a Necessitarian; but by taking up the spirit of liberty, in its best state, we should work it to the subduing of the ills of necessity as far as possible'.[49] Yet, as we have already seen, 'Liberty' and 'Necessity' were gendered concepts for Sharples. Slipping between 'Liberty' as 'Eve' and 'Eve' as 'Woman', Sharples argued that women's emancipation was necessary for men's defence against the tyranny of systems. Suspicious of the new social systems put forward by the Owenites, Sharples looked to the family as a natural form of social organisation and as a site of liberty. Paradoxically, she offered a patriarchal vision of the family:

> Man is nowhere more dignified than as the moral master of his own family, surrounded by a kind wife, affectionate children, and assistants, who love and respect him for his care of their welfare … The family man is like a solar system, the sun and its planets. He may move in the space required, without clashing with any other family man; but to make a uniformity of motion in each family, appears to me as impracticable, as to make a uniformity of motion in the varied solar system.[50]

Whilst insisting on women's rights to education and full citizenship, Sharples ultimately reduced all political and social identities to the level of the family. By rejecting the ideal of union Sharples

provided no collective aims, model or forum by which women
could associate together except as her disciples.

## Isis: women in public

Like other female freethinkers Sharples was subjected to a barrage
of personal attacks. *The Times* ridiculed her 'new line' in public
speaking, casting aspersions on her respectability, asking 'Would
not the place of housemaid, or servant of all work in some decent
family, serve her purpose better?' Sharples deflected such criticism
by appealing to conventional etiquette. She refused to respond to
public criticism despite her commitment to free enquiry and
rebuked one man who dared to question her: 'I do not feel bound
to hold conversation with any persons upon what I may or may not
advance upon this stage, and much less shall I be disposed to put
myself on a level with bad manners. I should have no objection to a
conversation with ladies; nor to answer in a subsequent discourse
written questions from any respectable person.'[51] Sharples
frequently called on women to join her lecturing mission but there
was a contradiction between her desire to empower and associate
with other women, and her self-presentation as a 'novelty among
women'.[52] In March she bragged to her readers:

> I now find a thousand [admirers], bowing like idolators to a
> goddess, and keeping at that respectable distance at which all idol-
> ators should keep from goddesses and from all such things sacred.
> I boast of this to encourage other ladies to come out from their
> common prison-house of religious or fashionable society, and
> assist me in doing that in which I am engaged. My business is not
> now to be coquetting every day for some new admirer; but to be
> much employed in keeping the multitude at a distance, and gently
> brushing them away, where they become a little too rash.[53]

However, Sharples' self-presentation as a goddess was in tension
with her democratic intentions and with the collective and egalitarian spirit of the contemporary reform movements. Her audiences
dwindled and, unable to maintain the rent on the Rotunda, she was
forced to move by the end of March to the Owenite lecture rooms
at Burton Street, only to find herself in competition with Robert
Owen. By the end of July she announced a break from lecturing
and from then on lectured only by invitation.[54]
Sharples began to channel her energies into her journal, but

despite contributions from the Owenite freethinkers Frances Wright and the Revd James Smith she failed to attract a wide readership. 'Printing is a peculiar trade', she confessed. 'There are not enough persons to whom *The Isis* is approachable, fond of such solid reading, to enable me to sell it cheaper.' Priced at sixpence, *The Isis* was beyond the reach of many of the plebeian radicals who provided the main constituency of freethought radicalism. Despite her support for the campaigns to abolish the stamp on newspapers, Sharples dismissed the cheap periodicals and working-class support in favour of a more wealthy and 'respectable' audience, contending, 'I do not much admire the cry for cheap publications. I pity but cannot appeal to poverty and misery for assistance.'[55] By the end of the year *The Isis* appeared fortnightly only and Sharples was unable to find sufficient subscribers to begin a cheaper, second volume. When Carlile was released from gaol in 1833 their limited resources were directed into his publishing ventures and Sharples appears not to have written for publication again.

Sharples also failed in her efforts to attract the support of other freethinking women. Helen, an advocate of co-operative association from London, welcomed the 'new and rational pleasure' Isis had given the ladies, and hoped to join her mission soon: 'I wait the opportunity of family arrangements to join you, to rival you, to excel you, if possible; for though I do not like much of the world's competition, I like it in matters of the mind. Moral rivalry cannot be too strong.'[56] There is no evidence that Helen succeeded in sorting out her family affairs or managed to join Isis. Few women with family or household commitments would have had the time or resources to devote themselves to public lecturing, as evidenced by Sharples' erratic lecturing career after 1832. Many women, no doubt, were unable to imagine themselves as a goddess, or as a female 'second coming'. The Editress was left musing: 'I verily believe that I stand alone in this country, as a modern Eve, daring to pluck the fruit of this tree, and to give it to timid, sheepish man. I have received kindnesses and encouragements from a few ladies since my appearance in the metropolis, but how few!'[57]

Through her moral union with Carlile, Sharples gained access to a public platform from which most other radical women were effectively barred. However, she was to pay heavily for her social deviance. Sharples was ostracised by her family in Bolton and her denunciation by her former Wesleyan minister presaged the attacks she received from anti-freethought Christians until her death. In 1832, however, she showed little regard for the material and ideological pressures which confined women to their 'prison-houses', or indeed of the investment that many women had in the ideal of 'separate spheres'. At the end of the year her younger sister Maria wrote to Sharples pointing out the damaging effects of Eliza's infidel status on her family. Sharples rebuked her sister in *The Isis*, lecturing her on the evils of the marriage market; the importance of basing marriages on reason; and her own good sense in choosing Carlile as a partner. In a reply that notably was not published by the Editress, Maria contested Sharples' brand of philosophy that divorced itself from the constraints of public opinion:

> But as I am no philosopher, as you profess to be, and therefore unable to judge of things as they really are, I am obliged to confine judgement to the nature of things as they appear to be, and as the judgements of society are necessarily governed by appearances, we surely claim too much from society when we expect its good opinions and its bestowal of confidence, without paying the compliment of our attention and regard to appearances.

Ignoring her sister's plea for privacy, Sharples published a further five letters to Maria in *The Isis*.[58] Tragically, the very 'judgements of society' which Sharples disowned were already raising conflicts within her own moral union, calling into question Sharples' and Carlile's views of philosophy, politics and love.

### Hypatia: mission and martyrdom

This chapter began with a reference to current debates on the role of discourse in the construction of 'experience'. These debates have been informed by Michel Foucault's understanding of knowledge as a technique of power. Foucault sees institutions as constructing and employing bodies of knowledge which position some people as subjects and others as objects of knowledge.[59] Radical politics can been seen as constructing its own body of knowledge, which frequently countered those of dominant institutions, such as the law, the clergy and the government. The authors of radical knowledge in the early nineteenth century were overwhelmingly men who constructed the radical actor, or subject, as male. The insistence within republican freethought on the limitless and emancipatory potential of reason, and the claim that knowledge was power, provided Sharples with the moral and political authority to question radical as well as dominant forms of knowledge. She subverted the rhetoric of 'woman's mission' to position woman as an author of and authority on radical knowledge. She devised new rhetorical strategies, particularly the voice of prophecy to envision the equality of the sexes. Her own experience, she contended, must surely be shared by other women and reason alone would dispel ignorance and superstition and liberate the suppressed desire and speech of all women. As a wife, mother and widow, however, she was to experience unforeseen obstacles to political engagement. Her vision of 'woman's mission' was challenged within radical culture, which in the 1830s and 1840s reasserted woman's auxiliary rather than equal status with man. This wider resistance to female autonomy was encountered unexpectedly from her philosophic partner who prioritised his own political ambitions over those of Isis. Sharples' ability to articulate and politicise 'experience' was contained by relations of authority in the private sphere as well as in the public arena of popular radicalism.

When Sharples fell pregnant the authorities attempted to stop her prison visits. She appealed to her husband to make the pregnancy public and to petition for the resumption of her visits but Carlile, fearful of public scandal, cautioned her to keep quiet and tetchily advised her to apply herself to her studies: 'Instead of growing in philosophical improvement, you are diverging from it. You do not act up to the promise of your Bolton letters ... I cannot degrade myself so far as to exhibit folly and madness about it, and to be food for the spirit of my enemies.'[60] In an impassioned response, Sharples pleaded for an intrepid, uncompromising declaration of love to match their radical politics: 'I want to become a scientific lover – not a philosopher ... When we talk of moderate love, philosophical love, etc., it amounts to nothing. There is no such thing as a moderate true lover. Pray tell me how do you like a moderate reformer?'[61]

The conflict between Sharples and Carlile over the pregnancy reflects increasing divisions among the reform movements over the issue of sexual radicalism. From the 1790s sexual radicals had often been tarred with the brush of 'free love', but in the early 1830s attacks on the morality of freethinkers intensified. In the same year that Sharples became pregnant the Parliamentary Commission into the operation of the Poor Laws was reviewing provision for single mothers with illegitimate children. In response the rules on bastardy were redrawn by the New Poor Law of 1834 to guard as a deterrent against non-marital sex. Unmarried mothers were unable henceforth to claim financial support by naming the putative father, a provision which the Commissioners argued encouraged women to have sex outside of marriage and to name whichever man could offer the most support. Unmarried mothers and their offspring were only to receive relief within the workhouse, so that the bastard should become 'what Providence appears to have ordained that it should be, a burthen on its mother, and, where she cannot maintain it, on her parents'.[62] The Bastardy Clauses were to have a profound influence on working-class courtship and marital practices, but they also had an important effect on radical discussions about marriage and gender relations. Rather than defending traditional plebeian courtship patterns, Anna Clark has suggested that radical movements were thrown on to the defensive. Women and men within the Anti-Poor Law and Chartist movements insisted that they, rather than the architects of the Poor Law, were the advocates of Christian morality and the family. Although Owenite freethinkers continued their attacks on the tyranny of marriage, most working-class radicals appealed to marriage as a mark of their own class respectability and increasingly championed the ideal of the male breadwinner and the domestic wife as the best solution to poverty and unemployment.[63] In this context the 'moral marriage' became a source of heated debate within the radical politics.

On Carlile's release from gaol early in 1833 his 'moral divorce' from his first wife Jane and his 'moral union' with Sharples fuelled a series of hostile exchanges between Carlile, Hetherington and Carlile's now rival, the Revd Taylor. Arguments over competing conceptions of politics and theology, democratic organisation and leadership were embroiled with personal attacks. All three men attempted to disparage their rivals' politics by castigating each others' marital affairs, paying scant regard for the reputation of the women involved. The Revd Taylor singled out the Carliles in a lecture on 'matrimony, harlotry, moral marriage, bastards'. Sharples urged Carlile to hit Taylor, but instead he chose to attack his former associate in his new journal, *A Scourge for the Littleness of*

'Great' Men, which was used mainly to slander other radical men. Hetherington and Carlile exchanged hostile editorials over Carlile's 'moral divorce' and 'moral marriage'.[64] Carlile defended female equality over conjugal duty, but in practice he expected male authority to be observed and denounced the complaints made by some radical women against his attacks on Mrs Hetherington:

> All these hags are annoyed and alarmed at my instance of spirited justice towards a troublesome and disagreeable wife. They know they deserve similar justice, so they decry it to frighten their unmanly husbands ... And to every woman who finds fault with me in what I have done, I have to say, conduct yourself as a wife ought to conduct herself, not in slavish submission to tyrannical will, but in pure equality and respect only of what is respectable, and you have nothing to fear.[65]

Given the ferocity of these attacks it is perhaps unsurprising that many working-class radicals fought shy of the marriage debates which occupied the Owenite and freethought movements.

Carlile's misogynistic attack on Mrs Hetherington and her friends reveals the limits of his attachment to the rights of women and deep anxieties about the nature of the radical marriage. Nevertheless, Carlile remained committed in principle to Sharples continuing her public career. They planned to lecture together but their aspirations were tragically defeated. Their first child died while they were engaged on a joint lecture tour of the north in 1833. The inscription on their baby's coffin bore testimony to his parents' grief and the price of dissidence: 'Thou hast not wanted parental affection, but, through vicious persecution, thou hast wanted parental care.'[66] From then on Carlile's political career was priori- tised over Sharples', who rarely lectured during their marriage, although she undertook a lecturing tour on phrenology in 1838.[67] By opposing the Chartists in the late 1830s Carlile lost much of his support and the couple were dogged by poverty. In 1840 Carlile bitterly reflected: 'Mrs. C. is heartily sick of the poverty of philoso- phy. You may be sure of that. She has had her martyrdom that way, as often without money as with it.'[68]

As a mother Sharples was to become acutely aware of the mat- erial and ideological constraints on female autonomy to which she had been largely indifferent in 1832. When Carlile died intestate in 1843 his business was taken over by the son of his first wife and as his marriage with Sharples had no legal status, she was left only the furniture and personal property. She fell back on her Owenite friendships and moved briefly to the Owenite community at Ham Common where she managed the sewing room. Dissatisfied with the community's vegetarian diet, Sharples returned to London to support her son and two daughters by needlework. It is ironic that having used the metaphor of needlework to convey to women the idea of knowledge as a form of labour, she was to reflect bitterly to the Chartist and secularist Thomas Cooper on the penury of needlework and the 'helplessness' of women 'who have only sorrow and labour as their portion'. She described to him the paralysing effect of poverty on her public career:

> Many have said: 'Why not devote yourself to public usefulness?' My answer is because my helpless family demanded all my attention: night and day I had to struggle for daily bread, and if the physical is weakened the mind is surely paralyzed. They are getting now beyond immediate care, and abler somewhat to assist themselves, which will leave me more able to combat the melancholy prospect before me, and I hope, perform a task, which is the first wish of my heart – to write the life of Richard Carlile. Nothing is wanting but the means of living to enable me to do this.[69]

Despite her social and political marginalisation, Sharples continued her missionary efforts. At the Owenite Literary and Social Institution in 1846 she gave a lecture 'on the Nature and Character of Woman and her Position in Society' and in 1849 made a few remarks at the birthday celebration of Paine, along with leading secularists like Hetherington, George Jacob Holyoake and a Miss Dyer, who was currently lecturing on women's rights. The same year, a group of freethinkers, who were 'energetic and enthusiastic disciples of Richard Carlile', invited Sharples to manage a secularist Temperance Hall at Warner Place.[70] These brief references to Sharples' public appearances indicate the continued interest in the rights of women among the Owenite, freethought and secularist circles in the 1840s and early 1850s.[71] Sharples' views on women's rights might have found a receptive hearing from the female Chartist organisations in London which were influenced by the freethought tradition. The Chartist East London Female Total Abstinence Society set up its own school as an alternative to those provided by the Church and state and promoted the intellectual emancipation of women as part of the 'cause of universal redemption'.[72] However, Carlile's hostility to the Chartist movement probably prohibited Sharples' involvement with these groups, even though they too deployed the rhetoric of 'woman's mission' to authorise women's political activism. In 1848 the Bethnal Green Female Chartist Association urged that woman 'will not only be social, but political – no longer stifle her miseries at home, but spread them abroad'. They attempted to define women's public role by asking:

> what power has woman and by what means can she assist in the redemption of her species? Time shall give the solution. It is enough for us to know that woman possesses an influence, that that influence has often been exercised for her own enslavement, and seldom for the advancement of her happiness. For the future let us strive to redeem the error of the past. We are acknowledged to be the most useful apostles in the promulgation of religion – in this walk our claim has never been disputed. What, then, shall prevent us being useful in the mission of politics, peace, virtue and humanity?[73]

As Michelle de Larrabeiti argues in this volume, the rhetoric of 'woman's mission' was deployed in complex ways by Chartist women to legitimise their entry into the public sphere, yet it seems that the assertion of sexual difference prohibited women from participating in the movement on the same terms as men. Dorothy Thompson has suggested that the decline of the Chartist mass platform with its appeal to the whole community and its replacement by an increasingly formalised, committee-based working-class politics in the 1840s discouraged the active involvement of women in radical movements.[74] Sharples' experience at the Warner Temperance Hall illuminates this process of marginalisation. In 1850 she informed Thomas Cooper of her plans for a series of lectures on the 'Rights of Woman'. These had been thwarted by 'unfair play' from men connected with the Hall who laughed at the idea that 'all Reform will be found to be inefficient that does not embrace the Rights of Woman', and who saw Sharples merely as a server of coffee. She resented this confinement since serving coffee was not her 'sphere' and described herself as the loneliest person in the world.[75] Although Sharples challenged radical men's definition of woman's sphere, in outlining her prospective lecture course to Cooper she presented her defence of women's rights in accommodating terms for men. She argued that women had power for good or evil; that 'If they advance not knowledge they will perpetuate ignorance'; that woman's position corresponded to the state of civilisation of a society.[76] Her invocation of 'woman's mission' reveals the similarities and differences between the women's rights discourses of the early 1830s and the 1850s. In 1850, Sharples still equated the intellectual emancipation of women with social and political progress, but where in 1832 she had defied male monopoly and celebrated the female intellect and spirit, she now seems more diplomatic, choosing her words carefully to solicit the approval of a radical man. Her tone might be seen as reflective of the tenuous position that women now held in radical movements.

In 1832 Sharples had proclaimed herself as the new Eve, as Liberty and as Isis yet, tragically, of all her personae, that of Hypatia, the Greek martyr, seems the one most fitting in the light of her poverty and isolation. In the late 1840s Sharples offered a home to the young Charles Bradlaugh, future leader of the secularist movement who, like her, had been disowned by his family because of his endorsement of freethought. It was as a martyr that Bradlaugh remembered Sharples, 'quiet and reserved'; 'a broken woman, who had her ardour and enthusiasm cooled by suffering and poverty'.[77] When she died in poverty in 1852, the Owenite and secularist societies paid for her children to emigrate to America.[78] On both sides of the Atlantic, members of her own and her adopted family continued to promote Sharples' claims for women's emancipation. Bradlaugh's advocacy of women's rights may well have reflected Isis' teachings. Sharples' daughter Theophilia finally produced the biography of Carlile that Sharples had hoped to write, paying tribute to Isis as well as her father. An active member of the American women's movement, Sharples' granddaughter wrote in 1918 to Hypatia Bonner, Bradlaugh's daughter, congratulating the British suffrage movements on winning the vote for women over thirty. Some of Eve's wisdom had borne fruit.[79]

## Notes

1  This chapter engages in particular with the following studies which have all been informed, although in different ways, by post-structuralist theory: G. Stedman Jones, *Languages of Class: Studies in English Working-Class History, 1832–1982* (Cambridge, Cambridge University Press, 1983); J. Scott, 'Language, Gender and Working-Class History', in idem, *Gender and the Politics of History* (Princeton, Princeton University Press, 1988); the work of P. Joyce, notably *Democratic Subjects: The Self and the Social in*

*Nineteenth-Century England* (Cambridge, Cambridge University Press, 1994); and J. Epstein, *Radical Expression: Political Language, Ritual, and Symbol in England, 1790–1850* (Oxford, Oxford University Press, 1994).

2 For a biographical sketch of Sharples see entry by E. Royle, in J. O. Baylen and N. J. Gossman (eds), *The Dictionary of Modern British Radicals*, vol. 2 (Brighton, Harvester, 1979). There is no full length biographical study of Eliza Sharples although most of Carlile's biographers make some reference to her, particularly: T. Campbell Carlile, *The Battle of the Press as Told in the Story of Richard Carlile* (London, Bonner, 1899); J. Weiner, *Radicalism and Freethought in Nineteenth-Century Britain. The Life of Richard Carlile* (London, Greenwood, 1983). For Richard Carlile see also G. J. Holyoake, *The Life and Character of Richard Carlile* (London, Austin, 1849); G. Alfred, *Richard Carlile, Agitator: His Life and Times* (Glasgow, Strickland Press, 1941); and G. D. H. Cole, *Richard Carlile, 1790–1843* (London, Gollancz, 1943). For Revd Taylor and his infidel partnership with Carlile see Weiner, *Radicalism and Freethought* and J. Epstein, 'Reason's Republic: Richard Carlile, Zetetic Culture, and Infidel Stylistics', in his *Radical Expression*, pp. 100–46.

3 *Isis*, 11 Feb. 1832, pp. 1–5.

4 'Dedication', folio volume of *Isis*, May 1834.

5 The Revd Taylor had deployed theatricality in his infidel sermons at the Rotunda, mimicking and subverting the rhetoric and form of Christian ritual. Epstein argues that in his use of metaphor and allegory, Taylor moved away from the strict rationalism and literalism of zetetic discourse. While Taylor dressed in bishop's robes to mock the pomp and ceremony of Established Christianity, Sharples used ritual and symbol more positively to elevate and sensationalise her public intervention. See Epstein, 'Reason's Republic', pp. 136–46 for his fascinating discussion of 'infidel sylistics'.

6 Informer's report, HO 64/12, cited by Weiner, *Radicalism and Freethought*, p. 181.

7 'Second Discourse of the Lady of the Rotunda', *Isis*, 11 Feb. 1832, p. 7; 'The Editress to her Sister Maria', 27 Oct. 1832, p. 545.

8 *Isis*, 31 Mar. 1832, p. 113, 27 Oct. 1832, p. 546.

9 'Moral Marriage', *The Gauntlet*, 22 Sept. 1833, pp. 521–2.

10 Weiner, *Radicalism and Freethought*, pp. 141–90.

11 *Report of the Trial of Mrs. Carlile* (London, Jane Carlile, 1821). For an analysis of women's participation in the zetetic movement see I. McCalman, 'Females, Feminism and Free Love in an Early Nineteenth Century Radical Movement', *Labour History* (Canberra), 38 (May 1980), pp. 1–25.

12 For Carlile's version of his separation from Jane see his 'A Statement of My Own Family Affairs', *A Scourge of the Littleness of 'Great' Men*, 18 Oct. 1834, pp. 17–21.

13 'Moral Marriage', *The Gauntlet*, 22 Sept. 1833, pp. 521–2. For a discussion of Wright's involvement with freethought movements, see B. Taylor, *Eve and the New Jerusalem: Socialism and Feminism in the Nineteenth Century* (London, Virago, 1983, pp. 65–70).

14 'Family Affairs', *A Scourge*, 18 Nov. 1834, pp. 46–7. For Sharples' vindication of the moral marriage, see the Preface to the folio edition of *Isis*, 29 May 1834.

**15** Sharples to Carlile, 11 Dec. 1831, in *The Gauntlet*, 22 Sept. 1833, p. 522.

**16** In a letter to Thomas Turton (28 Nov. 1833) Carlile claimed that *The Isis* was his own work: see, Campbell Carlile, *Battle of the Press*, pp. 201, 159.

**17** 'Isis' to Richard, undated letter, cited in *ibid.*, p. 173.

**18** *Isis*, 5 May 1832, pp. 200, 202–3.

**19** Printed circular advertising Taylor and Carlile's 'atheist mission', May 1829, cited by Weiner, *Radicalism and Freethought*, p. 157. See his chapter 'Infidel Missionaries', pp. 141–63 and Epstein, 'Reason's Republic' for the changes in Carlile's theological views in the late 1820s.

**20** For a useful introduction to biblical criticism in the eighteenth and early nineteenth centuries, see E. Royle, *Victorian Infidels: The Origins of the British Secularist Movement, 1791–1866* (Manchester, Manchester University Press, 1980), pp. 9–23. For criticisms of Sharples' notion of moral allegory, see J. Hibbert's advocacy of an 'astronomical solution', *Isis*, 12 May 1832, pp. 218–19; Lyon's support of historical criticism, 19 May 1832, p. 235; and letter from 'A', 26 May 1832, pp. 255–6.

**21** 'First Discourse on the Bible', *Isis*, 28 Apr. 1832, pp. 177–83; 'Second Discourse on the Bible', 5 May 1832, pp. 193–9.

**22** *Isis*, 28 Apr. 1832, p. 177.

**23** Sharples produced a 'Glossary' to explain the meaning of the principal characters of the Bible, but curiously she refers to very few female characters. She described the Virgin Mary as 'the second birth of Eve', but provided no interpretation of Mary Magdalen. See *Isis*, 7 July 1832, pp. 338–40. Carlile extended Sharples' glossary in *A Dictionary of Some of the Names in the Sacred Scriptures Translated into the English Language* (Manchester, Thomas Paine Carlile and London, Alfred Carlile, n.d.).

**24** D. Valenze, *Prophetic Sons and Daughters: Female Preaching and Popular Religion in the Industrial Revolution* (Princeton, Princeton University Press, 1985), pp. 35–7.

**25** For example, Mary Hays, friend of Wollstonecraft, argued that the story of the Fall was allegorical and that reason and religion opposed the subjection of one sex to another. See G. Kelly, *Women, Writing and Revolution, 1790–1827* (Oxford, Clarendon Press, 1993), p. 114.

**26** 'Who Are the Sinners?', *Isis*, 25 Feb. 1832, pp. 34–9.

**27** 'Glossary', *Isis*, 7 July 1832, pp. 338–40.

**28** 'Liberty and Necessity', *Isis*, 7 Apr. 1832, p. 132.

**29** For Macauley's discussion of original sin, see her 'Essay on Religious Responsibility', *The Crisis* (June 1832), pp. 42, 64, 66. For Owenite interpretations of Scripture see Taylor, *Eve*, pp. 118–82, especially pp. 143–8.

**30** 'Who Are the Sinners?', *Isis*, 25 Feb. 1832, p. 36.

**31** 'Editress to Her Readers', *ibid.*, p. 39.

**32** 'On Words', *Isis*, 18 Feb. 1832, pp. 17–23.

**33** *Ibid.* The problem of interpretation had long vexed the zetetics and in the early 1820s both Carlile and Allen Davenport urged rationalists to avoid word-play and carefully choose words for their strictly literal sense. See Epstein, 'Reason's Republic', pp. 112–13.

**34** [R. Carlile], *Every Woman's Book, or What is Love?*, pp. 2, 5 (abridged from *The Republican*, 6 May 1825). For Carlile and the sexual radicalism of the 1820s, see McCalman, 'Females', pp. 14–24.

35  See C. Kaplan, 'Wild Nights: Pleasure/Sexuality/Feminism', in her *Sea Changes: Culture and Feminism* (London, Verso, 1986); Taylor, *Eve*, p. 214.

36  'Editress to Her Readers', *Isis*, 24 Mar. 1832, p. 101.

37  The Editress, Dedication of folio volume of *Isis*, May 1834.

38  See Taylor's analysis of the tailoring dispute in *Eve*, pp. 83–117.

39  *Poor Man's Guardian*, 21 July 1832, pp. 469–70; 19 Apr. 1834, p. 88.

40  *Ibid.*, 24 Mar. 1832, p. 321.

41  No reliable figures exist recording the size of the Friends. I. Prothero refers to a fifty-strong radical female society at the Theobald's Institution and at Kings Cross, led by William Benbow's wife; see Prothero, *Artisans and Politics in Early Nineteenth-Century London* (Folkestone, Dawson, 1979), p. 294. One hundred women assembled at short notice to welcome the release of Mary Willis from imprisonment for selling copies of the *Poor Man's Guardian*, but it is unclear how far this number reflected the strength of the Society. See *Poor Man's Guardian*, 6 Oct. 1832, p. 599.

42  *Ibid.*, 26 May 1832, p. 403; 3 Mar. 1832, p. 303.

43  For women's appropriation of the constitutionalist and patriotic discourses in the early reform movements, see Epstein, *Radical Expression*, pp. 80–92.

44  *Poor Man's Guardian*, 4 Aug. 1832, pp. 482–3, 487–8; *Isis*, 4 Aug. 1832, pp. 385–7.

45  For a discussion of radicalism and the language of class, see G. Stedman Jones, 'Rethinking Chartism', in his *Languages of Class*.

46  *Isis*, 4 Aug. 1832, pp. 385–7.

47  *Ibid.*, 7 Apr. 1832, p. 159. For a useful discussion of similar arguments deployed by female suffragists in the mid-Victorian era, see J. Rendall, 'Citizenship, Culture and Civilization: The Languages of British Suffragists, 1866–1874', in M. Nolan and C. Daley (eds), *Suffrage and Beyond: International Feminist Perspectives* (Wellington, Auckland University Press, 1993).

48  The Editress's comments on *The New Charter* in *Isis*, 14 Apr. 1832, p. 159.

49  'Liberty and Necessity', *Isis*, 7 Apr. 1832, pp. 129–34.

50  *Ibid.* For the influence of necessitarian philosophy on nineteenth-century infidel and secularist thought, see Royle, *Victorian Infidels*, pp. 9–58, especially pp. 21–3.

51  *Isis*, 11 Feb. 1832, p. 7; 'On the Importance of Philosophical Lecturing Institutions', *Isis*, 31 Mar. 1832, p. 117.

52  *Ibid.*, 26 May 1832, p. 246; 11 Feb. 1832, p. 2.

53  *Ibid.*, 10 Mar. 1832, p. 71.

54  *Ibid.*, 24 Mar. 1832, p. 97; and *ibid.*, 28 July 1832, p. 372.

55  *Ibid.* and *Isis*, 11 Feb. 1832, p. 5.

56  'Helen', *ibid.*, 25 Feb. 1832, pp. 47–8.

57  *Ibid.*, 31 Mar. 1832, p. 128.

58  'The Editress to Her Sister Maria', Letters I–VII, *ibid.*, nos 34–39, 20 Oct. 1832–15 Dec. 1832; Campbell Carlile, *Battle of the Press*, pp. 181–5.

59  M. Foucault, 'The Order of Discourse', inaugural lecture at the Collège de France, 2 Dec. 1970, reprinted in R. Young (ed.), *Untying the Text: A Post-Structuralist Reader* (London, Routledge & Kegan Paul, 1988), pp. 48–78.

60  Carlile to Sharples, undated 1832, in Campbell Carlile, *Battle of the Press*, p. 188.

61  Sharples to Carlile, undated letter, in *ibid.*, p. 175. Sharples' celebration of

desire, and attempts to make politics a passionate affair, in public and private, set her apart from most nineteenth-century female advocates of women's rights. Barbara Taylor has argued that feminists, from Wollstonecraft onwards, were cautious about adopting the tenets of free love, and emphasised the importance of reason in guiding the passions, rather than elevating the sex drive; see *Eve*, ch. 6, especially p. 214.

**62** *Report from H.M. Commissioners for Inquiring into the Administration and Practical Operation of the Poor Laws*, London, 1834, cited by U. R. K. Henriques, 'Bastardy and the New Poor Law', *Past and Present*, 37 (1967), p. 109.

**63** A. Clark, *The Struggle for the Breeches: Gender and the Making of the British Working Class* (London, University of California Press, 1995).

**64** For Carlile's attacks on Taylor and Hetherington and defence of his own marital relations, see *A Scourge*, 4, 11, 18 Oct. 1834, pp. 1–8, 9, 11, 12, 14, 15, 17–30; 8, 29 Nov. 1834, pp. 41–7, 67; 13 Dec. 1834, pp. 67–8, 87. For Hetherington's criticisms of Carlile see *Poor Man's Guardian*, 1, 15 Nov. 1834, pp. 308–10, 326–7; 6 Dec. 1834, pp. 347–9.

**65** *A Scourge*, 29 Nov. 1834, pp. 67–8.

**66** *Gauntlet*, 3 Nov. 1833, pp. 609–10; Campbell Carlile, *Battle of the Press*, p. 194. Carlile's son's illness reaffirmed his commitment to birth control, see *Gauntlet*, 27 Oct. 1833, p. 592.

**67** Campbell Carlile, *Battle of the Press*, p. 210.

**68** Carlile to T. Turton, 1 Dec. 1840, in *ibid.*, pp. 195–6.

**69** Eliza Sharples to Thomas Cooper, 28 July 1849, in Bradlaugh Papers, ed. E. Royle (Wakefield, Microfilm Ltd, 1977), Additional Papers, 18e. Thanks to Edward Royle for referring me to Bradlaugh's papers.

**70** *The Reasoner*, 18 Nov. 1846, p. 304 and 3 Jan. 1849, p. 79; H. Bradlaugh Bonner, *Charles Bradlaugh: A Record of his Life and Work by his Daughter* (London, Unwin, 1902), p. 9.

**71** See Taylor, *Eve*, pp. 275–85 for a discussion of women's rights and the mid-nineteenth-century secularist movement.

**72** 'Address of the East London Female Total Abstinence Association', *Northern Star*, 30 Jan. 1841, p. 1.

**73** 'Address from the National Female Chartist Association (Branch no. 2) to the Women of Bethnal Green', *ibid.*, 8 July 1848, p. 1.

**74** D. Thompson, *The Chartists: Popular Politics in the Industrial Revolution* (London, Temple Smith, 1984). On the question of women's marginalisation in the Chartist movement, see Taylor, *Eve*, pp. 265–75; S. Alexander, 'Women, Class and Sexual Differences in the 1830s and 1840s: Some Reflections on the Writing of a Feminist History', *History Workshop*, 17 (1984), pp. 135–48; J. Schwarzkopf, *Women in the Chartist Movement* (Basingstoke, Macmillan, 1991), pp. 283–8.

**75** E. Sharples Carlile to T. Cooper, Temperance Hall, 1 Warner Place, Hackney, 23 Apr. 1850, Bradlaugh Papers, 19a.

**76** Sharples to Cooper, *ibid.*

**77** Bradlaugh Bonner, *Charles Bradlaugh*, p. 15.

**78** See *The Reasoner*, 31 Mar. 1852, pp. 305–6.

**79** T. Campbell Bassett to H. Bradlaugh Bonner, 2 Apr. 1918, Bradlaugh Papers, 3056(A).

# 3

# Images of femininity in the Royal Commissions of the 1830s and 1840s

SOPHIE HAMILTON

The state has always played an important role as a powerful cultural agency helping to shape gender practices and expectations. In the early nineteenth century, the state made unprecedented investigations into working-class life and as a direct result, parliament passed legislation which impacted strongly on working women in the 'public' and 'private' spheres. Any attempts by women to represent themselves in social movements would have to manoeuvre within the constraints erected by state representations of femininity and the laws which embodied these. Through a detailed textual study of the Children's Employment Commissions Inquiring into the Factories (1833) and the Mines (1842), as well as the Royal Commission on the Poor Laws (1834), this chapter examines the various stages of these inquiries and critically analyses the relationship between the original depositions taken by the Commissioners and the evidence they then chose to include in the *First Report*.

The analysis of the role played by gender is crucial for an understanding of the selection process.[1] The Commissioners, who are best described as rising professional men, either unconsciously or deliberately selected negative images of female sexuality which reinforced their middle-class domestic ideology. As a result two powerful images of working-class female sexuality emerge from a reading of the *First Report*: women are either sexually voracious or vulnerable and therefore in need of regulation or protection. These images were mobilised to justify legislation which moved women closer towards married domesticity where their 'natural' sexuality could once again be restored.[2] However, while appearing to protect women the Commissioners were also safeguarding male interests in the workplace or, in the case of the Bastardy Clauses in the Poor Laws, removing the financial onus of responsibility from the man to the woman.

## A general introduction to the Royal Commissions

The Royal Commission was an investigatory body which was revived and further developed in the 1830s and which then 'spread like a contagion' over the next two decades: more than 100 such inquiries set to work between 1832 and 1846. The major Commissions followed the pattern established by the Poor Law inquiry; three Commissioners, forming a Central Board, stayed in London, overseeing the operation and often devising the question-naires, while itinerant Commissioners called Assistant, District or Sub-Commissioners collected evidence in a designated geographi-cal area. Each Royal Commission inquiry divided into three main sections. First, there were the thousands of testimonies taken from individuals of 'all classes'[3] by the Sub-Commissioners which made up the Minutes of Evidence; this constituted the raw material of the Commissions. Yet even these depositions did not necessarily give a true representation of the working-class woman. It must be remem-bered that the Commissioners presided over the interviews; they asked the questions, they chose the subjects for discussion and dictated the course the interview took. Then came the second stage, when each Sub-Commissioner drew up a *Report* bringing together the most 'relevant' evidence from the original testimonies. Finally the Commissioners used this information to write the *First Report* of the Commissions, which was described as 'a digest of the whole matter returned'. The purpose of the *First Report* was to make 'sense' of the 'voluminous evidence' by exhibiting it in 'a condensed and connected form'.[4] This chapter examines how objectively the Commissioners made sense of this evidence.

The key Commissioners were largely men from secure middle-class and professional backgrounds who tried to bring into being a new-style civil service. Edwin Chadwick (1800–90), who presided over the Poor Law and Factory Commissions, was the exemplary figure. From an affluent Manchester Unitarian family, having trained as a barrister and having served as Jeremy Bentham's last secretary, this Utilitarian used old channels of aristocratic patronage to try to transform the civil service from the 'Old Corruption' of jobs for friends and kin, to a neutral body of professionals who brought science and a sense of service to their work. Investigation was integral to Chadwick's idea of science; investigations, like those carried out by Royal Commissions, would precede legislation which in turn would create inspectorates to keep the process of investigation ongoing. Jellinger C. Symons (1809–60), perhaps the best known of the Sub-Commissioners investigating the mines, followed this new career track. The son of a vicar, Symons served as a Commissioner on the inquiry into the condition of the hand-loom weavers, then became a tithe commissioner. After working on the mines inquiry and becoming a barrister, he investigated the state of education in Wales, and finally ended up as an HM Inspector of Schools, a post which he held from 1848 until his death. Significantly, Frank Mort has argued that these new-type professional men made a concern with 'proper' gender division and sexual conduct as much a part of their masculine identity as scrupulous professional probity.[5] It is not surprising that these men were also concerned with gender issues in their investigative work.

## The Children's Employment Commission Inquiring into the Factories (1833)

This Commission was very controversial and addressed one of the most hotly debated issues of the day: the tendency of the factory system and especially its effects on child labour. To some, this Royal Commission seemed a political ploy, fuelled by the 'mercenary influence of the mill-owners', to derail a Ten Hour Bill which had already received its second reading and to overturn the findings of a Select Committee investigation, which had been sympathetic to the demands of the working-class movement agitating for a Ten Hour factory day. Parliamentarians like Michael Sadler, the chair of the earlier Select Committee, and Lord Ashley refused point-blank to have anything to do with the new inquiry, as did many working people in the factory districts.[6] The Central Commissioners, with Chadwick in charge, gave instructions about the subjects to be covered and supplied a detailed questionnaire to be filled in by employers of labour. This part of the inquiry has received attention from historians.[7] What has been less noticed is how some of the itinerant Commissioners implemented the more general instructions in ways which had clear gender implications. This section critically analyses the questionnaire used for interviewing the factory workers by John Spencer, Commissioner for the Western District of Newcastle under Lyme and the Staffordshire Potteries (see Appendix),[8] and examines how women were forced to take on a helpless, childish identity.

Spencer compiled two questionnaires, one for adults and one for children. Significantly, women were classified in the same category as children. Consequently Jane Apsley, a married woman of twenty-four, was asked the same questions as Joseph Heath, who was 'near nine', while Thomas Marks, aged sixteen, was asked the same questions as the adult men.[9] Spencer evidently perceived women in the same way as children. They both needed to be protected and had no place in the workplace. Consequently when he questions the children about their parents' work he asks: 'What is your father?', while he then asks: 'Does your mother work?'. The different phraseology is crucial to the historian interested in gender. The use of the verb 'is' in relation to the father's occupation suggests that men are defined by their work. A man's identity is established through his work and Spencer automatically assumes that the father would be working. Women on the other hand, gaining their 'femininity' from their roles as housewives and mothers, should not work. By asking 'Does your mother work?' rather than 'What is your mother?', Spencer reveals his belief that a woman's place is in the home and work is an undesirable extra.

Spencer, perceiving women to be the property of men as opposed to autonomous beings, asks who sent them to the factory. Jane Apsley, the married woman referred to above, replies, 'myself', which highlights how ridiculous his assumption is. By conceptualising women as children, Spencer's questions are often inappropriate and ludicrous. For example, Margaret Jackson (18 years), Ann Cook (23 years), Jane Apsley (24 years and married) and Mary Bullock (24 years) are asked whether they have a play-ground and how many hours they are allowed for 'play'. At another point he asks 'Are you, or other children in your work in the habit of frequenting public houses?'. Using the word 'you' in conjunction with the word 'children' reinforces the characterisation of women as children.[10] Significantly men are not asked this question. Spencer evidently thought women and children were a disruptive, immoral force in the workplace, as is shown by the question put to the men about the children. They are asked if there is any 'restraint or regulation imposed by the proprietor of your works, to prevent any obscene conduct on the part of girls?'. Women and children are also assumed to be idle and irresponsible, which prompts the questions: 'When you are idle, or behave ill, at the factory, what do they do to you?'. Similarly they are asked whether they are fined for 'committing any error, or spoiling the work'. Again, the men are not asked these questions.

Spencer questions the women about their personal experiences in the workplace, wanting to know whether they can wash themselves every day, what time they go to bed and whether the boys and girls share the same water closet. In contrast the men are asked to give their opinions, crediting them with greater status. He assumes the male factory workers to be autonomous, thinking individuals who are capable of assessing and commenting on the general running of the mill, the effects of the Ten Hour Bill being put forward and, most significantly, the experiences of women and children in the factories. Spencer asks 'how many children are employed and from what age?'; he wants to know whether the children are 'kept longer at work than is suitable to their age' and what the effects of preventing child labour would be for the factories. While the men are asked to comment on the plight of women and children: 'Do the children appear much tired after they leave work?', women and children are only asked about their direct experience: 'Are you very tired after a day's work?'. Spencer never asks women to comment on the problems of child labour, primarily because they are seen as part of the problem.

Linguistically and conceptually women are classified as children by Spencer's questionnaire. This forces women to present themselves in a certain light, i.e. as weak, vulnerable and in need of protection through legislation. In fact, the Central Commissioners did not propose a curb on women's working hours in their recommendations at this time. But the groundwork had been laid. Interestingly, it was when the arch-enemy of the Factory Commission, Evangelical Lord Ashley, got control of the investigative process with his Select Committee on Children's Employment of 1840 that the spotlight was turned more deliberately on to women. The resulting Factory Act of 1844 extended the young person's 69-hour working week to women as well, and became the first piece of legislation to regulate the hours of adult working women. The state, containing clear religious as well as utilitarian elements, had infantilised women in order to justify protecting them.

## The Royal Commission on the Poor Laws (1834)

This Royal Commission addressed an issue which had been seething from the period of the 1790s when a cycle of food shortages and political unrest had put the Poor Laws into the centre of political discussion and when some new and startling voices from political economy and religion had argued that the Elizabethan framework needed to be drastically reformed. Combining the two voices, the Revd Thomas Malthus, the first professional political economist, had issued the brutal dictum in 1803 that if a labourer could not feed his family 'they must starve'. Although his advice did not prevail, the Poor Laws continued to be problematic and the Royal Commission set up in 1832 was to be the opportunity to take a comprehensive view of their 'Administration and Practical Operation'. This section concentrates on the evidence pertaining to the Bastardy Laws collected by the Poor Law Commissioners for the *First Report*. The evidence amassed from the twenty-two volumes of the Sub-Commissioners' Reports and Evidence is a catalogue of sensational statements denouncing the immorality of the female labouring population. Image after image of wild, wanton and debased womanhood is detailed to ensure the repeal of the existing Bastardy Laws. The masculinity of the discourse is indisputable; no female statements are quoted and we only hear what women have allegedly said or done from male interviewees. The evidence condensed in the *First Report* of the Poor Law Commission unanimously advocates the repeal of the Bastardy Laws. This was the favoured male outcome, for under the existing laws the reputed father of a child was responsible for its maintenance. Once named as the father, a man had three options – either he married the woman or agreed to pay the child's allowance or he went to prison.

A passage at the beginning of the *First Report* unequivocally demonstrates where the Commissioners' sympathies lie. It states nothing could be 'more revolting' than a law which compels the oppression of men by placing them at the 'mercy of any abandoned woman' who wishes to swear them as the reputed father of her bastard. An example is cited where a young apprentice, a mere 'boy', had been committed to a house of correction for want of security after being named by a woman as the father of her child. Ironically the Commissioners use language more usually employed in middle-class rhetoric to describe the fall of an innocent girl. The Commissioners bewail the fact that he has been 'ruined' by the oath of a person with whom he denied having intercourse. They demand to know for what he is being punished, as sexual intercourse is not an offence in law.[11] Yet from a reading of the *First Report* it becomes clear that the Commissioners felt that while sexual intercourse outside marriage was a 'mere delinquency'[12] for a man, it was a punishable crime for a woman. In fact numerous male witnesses quoted in the *First Report* were extremely critical that, to use the words of Assistant Commissioner Captain I J. Chapman, there was a 'general disinclination ... on the part of the overseer to punish the mother'.[13] A woman, they argued, should be punished harshly for her transgression.

The laws on bastardy were cited as the major cause for the demoralisation of working-class women's characters. According to Alfred Power, the Assistant Commissioner studying Cambridge, they were 'the most active inducement to incontinence in the female'.[14] The certainty of an allowance, it was argued, removed those 'checks to irregular intercourse'[15] which women usually and naturally exercised. The Commissioners believed that working-class women, having realised that remaining 'virtuous and modest' would not secure them either 'the greatest prize – a husband'[16] or a little fortune,[17] that is a maintenance fee, were tempted to renounce a life of virtue or monogamy in favour of promiscuity and immorality. The laws too had 'abolished female chastity, self-respect, proper pride, and all the charities of domestic life'.[18] For John W. Cowell, investigating Norfolk and Nottingham, they were 'the most effective instrument for extinguishing every noble feeling of the female heart – for blighting domestic affections'.[19]

Women are depicted as seductresses who prey on innocent young boys and who will stop at nothing to ensure a husband or an allowance. Berkshire magistrate Colonel A'Court's description of women's behaviour is typical of many statements. He argues that '*middle aged women* will sometimes unblushingly swear *mere lads* to be the fathers of their bastard children; *lads* whom they have *enticed* to the commission of the offence' [my italics].[20] Significantly the women who are seducing 'mere lads' are middle-aged. The naivety and innocence of the boys is emphasised by the reiteration of the word 'lad' which makes the women's offence seem all the more heinous. The women are seen as cunning and brazen, being prepared to 'unblushingly swear', without remorse, young boys to be the fathers of their bastard children. The use of the word 'enticed' conjures up the image of the seductress. Mr Simeon uses equally charged language when criticising the practice which allows 'a woman of dissolute character to pitch upon any unfortunate young man, who she has *inveigled* into her net, and swear that child to him' [my italics].[21] Here the notion of the temptress turned captor is vividly conveyed through the verb 'inveigle' and the image of the net. Some of the witnesses speak as if there was a female plot to 'ruin' young men. Mr Simeon, for example, knows of instances where 'mothers have been instrumental in having their daughters seduced for the express purpose of getting rid of the onus of supporting them and saddling them upon any unfortunate young man of the neighbourhood whom they could get to the house'.[22] Women of all ages, mothers and daughters, are portrayed as conspiring to bring about man's downfall.

The *First Report* details endless statements testifying to women's alleged deceit and immorality while men are repeatedly characterised as their helpless victims. A Lambeth contractor, Charles Mott, relates to Chadwick how one girl, on being pressed by a committee to name the father, had the audacity to suggest that 'she would make one of them ... look foolish if she did'.[23] Men are seen as completely powerless; even the law cannot protect them, for the magistrates had 'no power to discriminate, no power to reject, no power to punish'.[24] According to one parochial officer at least nine out of ten bastards are falsely sworn from 'ignorance and willful perjury'[25] – the former implying promiscuity, the latter deceitfulness. Women, the Commissioners argue, have rejected their natural sympathies and sentiments; greed usurps their true maternal feelings, which causes them to favour the bastard, who is 'a means to extort money',[26] over the child born in wedlock. One woman allegedly stated gleefully on leaving the workhouse after her fourth confinement, that if she had 'the good luck to have another child', she would be able to 'draw a good sum from the parish' which would make her 'better off than any married woman in the parish'.[27]

The demand for the repeal of the Bastardy Laws can be seen as an element in the state's normalising drive, for, significantly, single women with children were stigmatised. The *First Report* condemns these women without contextualising their sexual behaviour within the working class's different set of sexual mores. In working-class communities a high premium was put on fertility as opposed to chastity and therefore pregnancy before marriage was not condemned. In fact pregnancy was often a prerequisite of marriage. Assistant Commissioner Captain Chapman refers to the practice of 'keeping company', but he denounces the practice because it destroys the distinction between vice and virtue, making 'the best careless about virtue' and giving 'an opportunity to the worst to carry on a career of more extended intercourse with impunity'.[28] Without attempting to understand the working-class sexual code, the Commissioners complain that women of 'lost virtue' are treated as if they have not 'committed the slightest offence against society'.[29] They argue that Britain could only become a country for the honest woman if the Bastardy Laws were repealed.[30] For only this measure would reverse the state of affairs whereby the 'brazen prostitute'[31] prospered at the expense of the 'honest widow'.

The Commissioners objected to the heavy financial burden incurred by the state if the father absconded. 'A bastard', the *First Report* stated in no uncertain terms, should be 'what Providence appears to have ordained that it should be, a burthen on its mother, and, where she cannot maintain it, on her parents'.[32] The Commissioners recommended stopping all maintenance money so women alone would be forced to take the whole onus of responsibility. Single mothers were vilified so the state could wash its hands of women who did not conform to the middle-class norm of monogamous, married relationships. As a close reading of the *First Report* shows, the Commissioners selected powerful images of wanton prostitutes, cunning temptresses and voracious crones to legitimise prompt legislative intervention which would restore the 'natural' sexuality of women as well as conveniently reduce state expenditure.

### The Children's Employment Commission Inquiring into the Mines (1842)

> Chained, belted, harnessed, like dogs in a go-cart – black, saturated with wet, and more than half *naked* – crawling upon their hands and feet and dragging their heavy loads behind them, they present an appearance indescribably disgusting and unnatural.[33]

This image of brutalised, debased, wretched womanhood is ubiqui-
tous in the *First Report* into the employment of children in the
mines. The demoralised state of the women is attributed to their
position as workers. Work, the Commissioners argue, has polluted
women's true femininity, and its immoral effects are unanimously
condemned by the evidence selected for the *First Report* of the
Commissioners. For Jellinger C. Symons, the Sub-Commissioner
investigating part of Yorkshire, it was a 'revolting abomination'
which was 'flagrantly disgraceful to Christians as well as to a civi-
lized country'. George Armitage, a Hoyland teacher, felt that
'nothing could be worse' while miner George Carr maintained that
he would rather 'live upon a meal a day' than make his daughter
work at such a 'shameful practice'.[34] By turn it was denounced as a
'disgusting', 'scandalous', 'brutalising',[35] practice that was unfit for
women, leading them to reject their natural roles of mother and
housewife. According to collier Matthew Lindley, 'not one in ten of
them ... know how to cut a shirt out or make one and they learn
neither to knit or sew',[36] while Matthew Fountain, an underground
steward, believed the work to be 'not proper for females at all'
because they were 'unfitted' by being at the pits from learning to
manage families.[37]

Yet while a reading of the *First Report* confirms the
Commissioners' statement that 'all classes of witness bear the
strongest testimony to the immoral effects of this practice',[38] a
study of the original depositions reveals that this statement needs
qualification. It is true that most of the miners, especially the
women, speak out against the work but they stress the physical
severity of the labour, and the appalling conditions for both sexes,
rather than emphasising its 'immoral effects'. The following statements are representative of the terms in which women discuss their
work: for example, Agnes Reid, a coal bearer aged fourteen, states
that 'it is very sore work, and makes us often cry; few lasses like
it',[39] while it is seventeen-year-old Anna Moffatt's belief that 'the
work is o'er sair for females'.[40] Jane Peacock Watson (coal bearer
aged forty, married with six living children) denounces the work as
'horse work' and feels it 'ruins the woman', not morally but physically, for 'it crushes the haunches, bends their ankles and makes
them old women at forty'.[41] Women, it seems, are not adverse to
work in itself, but as Isabel Hogg aged fifty-three comments, 'they
object to horse work'. Women complain that they are given the

most strenuous jobs, for example the winching up of miners from the bottom of the pits, and are made to 'submit to work in places where no man, or even lad, could be got to labour'. Women, it seems, did not shrink from the hard grind; they needed to work because the domestic existence which the middle classes advocated was not economically viable. Hence Isabel Hogg asks Queen Victoria to remove them from the pits and send them to 'other labour' rather than back into the home.[42] The women emphasise the unsuitability of the work for men and women alike. As Anne Harris, aged fifteen, correctly states, the work in the mines 'is no woman's work nor is it good for anybody'.[43]

A comparison of the testimonies given by a 'respectable' woman from Silkstone and by Benjamin Mellor, a miner, illustrates the factors that influenced the Commissioners' selection process. The 'respectable' woman's statement is included, although its reliability is contestable, being based solely on hearsay. She claims that she has been 'credibly informed' that scenes take place in the pit 'which are bad as any house of ill-fame'. She denounces the work on account of its 'injurious' moral effects rather than its physical hardship; in fact she claims that 'the work in the pit does not hurt them'.[44] In contrast, Mellor does not think the work 'at all objectionable on account of morals' and argues that there is 'less immorality' in the pits than in service. He also sees the mining women as active and capable of robust self-protection: 'if a man was to offer any insult to a girl in a pit, she would take her fist and give him a blow in his face'. Mellor's comment is omitted, no doubt because it contradicted middle-class notions about the appropriate spheres of work for women.

In the *First Report*, evidence contradicting the claim that 'where girls are employed the immoralities practised are scandalous'[45] is conspicuous by its absence. The Commissioners refuse to recognise evidence detailing a strict moral code down the mines. For example, Selina Ambler's statement that 'the boys never dare touch us, if they did my brother would plump them'[46] is omitted, as is Esther Craven's comment that although she worked 'in trousers bare-legged, and a pair of old stays; the men never meddle with us'.[47] The conditions of employment, the darkness, the nakedness of the workers and the isolated nature of the work made it impossible for the Commissioners to believe Elspee Thompson's comment that colliers' daughters were as 'full virtuous as other women, only their habits are so different from being taken down so early'.[48] The Commissioners judged the mining women by their own value system, refusing to accept that the working-class moral code, although different, was as legitimate as their own. As Elspee points out, just because the miners' habits were different this did not automatically mean that they were all less moral.

Sometimes crucial sentences from the original depositions are deleted when cited in the *First Report*. For example the Revd Oliver Levey Collins was quoted as saying in the *First Report*: 'There is a good deal of drunkenness and sensuality. Bastardy is sadly too common; they look on it as a misfortune and not as a crime.'[49] The original statement read: 'There is a good deal of drunkenness and sensuality *but in point of honesty they are astonishing*. Bastardy is sadly too common' [my italics].[50] Significantly the only positive comment about the women is omitted. Similarly, the exclusion of Mary Barrett's last sentence in the *First Report* changes the whole sense of the passage. In her original statement she comments: 'I wear nothing but my chemise; I have to go up to the headings with the men; they are all naked there; I am got well used to it; I was afraid at first, and did not like it; *they never behave rudely to me*' [my italics].[51] The words in italics are not quoted in the *First Report*, which leaves the reader assuming that immorality inevitably takes place.

Many of the original depositions vouch for the women's morality and domesticity. Yet these comments, along with evidence stating that women carried out their double burden efficiently and conscientiously, are absent from the *First Report*. Dr Charles Barham, Sub-Commissioner for Devon and Cornwall, for example, believes that the 'hearts' of the pit women are in 'their homes', and that they make for the most part 'tender mothers and industrious wives';[52] collier George Hirst states that many mining girls become 'respectable women' and most probably 'useful wives', rejecting the view that they 'have any more impudence than the other girls that are brought up in other ways'.[53] Importantly Esther Craven maintains that the work in the pits does not prevent her from carrying out her domestic chores: 'I can hem and sew, and mend my stockings'. She comments also that she liked the work 'very well' and that she would rather be in the pit than 'nought else' as she preferred it to 'nursing or any other kind of work'.[54] Unsurprisingly this was not included in the *First Report*, presumably because it contradicted the prevailing middle-class belief that women should only work in the home, in domestic service or in caring jobs which were extensions of the female sphere. Employment such as mining 'brutalised' a woman and was therefore unsuitable. However, conditions for the needlewomen employed in the sweatshops, although seen as 'feminine' work were equally arduous and exploitative.

A powerful image of the mining women as debased, voracious and depraved emerges from a reading of the *First Report*. The mining women are 'bold', 'brutish', 'degraded and dejected'.[55] According to John Thorneley, a Yorkshire magistrate, 'women brought up in this way lay aside all modesty, and scarcely know what it is by name'.[56] George Armitage of Hoyland attributes the women's immorality to the work environment and the 'company' which make it 'scarcely possible for girls to remain modest'.[57] He is not alone in citing work as the primary reason for the mining women's debasement. David Forrester, another teacher from near Kilkady, describes them as 'a separate and lower caste'[58] on account of their degrading work. For Sub-Commissioner Scriven the mining women 'are vulgar in manner and obscene in language' on account of 'living and labouring' with men in a 'state of disgusting nakedness'.[59] Barnsley surgeon Michael Sadler felt 'the female character is totally destroyed' by the work which renders the women's 'habits and feelings … altogether different' so that they become unable to discharge their 'duties of wives and mothers'.[60] Typically, 'true' and 'natural' femininity is inextricably linked to the way women execute their domestic tasks. For John Ambler the female miners are 'worse than the worst' because they are 'degraded and dejected creatures' who make 'bad wives' bringing up their children in a state of 'ignorance and depravity'.[61] Women's immorality is seen as a major cause of the demoralised state of the whole mining community. The Commissioners argued that many men finding their homes neglected, dirty and unkempt turned to the public house for solace, in order to find that 'cheerfulness and physical comfort which his own fire-side does not afford'.[62]

According to the Sub-Commissioner for East Scotland, Robert Hugh Franks, the 'cleanliness and decent properties of person and home' are 'invaluable as a means of keeping the tone of the labouring population from sinking into grossness'.[63] Women had to be forced back into the home from where they could exude a moral influence over the mining community. Women hold a paradoxical position in the middle-class domestic ideology, for they can be both the agent of society's regeneration, or conversely of its degeneration. So although they are characterised as being the cause of the mining community's degraded state, they are simultaneously seen as its only hope for redemption. Thus the middle classes use these emotive images of debased femininity to detract from the real causes of the wretched situation of the labouring poor – exploitation, low wages, long hours and bad conditions of work.

Many of the middle-class testimonies are more supposition than fact. The darkness, the isolation of the work, and the half-naked state of the miners fires the middle-class informants' imaginations and arouses the certainty that sexual intercourse must be rife. Hence John Thorneley claims that 'sexual intercourse decidedly frequently occurs' as young children of both sexes work together in 'a half naked state' which means 'the passions are excited before they arrive at puberty'.[64] Similarly, Mr George Armitage is in 'no doubt that debauchery is carried on, for which there is every opportunity; for the girls go constantly when hurrying to the men who often work alone in the bank-faces apart from everyone'.[65] The Revd Hand, vicar of Handworth and also a magistrate, believes the morals of the women who work in the pits are worse than those of female agricultural workers 'because they work at night';[66] while Edward Newman, a Barnsley solicitor, feels that the women who work at the furnaces are probably more moral than those who work underground because they 'dress better' and 'work by daylight', which does not 'create in one's mind so revolting an effect'[67] – a comment that reveals more about his prurient imagination than it does about the character or work habits of the mining women.

For Commissioners, like Symons, gathering evidence seems to be both titillating and voyeuristic. For example, he repeatedly asks questions about the straps of the courbes which passed between the girls' legs. He lingers over the descriptions of the wounds these straps made, and the holes they made in the girls' trousers. He, like the majority of the Commissioners, attaches sexual connotations to the women's appearance and behaviour. Newman, a middle-class informant, is obviously fascinated by the women washing themselves: 'at Silkstone there are a great many girls who work in the pits, and I have seen them washing themselves naked much below the waist as I passed their doors, and whilst they are doing this they will be talking and chatting with any men who happen to be there'. However, this description of them washing themselves reveals more about his voyeurism than the women's supposed immorality.[68] He is surprised by their uninhibited behaviour, which reveals his misunderstanding of the more open sexual, but not necessarily more immoral, behaviour of the working classes.

The way in which women are depicted in the *First Report* is part of a wider set of images working along class lines. Domestic ideology worked to control women through pairs of antithetical images, showing women as either mothers or whores, Madonnas or Magdalenes.[69] From reading the *First Report* of the Children's Employment Commission inquiring into the mines it is clear that working-class women are the whores. The message is in keeping with middle-class ideology. Women must be removed from the workplace, which is little better than a brothel, and returned to the home so that moral order can be restored to the labouring population.

## Conclusion

The language of the Commissioners and, in particular, these debased images of femininity informed the parliamentary debates on the mines and the Poor Law, thereby shaping and justifying legislation which impacted significantly on the lives of women in the public and private spheres. It is unclear whether moral outrage or Malthusian fears most informed the Commissioners' recommendations for the Bastardy Clauses but, whatever the underlying imperative, the hysterical language of the *First Report* was exploited by supporters in both the House of Commons and the House of Lords.[70] Although the Commissioners did not achieve the complete withdrawal of a maintenance grant, the New Poor Law removed moral and financial responsibility from the man and placed the whole burden of responsibility on the woman. Reflecting the Commissioners' recommendations, the legislation aimed to curb women's supposedly manipulative use of sexuality to secure a maintenance. Affiliation orders could still be placed but the action was costly and a woman's evidence had to be corroborated. Significantly, even if affiliation was proven, the money went to the parish, not to the mother. From this time onwards illegitimacy carried more of a stigma; unmarried mothers were identified as sexual outlaws and a dangerous moral threat.[71] As one woman stated when commenting on the workings of the New Poor Law, 'it is a fine time for the boys now ... It is a bad time for the girls, Sir, the boys have their own way'.[72]

The parliamentary debates about employment in the mines stressed just what the investigators had highlighted, namely rampant sexuality on the one hand and ignorance of domesticity on the other. The Mines Act of 1842 banned women altogether from working underground in the dark eroticised spaces which the investigators invariably exposed. In the wake of the moral outrage unleashed by the mines debate, new factory legislation which included women within the twelve-hour limit for young persons was pushed through Parliament. Couching the debate in moral terms similar to those used in the mines debate, Lord Ashley stressed not only the gender disorder of women who replaced men as breadwinners but the undermining of civilisation brought about by imposing 'on the wives and daughters of England a burthen from which, at least during pregnancy, they would be exempted even in slave-holding states, and among the Indians of America'.[73] A convergence was also taking place between the parliamentarians obsessed by social order and working-class men, who, in movements like Chartism and the Ten Hours campaign, were trying to protect class interests by championing their own version of 'domesticity for women and breadwinning for men'.[74] A powerful common sense was being constructed which held that women could only be restored to their true sexuality if they were returned to their natural and rightful position in the home.

# Appendix: Sample of John Spencer's Questionnaire

| QUESTIONS | ANSWERS | | | |
|---|---|---|---|---|
| PUT TO JOHN JAMES, JOHN COWARD, WILLIAM GIBBS, and THOMAS MARKS. (June 1833.) | JOHN JAMES, employed by MESSRS. SAMUEL MUNDY and CO. *Bradford.* | JOHN COWARD, employed by MESSRS. SAUNDERS, FANNER and CO. *Bradford.* | WILLIAM GIBBS, employed by JOHN PHILIPS Esquire, *Melksham.* (About 300, all Men and Boys.) | THOMAS MARKS, employed by MESSRS. YERBURY, EDMONDS, and CO. *Bradford.* |
| 1. What is your name and age? | 1. Forty-four years. | 1. Fifty-six years. | 1. Willam Gibbs; twenty-seven | 1. Sixteen years. |
| 2. Where do you work, and what is your employment? | 2. At Messrs. Mundy's; dresser and cutter. | 2. At Messrs. Saunders; a scribbler. | 2. Mr. Philips; a slubber. | 2. Feeds a double. scribbler. |
| 3. What is the sort of manufactory at which you are employed? | 3. Cloth manufactory. | 3. Cloth work. | 3. Cloth manufactory. | 3. Cloth works. |
| 4. Is your work done by water or steam? | 4. By steam. | 4. By both. | 4. Steam. | 4. Steam. |
| 5. Any children employed? | 5. Yes. | 5. Yes. | 5. Yes. | 5. Yes, sir. |
| 6. How many under eighteen years of age? | 6. Twelve under eighteen. | 6. Forty. | 6. Thirty. | 6. About twenty-four. |
| 7. How many under twelve years of age? | 7. Eight under twelve. | 7. Twelve. | 7. Six. | 7. About twelve. |
| 8. How many women and girls employed? | 8. Five women; eight girls. | 8. Forty-five. | 8. None. | 8. 100. |
| 9. How many men and boys? | 9. Eighteen men; ten boys. | 9. About sixty. | 9. Three hundred. | 9. A great many. |
| 10. How many hours do you work? | 10. We, the dressers, work thirteen hours, but the younger hands only ten. | 10. Ten hours work. | 10. From six to seven at night. | 10. Ten hours.* |
| 11. What are the hours for meals? | 11. Two hours. | 11. And two hours meals. | 11. Two. | 11. Two hours. |

| QUESTIONS | ANSWERS | | | |
|---|---|---|---|---|
| | JOHN JAMES | JOHN COWARD | WILLIAM GIBBS | THOMAS MARKS |
| 12. Are all the six working days alike? | 12. Yes, excepting Saturdays we leave at two. | 12. Yes, except Saturdays, then leave at two. | 12. Yes, except Saturday, and that day we leave at two o'clock. | 12. No, Saturday we leave at two. |
| 13. Do the children at the end of the day appear much fatigued? | 13. Yes, when it is warm. | 13. No, they are quite lively. | 13. No, sir. | 13. Some of them do. |
| 14. Do you think the children that are employed in a factory are as healthy and as strong as those of the same age, and who are not employed in a factory? | 14. I think they are not. | 14. No, I see no difference, except in weakly cases. | 14. I see no difference. | 14. No, I don't think they are. |
| 15. Are all your workpeople paid by the piece? | 15. No, except the slubbers, and those are three only. | 15. Mostly by the piece. | 15. Mostly paid by the piece. | 15. The slubbers are paid by the piece, we by the week. |
| 16. Is your manufactory well ventilated? | 16. Yes, sir. | 16. Yes. | 16. Yes. | 16. There are casements. |
| 17. Are all the dangerous parts of the machinery well guarded? | 17. No, not at all. | 17. Yes. | 17. Yes. | 17. Not very well guarded. |
| 18. Do you think that the children are kept longer at work than is suitable to their tender years? | 18. No, I don't think they are. | 18. No, I don't think they are. | 18. No, sir. | 18. No, sir. |
| 19. Do you think in general the children have plenty of food? | 19. No, they have not. | 19. Yes, they have. | 19. I think they have. | 19. No, I don't think they have. |
| 20. Would their parents wish for an abridgement of the hours of labour? | 20. No, I think not. | 20. No, I never heard of any thing of the sort. | 20. No, sir. | 20. No, not unless they had the same money. |
| 21. Would the stopping of the children working necessarily stop the whole work? | 21. Yes, it would. | 21. A great part of it. | 21. Yes, sir. | 21. Yes. |
| 22. Did you ever work at any other factory? | 22. No, not any. | 22. Yes, at Dunkirk, because my master gave over trade. | 22. – | 22. – |

| QUESTIONS | ANSWERS | | | |
|---|---|---|---|---|
| | JOHN JAMES | JOHN COWARD | WILLIAM GIBBS | THOMAS MARKS |
| 23. Have you observed whether grown-up men and women who have worked in these factories are less strong and well-grown than other workpeople not employed in factories? | 23. Yes, they are just as well. | 23. I don't think they are. | 23. I see no difference. | 23. Yes, I think they are. |
| 24. Do all or most of the children in your manufactory attend a Sabbath-school? | 24. Yes, sir. | 24. A great part of them. | 24. Yes, all that are able. | 24. Yes, sir. |
| 25. Do you think those children more controllable and better behaved that have regularly attended a Sunday-school than those who have not attended any school? | 25. Yes. | 25. Yes, I think they are. | 25. Yes, sir. | 25. Yes, sir. |
| 26. Do you take any apprentices? | 26. No. | 26. No, sir. | 26. No. | 26. No. |
| 27. Do your workpeople in general have animal food three or four times a week? | 27. I can't say. | 27. I think the greater part of them have. | 27. Yes, every day. | 27. No. |
| 28. Do you think that if the labour of persons under the age of eighteen years was limited to ten hours, it would entail in practice a limitation of the labour of adults to the same hours; or in other words, would the whole of the working hours of the factory consequently be limited to ten hours? | 28. In our works it would not, because we have not many young hands. | 28. Yes, it must follow. | 28. Yes, it must. | 28. Yes, it would. |
| 29. At what age do boys and girls commonly begin to exercise their own discretion in engaging their services, and receiving and appropriating their earnings? | 29. Eighteen. | 29. About eighteen. | 29. About sixteen. | 29. About eighteen. |
| 30. At what age do young persons in factories commonly enter into a contract of matrimony? | 30. About twenty. | 30. About twenty. | 30. Nineteen to twenty-one. | 30. About twenty. |
| 31. Is there any regulation or restraint imposed by the proprietor of your works, to prevent any obscene conduct of the girls, or bad language on the part of any? | 31. The foreman would check any bad conduct. | 31. Any impropriety is checked. | 31. We have no girls. | 31. The foreman checks any thing of the sort. |

## ANSWERS

| QUESTIONS | JOHN JAMES | JOHN COWARD | WILLIAM GIBBS | THOMAS MARKS |
|---|---|---|---|---|
| 32. Does a practice prevail among the workmen in your employ, when they are engaged upon piece-work, of bringing with them to the factory one or more of their children of tender age, to assist them during the whole time that they themselves are at work, even to extra hours? | 32. In our works we have none work by the piece. | 32. No. | 32. No, not here. | 32. There is no piece-work here. |
| 33. At the factory you formerly worked, were you treated equally as well there as here? | 33. – | 33. Yes. | 33. – | 33. – |
| 34. If some or all of your workpeople stop longer to do over-work at the factory, is it optional on their part whether they do so? | 34. Yes, it is optional. | 34. It is optional. | 34. We wish it, but it is optional. | 34. Yes, it is optional. |
| 35. Are any of the children kept after the usual hours, to clean the rooms or machinery, or any other work? | 35. Yes, a short time to clean about their own places. | 35. No. | 35. No, sir. | 35. Yes, for a few minutes. |
| 36. If from any cause the works are stopped for a lengthened or short period, is that lost time always or mostly regained by additional hours of over-work? | 36. No. | 36. If our orders are heavy, we generally fetch up the time. | 36. – | 36. Yes, sometimes it is so. |
| 37. Have any persons been lately discharged from your manufactory, if so for what cause? | 37. Yes, some from our works, in consequence of the improved machine for cutting. | 37. No, I don't recollect any. | 37. – | 37. No. |
| 38. Are you quite sure that no alterations whatever have been made recently in the mode of conducting your works, either as to shortening the hours or otherwise? | 38. No alteration whatever. | 38. No sir. | 38. – | 38. No. |
| | JAMES ALDERWICK, You have heard the questions put, and answers given by John Coward, and believe them correct? – Yes. | | JOHN JONES, 27, THOMAS JONES, 30, STEPHEN JAMES, 35, { You have heard the questions put, and the answers given by William Gibbs, and believe them correct? – Yes. | SILAS LAND, You have heard the questions put, and answers given by Thomas Marks, and believe them correct? – Yes. |

* The ten hours is the real full hours of work.

# QUESTIONS

## ANSWERS

| QUESTIONS PUT TO MARGARET JACKSON, ANN COOK, JANE ASPLEY, MARY BULLOCK, and ELIZABETH SILVESTER. (May 1833.) | MARGARET JACKSON, employed by Messrs. LESTER & CO., Newcastle. | ANN COOK, employed by Messrs. LESTER & CO., Newcastle. | JANE ASPLEY, employed by Messrs. TODD & CO., Newcastle. | MARY BULLOCK, employed by Messrs. TODD & CO., Newcastle. | ELIZABETH SILVESTER, employed by JOHN RIDGWAY, Esq., Cauldron Place, near Newcastle. |
|---|---|---|---|---|---|
| 1. How old are you? | 1. Eighteen years of age. | 1. Twenty-three years. | 1. Twenty-four. | 1. Twenty-four. | 1. Fifteen. |
| 2. Where do you work? | 2. At Mr. Lester's silk-works. | 2. At Mr. Lester's silk-works. | 2. Messrs. Todd and Co's silk-works. | 2. Messrs. Todd and Co's silk-works. | 2. Mr. Ridgway's. |
| 3. What is your father? | 3. My father is dead. | 3. My father is dead. | 3. Potter. | 3. A saddler. | 3. He is dead. |
| 4. Does your mother work? | 4. No. | 4. My mother is dead. | 4. No. | 4. No. | 4. She is dead. |
| 5. How long have you been at the factory? | 5. About eight years. | 5. Thirteen years. | 5. From the first, when it was erected. | 5. About eight years. | 5. Four years. |
| 6. Are you paid by the week or by piece? | 6. By the piece. | 6. I have 6s. wages, and am allowed to get over work. | 6. By the piece. | 6. By the piece. | 6. By the week. |
| 7. Who sent you there? | 7. My mother sent me there. | 7. My mother. | 7. Myself. | 7. My parents. | 7. My mother, before she died. |
| 8. How soon do you go in the morning, and how late do you stay in the evening? | 8. Six in the morning until seven at night. | 8. From six to seven. | 8. Go at six and work till seven. | 8. Six o'clock. | 8. Half-past six morning, and six night. |
| 9. Summer? | 9. Same. | 9. The same. | 9. Same. | 9. Same. | 9. Same. |
| 10. Winter? | 10. Same. | 10. The same. | 10. Same. | 10. Same. | 10. At seven in the morning and six evening. |
| 11. How long are you allowed to get your breakfast? | 11. Twenty minutes. | 11. Twenty minutes. | 11. Twenty minutes. | 11. Twenty minutes. | 11. Half an hour. |
| 12. What do you get for breakfast generally? | 12. Tea. | 12. Coffee. | 12. Coffee. | 12. Coffee in general. | 12. Sometimes bread and butter, and sometimes bread and cheese. |
| 13. How long are you allowed for dinner? | 13. One hour. | 13. One hour. | 13. One hour. | 13. One hour. | 13. An hour. |
| 14. How many of your family are employed? | 14. Three. | 14. A sister. | 14. Only myself and husband. | 14. Only myself. | 14. Only myself and sister. |
| 15. How much do they all get in wages? | 15. About nine shillings. | 15. 11s., besides a little over-work. | 15. About twenty shillings. | 15. – | 15. I get two shillings and sixpence; my brothers work at other places. |
| 16. What do you usually get for dinner? | 16. Sometimes beef. | 16. Sometimes beef. | 16. – | 16. Meat and vegetables. | 16. Potatoes, and some-times minced meat. |
| 17. Do you get any thing to eat after dinner, before going to bed? | 17. Yes; tea. | 17. Yes; tea. | 17. Tea. | 17. Tea. | 17. Yes; coffee. |

## QUESTIONS / ANSWERS

| QUESTIONS | MARGARET JACKSON | ANN COOK | JANE ASPLEY | MARY BULLOCK | ELIZABETH SILVESTER |
|---|---|---|---|---|---|
| 18. At what hour do you generally go to bed? | 18. About ten, or soon after. | 18. At ten. | 18. Ten or thereabout. | 18. About ten. | 18. About ten. |
| 19. Are you washed every day? | 19. Yes. | 19. Yes. | 19. – | 19. Yes. | 19. Yes. |
| 20. When do you take your meals? | 20. Half past eight morning, one at dinner, and five at night. | 20. Half past eight morning, and one, dinner. | 20. Twenty minutes before nine for breakfast, and one dinner. | 20. Twenty minutes to nine for breakfast, at one for dinner, five tea. | 20. At nine breakfast, two dinner, tea about seven. |
| 21. Have you ever been at school? | 21. Yes. | 21. Yes. | 21. Yes. | 21. Yes. | 21. Yes. |
| 22. Can you read and write? | 22. Read, but not write. | 22. Read, but not write. | 22. Read, but not write. | 22. Read, and write a little. | 22. Read, but not write. |
| 23. Do you go to any school now whilst you are at the factory; if you do, what do you learn? | 23. I go to a Sunday-school, and I am a teacher. | 23. I go to a Sunday-school and I am a teacher there. | 23. No. | 23. No. | 23. On Sunday; I am in the Testament. |
| 24. If you do not go to school, what is the reason? | 24. Because I am obliged to work. | 24. Because I am obliged to work. | 24. – | 24. Because I am obliged to go to work. | 24. Because I am employed at the factory. |
| 25. Do you go to a Sunday-school? | 25. Yes. | 25. Yes. | 25. No. | 25. No. | 25. Yes. |
| 26. When you are idle, or behave ill, at the factory, what do they do to you? | 26. I can't say that they do anything. | 26. They never use any punishment to me. | 26. Nothing. | 26. Send for us into the office and reprove us, and then discharge us if repeated. | 26. They hit me sometimes with their hand, but it is seldom. |
| 27. Are you very tired after your day's work? | 27. Sometimes. | 27. Sometimes more tired than at others. | 27. Sometimes, but not much. | 27. Sometimes. | 27. Sometimes. |
| 28. Is the place you work in very warm? | 28. In summer it is. | 28. Yes, very warm in the summer. | 28. Not very warm. | 28. No. | 28. Yes, but not more than I like. |
| 29. Have you ever any pains when you are at work? | 29. Sometimes the headache. | 29. No. | 29. No, sir. | 29. No. | 29. No, sir. |
| 30. What wages do you get, and do you receive them yourself? | 30. Yes, I receive them myself; and sometimes 6s., sometimes 7s. | 30. Yes, 6s. and over-work. | 30. About 8s., and I receive my own. | 30. Yes, I receive them myself; sometimes I get 8s., and sometimes a little more. | 30. Yes, I receive 2s. 6d., give it my brother. |
| 31. Do you stand the whole time you are in the factory? | 31. Yes, all the working hours. | 31. Yes, all the working hours. | 31. Yes. | 31. Yes. | 31. I sit. |
| 32. Have any workpeople been lately removed from the factory? | 32. Not any. | 32. Not that I know of. | 32. No. | 32. Not since the present partners came to the works. | 32. Not any. |

| QUESTIONS | ANSWERS | | | | |
|---|---|---|---|---|---|
| | MARGARET JACKSON | ANN COOK | JANE ASPLEY | MARY BULLOCK | ELIZABETH SILVESTER |
| 33. What is the distance at which you reside from the factory you are employed at? | 33. About half a mile. | 33. Quarter of a mile. | 33. Not a quarter of a mile. | 33. A quarter of a mile. | 33. Two miles. |
| 34. During the day what hours are allowed for meals and for play? | 34. One hour and forty minutes. | 34. One hour and 40 minutes. | 34. One hour and forty minutes. | 34. One hour and forty minutes. | 34. Half an hour at breakfast, and one hour at dinner. |
| 35. Have you any play-ground? | 35. None. | 35. No. | 35. No. | 35. No. | 35. No. |
| 36. If you are a little after the time you ought to attend your employment, are you chastised, and if so, in what manner? | 36. I work by the piece, and am not liable to be chastised. | 36. No. | 36. No. | 36. Working by piece-work, they don't notice us. | 36. No, but scolded. |
| 37. If you are later in attendance than the hour appointed, are you abated, or is any money stopped from your wages at the end of the week? | 37. No, because I am at piece-work. | 37. Yes. | 37. No. | 37. It makes no difference to me, working by the piece. | 37. No, sir. |
| 38. If you are abated or stopped in your wages, to whom does that stoppage go? | 38. To the master. | 38. To the master. | 38. Never are abated. | 38. – | 38. I am never abated. |
| 39. Are you paid your wages in money? | 39. Yes. | 39. Yes. | 39. Yes. | 39. Yes. | 39. Yes. |
| 40. Are you or your parents obliged to purchase provisions, or other articles, at any particular shop, by the owner of your factory? | 40. No. | 40. No. | 40. No. | 40. No, sir. | 40. No. |
| 41. If you are abated in your wages for being too late in your attendance, or for committing any error, or for spoiling the work on which you are employed, who is it that puts you under those abatements? | 41. The steward. | 41. The steward. | 41. I am never abated. | 41. – | 41. I am never abated. |
| 42. Do you clean the rooms in which you are employed, and how often? | 42. No. | 42. No; there are boys on purpose to clean them. | 42. No. | 42. No, a girl is hired for that purpose. | 42. We take this in rotation; my turn is about once a fortnight. |
| 43. Have you any seats to rest upon during your working-hours? | 43. None but the skips. | 43. Yes, the skips that we use. | 43. No. | 43. No. | 43. – |

| QUESTIONS | | ANSWERS | | | |
|---|---|---|---|---|---|
| | MARGARET JACKSON | ANN COOK | JANE ASPLEY | MARY BULLOCK | ELIZABETH SILVESTER |
| 44. Do the boys and girls go to the same water-closet? | 44. No. | 44. No. | 44. No. | 44. No. | 44. No; different for each. |
| 45. Have you any Irish children employed in your factory? | 45. A few. | 45. Yes, one family, but I don't know of any more. | 45. Several. | 45. Yes, several. | 45. Not any. |
| 46. Are you, or other children in your works, in the habit of frequenting public-houses? | 46. No, sir. | 46. No; the master won't allow it. | 46. Never. | 46. Not that I know. | 46. No, sir. |
| 47. Are you instructed in reading and writing after you have left your employment? | 47. No. | 47. No. | 47. No. | 47. No, sir. | 47. No, but I go to a Sunday-school. |

## Notes

1 For gender, see U. R. O. Henriques, 'Bastardy and the New Poor Law', *Past and Present*, 39 (1967); J. Humphries, 'Protective Legislation, the Capitalist State and Working-Class Men: The Case of the Mines Regulation Act', *Feminist Review*, 7 (1981).

2 A. John, *By the Sweat of their Brow: Women Workers in Victorian Coal Mines* (London, Croom Helm, 1980), p. 44.

3 Children's Employment Commission (Mines), *First Report, Parliamentary Sessional Papers* (1842), vol. xv, p. 5.

4 *Ibid.*

5 F. Mort, *Dangerous Sexualities: Medico-Moral Politics in England since 1830* (London, Routledge and Kegan Paul, 1987), pp. 51–3; for the civil service, see P. Corrigan and D. Sayer, *The Great Arch: English State Formation as Cultural Revolution* (Oxford, Blackwell, 1985), pp. 159, 123; for Chadwick, S. E. Finer, *The Life and Times of Sir Edwin Chadwick* (London, Methuen, 1952); for J. C. Symons, see the *Dictionary of National Biography*.

6 See C. Driver, *Tory Radical: The Life of Richard Oastler* (Oxford, Oxford University Press, 1946), chs 18–20 for the opposition.

7 See R. Gray, *The Factory Question and Industrial England, 1830–1860* (Cambridge, Cambridge University Press, 1996), p. 88; also 'Instructions to Commissioners', Factories Inquiry Commission, *First Report of the ... Commissioners for Inquiring into the Employment of Children in Factories, British Parliamentary Papers* (1833), vol. xx, pp. 79–94.

8 'Examinations taken by Mr Spencer', *First Report ... Factories, Appendix B.2* (1833), vol. xx, pp. 1–85.

9 'Examinations by Spencer', pp. 22–5, 30–2, 54–7; see Appendix, pp. 91, 95.

10 'Examinations by Spencer', pp. 22–5 for the women; see Appendix, pp. 95–102.

11 Poor Law Commission, *Report from H.M. Commissioners on the Administration and Practical Operation of the Poor Laws, Parliamentary Sessional Papers* (1834), vol. xxvii, p. 93. Hereafter called *Poor Law First Report*.

12 *Ibid.*

13 *Poor Law First Report, Appendix A, Reports from Assistant Commissioners, British Parliamentary Papers* (1834), vol. xxviii, p. 450.

14 *Poor Law First Report*, vol. xvii, p. 96.

15 *Ibid.*, p. 94.

16 Quoting the evidence of Mr Simeon before the House of Lords Committee on the Poor Laws, 1831, *ibid.*, p. 98.

17 *Reports from Assistant Commissioners*, vol. xxix, pt III, p. 216.

18 *Ibid.*, vol. xviii, p. 650.

19 *Ibid.*, p. 646.

20 *Poor Law Report*, vol. xxvii, p. 94.

21 *Ibid.*, p. 98.

22 *Ibid.*

23 *Reports from Assistant Commissioners*, vol. xxix, pt III, p. 202.

24 *Ibid.*, vol. xxviii, p. 452.

25 *Poor Law Report*, vol. xxvii, p. 94.

26 *Ibid.*, pp. 93, 196; also *Reports from Assistant Commissioners*, vol. xxviii, pp. 453, 451.

27 *Poor Law Report*, vol. xxvii, p. 95.
28 *Reports from Assistant Commissioners*, vol. xviii, p. 451.
29 *Ibid.*
30 *Ibid.*, p. 650.
31 *Ibid.*, p. 453.
32 *Poor Law Report*, vol. xxvii, p. 197.
33 'Report by Samuel S. Scriven' (on a part of the West Riding of Yorkshire), Children's Employment Commission, *First Report of the Commissioners. Mines*, Appendix, pt II, *British Parliamentary Papers* (1842), vol. xvii, p. 75.
34 *First Report ... Mines* (1842), vol. xv, pp. 32–3; 'Evidence collected by J. C. Symons', *ibid.*, Appendix, pt I, vol. xvi, witness no. 131, p. 261; witness no. 233, p. 284.
35 'Evidence collected by Scriven', vol. xvii, witness no. 49, p. 115; 'Evidence collected by Symons', witness no. 142 (meeting of 350 working colliers), p. 262; witness no. 139 (Barnsley surgeon Michael Sadler), p. 261.
36 'Evidence collected by Symons', vol. xvi, witness no. 109, p. 251.
37 *Ibid.*, witness no. 119, p. 254.
38 *First Report ... Mines*, vol. xv, p. 33.
39 'Evidence collected by Robert Hugh Franks' (East of Scotland), *First Report ... Mines*, Appendix, pt I, vol. xvi, witness no. 2, p. 436; also quoted *First Report ... Mines*, vol. xv, p. 29.
40 'Evidence collected by Franks', vol. xvi, witness no. 23, p. 440.
41 *Ibid.*, witness no. 117, p. 458; also *First Report ... Mines*, vol. xv, p. 30.
42 'Evidence collected by Franks', witness no. 131, p. 461; also *First Report ... Mines*, p. 30.
43 'Evidence collected by Franks', witness no. 193, p. 472; also *First Report ... Mines*, p. 29.
44 'Evidence taken by Symons', vol. xvi, witness no. 100, 101, p. 248; also *First Report ... Mines*, vol. xv, p. 32.
45 *First Report ... Mines*, p. 32, quoting evidence from Poor Law Guardian Joseph Ellison of Birkenshaw.
46 'Evidence collected by Scriven', vol. xvii, witness no. 79, p. 124.
47 *Ibid.*, witness no. 75, p. 123.
48 'Evidence collected by Franks', vol. xvi, witness no. 73, p. 450.
49 *First Report ... Mines*, vol. xv, p. 32.
50 'Evidence collected by Symons', vol. xvi, witness no. 236, p. 285.
51 'Evidence collected by Scriven', vol. xvii, witness no. 72, p. 122.
52 'Evidence collected by Charles M. D. Barham', *First Report ... Mines*, Appendix, pt I, vol. xvi, p. 806.
53 'Evidence collected by Symons', vol. xvi, witness no. 294, p. 297.
54 'Evidence collected by Scriven', vol. xvii, witness no. 75, p. 123.
55 'Evidence collected by Symons', vol. xvi, witness no. 146, p. 264; *First Report ... Mines*, vol. xv, p. 35; 'Evidence collected by Scriven', vol. xvii, witness no. 60, p. 119.
56 *First Report ... Mines*, vol. xv, p. 33, quoting 'Evidence collected by Symons', vol. xvi, witness no. 96, p. 246.
57 *First Report ... Mines*, vol. xv, p. 31, quoting 'Evidence collected by Symons', vol. xvi, witness no. 138, p. 261.
58 'Evidence collected by Franks', vol. xvi, witness no. 412, p. 508.

59 'Report by Scriven', vol. xvii, p. 73.
60 'Evidence collected by Symons', vol. xvi, witness no. 139, p. 261.
61 'Evidence collected by Scriven', witness no. 60, p. 119.
62 *First Report ... Mines*, vol. xv, p. 33.
63 'Report by Robert Hugh Franks', vol. xvi, p. 399.
64 'Evidence collected by Symons', vol. xvi, witness no. 96, p. 246, quoted in *First Report ... Mines*, vol. xv, pp. 32–3.
65 'Evidence collected by Symons', vol. xvi, witness no. 138, p. 261, quoted in *First Report ... Mines*, vol. xv, p. 31.
66 'Evidence collected by Symons', vol. xvi, witness no. 79, p. 242.
67 *Ibid.*, witness no. 108, p. 250.
68 *Ibid.*
69 L. Davidoff, 'Class and Gender in Victorian England', in J. Newton *et al.* (eds), *Sex and Class in Women's History* (London, Routledge and Kegan Paul, 1983), pp. 21–3.
70 See Henriques, 'Bastardy and the New Poor Law', pp. 109–14 for a discussion of Malthusian ideas and parliamentary debates. For parliamentary debates on employment in the mines, see John, *By the Sweat of their Brow*, pp. 48–9.
71 Henriques, 'Bastardy and the New Poor Law', p. 114.
72 Quoted in *ibid.*, p. 119.
73 Ashley quoted in J. Lewis and S. O. Rose, '"Let England Blush". Protective Labor Legislation, 1820–1914', in U. Wiklander *et al.* (eds), *Protecting Women: Labour Legislation in Europe, the United States, and Australia* (Urbana, University of Illinois Press, 1995), p. 99, which also discusses the parliamentary debates; see R. Gray, 'The Languages of Factory Reform in Britain, *c.* 1830–1860', in P. Joyce (ed.), *The Historical Meanings of Work* (Cambridge, Cambridge University Press, 1987) for the wider debates.
74 Lewis and Rose, '"Let England Blush"', p. 100; also J. Humphries, 'Protective Legislation' and A. John's reply in *Feminist Review*, 9 (1981), pp. 106–9.

# 4

# Conspicuous before the world: the political rhetoric of the Chartist women

## MICHELLE DE LARRABEITI

During the miners' strike of 1984/85 women from the mining communities became 'conspicuous before the world'. They entered the glare of the public political sphere in all-women support groups. The languages the women used to express their political activity were contradictory in the sense that, in the media at least, the women's actions were seen as emerging out of their 'roles' as wives and mothers, as supporters of their men. At the same time the women spoke of their *own* political development, coming from behind the kitchen sink, which led them to consider issues around gender as well as class, and to take part in the most 'masculine' aspects of the strike such as picketing. In her strike diary Iris Preston described her moment of political involvement like this: 'I had responsibilities not just as a housewife and working mother, but to workers everywhere, it is now time to "stand up and be counted"'.[1] During the early 1990s a smaller but active group of women from Women Against Pit Closures (WAPC) staged dramatic sit-downs at every pit due to be shut down. These women's political involvement as wives and mothers cannot be seen solely as arising out of a 'radical conservatism'[2] or a desire to defend things as they were. The women's support groups led, after the strike, to women demanding voting powers in the National Union of Mineworkers (NUM) itself.[3] Alongside a desire to keep their communities intact, the women discussed ways of continuing changes in the division of labour which had occurred in their homes during the strike.

Suddenly a group of women normally concealed from public view were seen and heard in both the NUM and the media. Their striking but relatively short-lived visibility led me to reassess the public stance of the Chartist women in the years 1838–42. Accused of using ultimately conservative discourses or languages of sub-ordination, of entering public politics only as wives, mothers and supporters of their men, the Chartist women have been blamed for holding back the early feminist politics developed by the Owenites.[4]

### History, discourse and the Chartist women

The few accounts written about the Chartist women depend largely on the addresses published in the Chartist paper, the *Northern Star*, between 1838 and 1842. The addresses were sent to the paper by female radical or Chartist associations from all over the country. Unlike the Owenite paper the *Pioneer*, the editorial board of the *Northern Star* was exclusively male, there was no women's page, and no institutional acknowledgement of the large numbers of female Chartists.[5] Unlike the Owenites, the Chartists appeared to address the 'woman question' not in feminist terms but as a problem arising out of the disruption of the 'natural' order of family life. Barbara Taylor has argued that the Chartists were concerned with the dislocation of familial relations, 'through the substitution of women for men as primary breadwinners and the introduction of the New Poor Law'.[6] She also argues that compared to the Owenite women the Chartist female activists' desire for a 'traditional' home-centred life helped to relegate feminist concerns below those of class for many decades. Similarly, Dorothy Thompson argues that working-class women disappear from public politics from the 1840s onwards – not to reappear until the 1880s. This is, she argues, largely due to the power exerted by domestic ideology over the working classes.

> The Victorian sentimentalisation of the home and family, in which all important decisions were taken by its head, the father and accepted with docility and obedience by the inferior members, became all-pervasive and affected all classes, including the working classes, where women who had previously been consid-ered economic helpmates to their husbands gradually acquired a sense of 'home-centredness and inferiority' very similar to that found among women of the wealthier classes.[7]

Again, Thomis and Grimmett's study of the Chartist women accepts that they not only described themselves as auxiliaries, but that that was how they saw themselves: 'it was an auxiliary, even a

subservient role that the women accepted'.[8] More recent accounts
such as Jutta Schwarzkopf's also take the language used by the
women at face value. Despite their avowed radicalism they
'stopped short of questioning the belief in women's home-
centredness'.[9] The tone of these accounts is pejorative. There is a
sense of disappointment in the failure of the Chartist women to
remain both feminist and politically visible into the mid-nineteenth
century. Worse still, the women's 'failure to question the validity of
domesticity on principle laid working-class women open ... to
increasing pressure to conform to middle-class standards'.[10]
Behind such readings lies the idea that complex identities can be
read off from highly stylised political rhetoric. A language of
domesticity and family was only one of many discursive strategies
which formed Chartist rhetoric. Little attention is paid to the multiple languages and selves jostling with each other as busy Chartist
women managed home, children, work and politics.

   The Chartist women went public at a time when evangelical religion and the state sought to restructure the nation's morals as well
as divisions of labour. Increasingly, the public and private became
gendered spheres. According to the prominent Evangelical Hannah
More, 'Women were naturally more delicate, more fragile, morally
weaker, and all this demanded a greater degree of caution, retirement and reserve. Men, on the contrary, are formed for the more
public exhibition on the great theatre of human life.'[11] Middle-class
women were withdrawing from their former activities as household managers and helpers in the family business. Meanwhile
working-class women left their homes for waged labour in factories, sweatshops and domestic service. The visibility of working
women coincided with bourgeois concerns over the moral corruption engendered by the expanding industrial urban centres. This
attention can be seen in the expansion of middle-class philanthropy, which set out to ameliorate poor living conditions, and in
state investigations, as chapter 3 has shown, which resulted in a
range of legislation which focused on the working-class family.[12]

   Middle-class concern concentrated on working women as the
bearers of 'purity and pollution, and indeed of projected male
sexuality'.[13] At this time a 'public woman' meant a prostitute.[14]
Because working women of necessity inhabited the public world
they were excluded by the bourgeois ideology of domesticity so
important to the Evangelicals, in which the home was 'a zone of

intimacy and refuge from the competitive world of work and politics'.[15] As both politics and an unrestrained sexuality were located in the public sphere, it is not surprising to find that the political discourses used by working-class women resisted the 'dominant' interpretation of their activities. In their addresses to the *Northern Star* the female Chartists appear anxious to deflect any slurs on their character. The addresses are full of apologies for boldness and often assert a 'purity' of purpose. A working-class female political activist had to be an exemplary figure, not only in the critical eyes of the middle class but in her own community. As Sophia of Birmingham wrote:

> We are careful that our houses be more clean, our children better instructed, our own persons scrupulously neat, and that *when in conversation*, they are gratified to perceive our taste improved, and never turn a frowning reproof upon any inattention to domestic comfort.[16] [my emphasis]

Sophia's language acknowledges the pressure these women were under to claim their space in the public arena. Chartist women were not just campaigning for the Charter but for their very identity against attack from a middle class determined to impose its ideology of separate spheres. Claiming a respectability for herself and fellow activists does not mean that Sophia's subjectivity can be read only in terms of the absence of a feminist 'consciousness'. This denies the women the complexity usually assigned to the bourgeois subject.[17] All subjectivities must be seen as unstable and, in Joan Scott's words, as 'processes of differentiation and distinction, requiring the suppression of ambiguities and opposite elements in order to assure (and create the illusion of) coherence and common understanding'.[18] The notion of the subject as unstable rather than unified is useful as it renders all subjectivities complex. For feminists it throws into question any idea of identities as given natural essences and allows for the notion of femininity and masculinity as constructed.

Language is central to the construction of gendered identity. French psychoanalyst Jacques Lacan has been appropriated by feminists because of his stress on the part played by language in the formation of sexual difference. Language structures experience, and it does so in a gendered way. When children enter the 'symbolic order' (through language), they are entering a gendered social and psychic order. Moreover, this is not a stable order as masculinity and femininity 'are positions which shift between and within discourses'. As Sally Alexander points out: 'both subjectivity and sexual identity ... involve antagonism and conflict in their very construction. Antagonism and instability are lived out, not only within the individual psyche and its history, they mediate all social relations between women and men; they prefigure and cohabit with class antagonisms; and as the history of feminism demonstrates may well disrupt class solidarities'.[19] Such antagonisms may also submerge solidarities among women in favour of class alliances, which is to say that the setting up of a binary opposition between masculinity and femininity enforces a rigid semantic antagonism which has worked to hold the two categories in place through history.[20] Sexual difference must be pushed beyond a containing fixity, and considered instead in the historical moment of its particular construction, and in all its discursive complexity. The instability of the gendered speaking subject posits a relationship between subjectivity and subjection, but includes the possibility of resistance to both forms: 'the individual subject is not a product of a single discourse, is not trapped in a prison of dominant meanings, but is in a sense "inter-discursive" with the potentiality for challenging and reversing forms of definition, deploying one system of meaning against another'.[21] Language itself is not a neutral set of signs, but is itself full of historically produced and contested meanings. The word is a site 'of struggle and contradiction ... [language is] a field of ideological contention'.[22]

Since we live in a culture that has and does exercise discursive powers which attempt to cast groups of people into silence, it is important that the study of both the silences and the precious moments of articulation of the marginalised become central projects for historians. The purpose of this chapter is to focus on the notion of a politics of language as contested, and to try and understand why and how a socially subordinate group such as the Chartist women chose to utilise the political rhetoric which represented them in the pages of the *Northern Star*.

The Chartist women used a variety of languages to represent themselves in the public domain. A close reading of these many idioms might help to liberate the women from readings which simplify their desires, both political and personal, for the Charter and, as they saw it, a decent life. I want to argue that the rhetoric employed by the Chartist women does not reflect a straightforward acceptance of a subordinate 'role'. Although they may have chosen to represent themselves as wives and mothers, they also managed to raise their political voices to question not only the oppressions of class and gender, but to articulate their own particular political sense of self.

Working-class women were largely absent from the political rhetorics that had developed in radical politics since the French Revolution. Mary Wollstonecraft's *A Vindication of the Rights of Woman* argued that, given a proper education, middle-class women should enjoy full political rights with men. Wollstonecraft also linked sexuality with politics. She argued that too many women suffered from a degenerate sexuality, which although culturally conditioned, served to make women unfit for the world of ideas and politics.[23] She argued against Rousseau's formulation of women's innate inferiority, but shared his belief that it was men's public activity which disciplined their libidinal excesses. This theoretical linkage between public/political activity and sexuality, combined with the notion of nature as the basis for sexual difference itself, forged a powerful discursive regime. The deployment of political discourse came to mean that if working-class women should venture into the political realm they would have to clean up their act, that is to choose a morally purified family discourse, which placed them as patriotic women and glorious auxiliaries to their men. Women had to elevate themselves in political discourse in ways that men did not.

The argument that women had a right to involve themselves in public politics for the sake of the family and moral justice was used by middle-class female abolitionists from the late eighteenth century onwards. These women further claimed that a moral crusade against slavery was their 'natural' sphere of influence, driven by horror at the 'unnatural' disruption of family life represented by slavery. Theirs was a rhetoric deeply rooted in Scripture:

> Be not turned aside by the often-repeated objection, that it is a *political question*, with which we *women* have nothing to do. *Nothing to do with Slavery?* Nothing to do in behalf of woman, scorned, polluted, ruined, both for time and eternity! *We* regard this as a cause *peculiarly woman's*. Hear the command of Scripture, *'Remember them that are in bonds as bound with them'* ... If *your*

parents, husband, children were bound with them, could you then
turn away from the subject as a *political* question, in which you
had no interest? Imagine your *own* mother on the treadmill – your
*own* innocent daughter chained to a vile wretch, sweeping the
streets for the alleged crime of *indolence* – your *own* cherished
infant left to die unattended. Cannot you bear the *thought*? Then
sign this petition in behalf of your negro sisters, who are experiencing the sad *reality*.[24]

A self-consciousness about their right to act politically pervades
the addresses and petitions of both the female abolitionists and the
women Chartists. Whereas the middle-class women can only speak
of the experience of oppression and poverty in terms of the 'other',
the Chartist women inflect the rhetoric differently as they had not
only personally experienced poverty and hardship but had been
the *object* of similar rhetorical descriptions. The high moral purity
of the abolitionist women's rhetoric matches their suspicion of
working-class women and, indeed, black female slaves.[25] While
middle-class female radicals could displace their anxiety about the
restrictions placed upon them on to slaves or working-class
women, Chartist women had to find a way of making an authentic
public space of their own.

These contradictions around femininity, sexuality and political
activity involved radical women in a complex set of relations, both
social and psychic. Female and male Chartists mobilised a
language of domesticity as part of a rhetoric, designed to persuade
others of the righteousness of their political aims and their equality. But the Chartist women were speaking from a different place.
When Chartist women demonstrated in Revd Close's church in
Cheltenham they were vilified from the pulpit in terms that left no
doubt that their transgressions made them more 'ferocious fiends'
than the men themselves.

> women now become politicians, they leave the distaff and the
> spindle to listen to the teachers of sedition; they forsake their fire-
> side and home duties for political meetings, they neglect honest
> industry to read the factious newspapers! and so destitute are they
> of all sense of female decorum, of female modesty and diffidence,
> that they become themselves political agitators – female dictators –
> female mobs – female Chartists![26]

The Chartist Women were also fighting for their own traditions of
political involvement. Although largely absent from the autobi-

ographies of Chartist and other male radicals, politically active women are mentioned as important influences during childhood. Benjamin Wilson remembers his aunt as 'a famous politician, a Chartist, and a great admirer of Fergus O'Connor'.[27] The radical James Watson was influenced by his mother's politics: 'I remember my mother being in the habit of reading Cobbett's Register, and saying she wondered people spoke so much against it.'[28] The *Northern Star* records the many and varied activities of the women from fund-raising tea parties and dances, to initiating the Exclusive Dealing campaign (which boycotted those shopkeepers who refused to support Chartism), and selling and distributing the paper itself.[29] David Jones disputes the claim that working-class women disappeared from politics during the 1840s. In his article 'Women and Chartism' he argues that women were politically active into mid-century in many different ways, including political clubs, unions and strikes. Jones points out that not enough questions have been asked of the political actions of working-class women and men during mid-century, so that different forms of political activity remain largely unknown.

The radical rhetoric of the 1830s and 1840s included the themes of a disrupted family and a threatened male wage (undercut by cheaper female and child labour). It was a 'language of grievance which embraced moral and sexual orders as well as economic discontents – social preoccupations, which became severed from political demands within the labour movement'.[30] The addresses demonstrate that rhetorical mix in which the family and sexual ordering operated alongside the more acknowledged 'political' issues of male labour and political representation. The addresses can be read as resisting emergent forms of male working-class organisation, rather than being wholly excluded or oppressed by them. Furthermore, as Sally Alexander indicates, women may have included a family discourse in their political rhetoric in *resistance* to the exclusion of the home from the world of politics.[31]

It is possible to look at the women's addresses to the *Northern Star* thematically, studying the various discourses that run through them. The women's rhetoric, deploys a range of discourses operating within and across different social groups.[32] The Bristol women strikingly use the metaphors of factory life and grim industrialisation normally associated with the north, while the Bradford women evoke a rural 'merrie England' and, whether they were married or not, they all call upon an idealised family life. I have chosen to concentrate on two themes which I have labelled the language of patriotism and a family discourse. Under these helpful but schematic headings the multiple languages of radicalism converge.

## The language of patriotism

The language of patriotism runs through all Chartist rhetoric. As Hugh Cunningham has said, 'The Chartists used the vocabulary of patriotism as a weapon of struggle, one which engaged with the enemy, and whose recollection of the past incorporated a vision of the future'.[33] Several of the women's addresses begin 'patriotically'. Mary Ann Moore from Perth calls upon 'Respected and honoured patriots; unflinching advocates of the people' while the Nottingham women address themselves 'To the patriotic women of England'.[34] The notion of the 'freeborn Englishman' was a commonplace among eighteenth-century middle-class radicals, but was swiftly mobilised by working-class radicals. To be a patriot was to gain access to a collection of 'civilising' rights. According to E. P. Thompson the freeborn Englishman should have:

> Freedom from absolutism (the constitutional monarchy), freedom from arbitrary arrest, trial by jury, equality before the law, the freedom of the home from arbitrary entrance and search, some liberty of thought and speech, and of conscience, the vicarious participation in liberty (or in its semblance) afforded by the right of Parliamentary opposition and by elections and election tumults ... as well as the freedom to travel, trade and sell one's own labour.[35]

Deprived as they were of these rights by the British Government, even slave-owning American revolutionaries could claim to be freeborn 'slaves'. This patriotic idiom was overlapped by the colonial usage employed by abolitionists in the later eighteenth and early nineteenth centuries. Words like 'tyranny', 'chains', 'bondage', 'slavery', 'liberty', 'justice' and 'rights' appear continually in the women's addresses, making the point that English people were slaves in their own land. The moral, scriptural usage of 'stand and fight' used by middle-class radicals in anti-slavery campaigns shifts to a political stance in Chartist rhetoric. For the women a further set of meanings recall Wollstonecraft's *Vindication*, where a language of colonial slavery is invoked to 'impugn female subjugation'.[36]

The language of patriotism not only drew upon constitutional rights and slavery but also upon the familiar radical metaphor of a Golden Age before the Norman Yoke, used by the Chartist women to evoke a lost English idyll and as a means of imagining a better future. When the women of industrial Bradford conjure up images of a rural paradise, 'Where are now the honest, independent artisans – the manly peasantry, and the small farmers, with their smiling wives and cheerful families of once merrie England?',[37] they may actually be recalling a time when their parents or grandparents were farmers or country town weavers. But the propaganda effect of their picture of rural health, the antithesis of the grimy city, conjures up a world turned upside-down by the 'slavery' of the factories and the separation of families under the New Poor Law. It was the duty of 'true' patriots, both male and female, to resist.

Many Chartist men employed a language of patriotism against the corruption of a social order which had reduced the English worker to a 'white slave'. One way of reversing such 'misrule' would be to pay men a wage on which they could keep their families, including their wives. T. C. Salt, a middle-class Birmingham manufacturer who defected from the Chartist movement in 1839, encouraged the Chartist women to their patriotic duty on the grounds of restoring the 'natural' family, in which the wife would be able to return to her rightful place in the home. He uses the same rhetorical devices as the women, but regards their political involvement as a necessary evil.

> They dragged the wife from her home, the child from its sport, to break down the wages of the husband and father. They made monopoly for themselves, and competition for us. They made laws to make *us* poor and then made poor laws to deprive us of relief. Therefore do the people gather together and therefore do the women leave their homes to attend political meetings.[38] [my emphasis]

Salt's 'us' is not the same as the women's, for as a Birmingham manufacturer his experience of poverty could never match that of the majority of Chartists. The discursive boundaries of the rhetoric seem to limit the women's political utterances along the lines of putting the world to rights and reinstalling a working-class family

of manly men and smiling wives. However, within those boundaries the language of slavery sanctioned a right to resistance, and
helped to create a place where the women exercised their own
notion of female power.[39]

Such a language involved them in constant negotiation with the
limits of acceptable femininity. The women of Nottingham felt able
to express 'unacceptable' militant aggression as they spurred the
men to action. 'Tis better to die by the sword than by famine, and
we shall glory in seeing every working man of England selling his
craft to buy a sword or a rifle to be prepared for the event.'[40] The
Chartist women knew full well that such excursions into public
rhetoric left them open to accusations of immorality and that they
would be seen as 'bad' women. As Agnes Lennox wrote from the
Gorbals, 'the time has now arrived when it becomes the duty of
everyone who wishes well to the country that gave her birth, to
come forward, casting aside all those feelings which *false* delicacy
and *mock* modesty give rise to – to take a prominent part in the
great movement for reform'.[41] Lennox rejects the idea that bourgeois prescriptions of feminine behaviour should limit the
women's activities.

What is further contested within languages of patriotism for
women is how to express themselves politically within the
constraints of the ideological conflation of woman's place and
nation. These constraints were compounded by the organic vision
of family life, natural order and nation so clearly pictured by
Hannah More:

> Now it is pretty clear, in spite of modern theories, that the very
> frame and being of societies, whether great or small, public or
> private, is jointed and glued together by dependence. Those
> attachments which arise from, and are compacted by, a sense of
> mutual wants, mutual affection, mutual benefit and mutual oblig-
> ation, are the cement which secure the union of family as well as of
> the State.[42]

But cement is also a containing substance designed to hold in place
those associations precisely criticised by the Chartist women.
Susanna Inge contested this version of woman's place as a measure
of civilisation:

> As civilisation *advances* man gradually becomes inclined to place
> woman on an equality with himself, and though *excluded* from

everything connected with public life, her condition is considerably improved; still she is regarded in an inferior light, her province being only to make a pudding, prepare a dinner, clean the house, tend to her children.[43]

As Inge notes, while women were seemingly being accorded a new 'respect', working-class women who entered the public world of politics were damned on grounds of sexual immorality. Any attempt to step outside her prescribed role of moral exemplar and nurturer meant that the women were seen as *more* dangerous than the men. The discourses of middle-class reformers and evangelicals sought to confine female sexuality within a *particular* kind of home, within which it was imperative that she had no time or mind for politics. As Revd Close of Cheltenham put it: 'A bad mother of a family is far more mischievous in the country than a bad father, because the infant children are entrusted to her ... What a curse such women are to the country! Their children must grow up revolutionists, for they have been taught revolution at home.'[44]

The female Chartists had good reason to be aware that the call for universal male suffrage was only part of a politics which sought to defend working-class culture on several fronts. Within the confines of both radical and conservative discourse, the Chartist women struck their pose as 'militant mothers',[45] whether they were mothers or not. They presented themselves as *centrally* important in formulating both active and rhetorical resistance to the 'uncalled for wretchedness of a people and nation'.[46]

### Family discourse

While Revd Close was accusing the Chartist women of being 'bad' mothers, they were using a 'family discourse' to defend themselves. I am using the notion of a family discourse to illustrate how complex and often contradictory radical languages, like those of slavery, religion and women's place, were intertwined but framed within particular notions of the family.[47] The women's use of rhetoric was bound up with their public image as political mothers and active members of families. As they resisted attacks on the working-class family – epitomised by the Poor Law – they placed themselves publicly as radical and influential people. The women of Nottingham exhorted other women to:

*Urge* on your husbands, fathers, brothers, friends and neighbours to be prepared and ready for the conflict. *Urge* upon them the necessity of calm reflection and duty to be sober, frugal, patriotic, and to consider themselves bound by the *sacred ties of nature* – to *protect* and *shield* their wives and children from that system of cruelty and starvation now stalking through the land.[48] [my emphasis]

Clearly this extends women's province to politically 'urge' others outside the family, to friends, neighbours and workmates, suggesting further that the working-class concept of family might easily slip into the broader nexus of street, community or workplace. Moreover, the women exhort men to be not only radical, but to be sober and do their duty by their families, suggesting that perhaps men might spend precious money on drink and, worse, desert their families altogether. While asking for protection the impression remains that this address comes from a group of strong, active women. Nevertheless, it was as man's 'helpmeet' that woman sanctioned her political activity. Her duty, according to leading Chartist R. J. Richardson, was to 'temper man'. Richardson was in favour of female suffrage, but only for single women as he saw married women's interests as at one with their husbands. Henry Vincent, on the other hand, pictured the Chartist home as a haven of radical politics: 'Talk of putting down the Chartists, forsooth, why every kitchen is now a political meeting house; the little children are members of the unions and the good mother is the political teacher.'[49]

Chartist rhetoric placed the family centrally as they saw it was under attack by the factory system and the New Poor Law. The Poor Law now treated poverty as a crime and created prison-like workhouses where families were forcibly segregated. Adapting anti-slavery discourse, the Chartists used Scripture to resist this perversion of 'the sacred ties of nature'.[50] The 'natural' family was posed against the 'unnatural' work and relief systems being imposed from above. While 'nature' here inserts these women into prescribed roles as mothers and nurturers, in the struggle with the oppressor 'nature' is a radical and on the women's side. This is what lies behind the Chartist women's claim for themselves as the 'better sex'. Women's qualities provide the basis for appealing to other women to join the fight. 'You, who possess the *finest sympathies* of our nature, will you refuse your *aid*, when the object sought is *yours* and your *children's* happiness and the complete *emancipation* of your country?'[51]

The *Northern Star's* male reporters repeatedly use the theme of woman as the 'better sex' as a justification for 'unbecoming' public activities. The occasion of a talk on the Charter by Mary Ann Walker was interesting because the audience heard 'the fundamental principles of the People's Charter defined and advocated by one of the *softer* and *better* sex.'[52] The propaganda value of these clichés was useful but the women themselves were clear in refuting such criticisms: 'It was a *bold thing*, she admitted, for woman to step out of her retirement; and of course there would always be found persons who would put *foul constructions* on her motives in order to deter and throw her back'.[53] [my emphasis].

As Sophie Hamilton has shown in chapter 3, the *First Report* on children's employment in the mines used imagery which marked out a literally dark, nether region of society as completely other. The Commissioners' use of languages of slavery slotted lower-class female sexuality into a highly political agenda where middle-class horror and fear of public women was equal to their loathing of working-class agitators. As radical female abolitionists had done, the Chartist women turned opprobrium into their own claims as righteous women with influence. A supporter of Chartism and one of the most radical abolitionists, Elizabeth Heyrick worked hard to use 'influence' as a radical force. She was instrumental in the campaign to stop women buying sugar produced by slaves and in bringing the abolitionists around to demand immediate rather than gradual abolition.[54] Similarly the Chartist women identified 'influence' as a source of female power, 'While others toil, she can persuade.'[55] The rhetoric of 'aiding', 'helping' and 'urging' was constantly used in the women's campaigns, particularly the Exclusive Dealing campaign.

The discourse of influence formed a paradoxical fusion which could mean restricting women to the home and family, or could be used as a basis for entry into the public sphere. A language of 'influence' is counterposed with a language of demands in political battle: 'we respectfully suggest that the shopocracy be left to their fate, and that no persons are so well qualified to bring these very important personages to their senses as the women of England'.[56]

While Chartist men were reassured that women's influence was strongest within the family, middle-class reformers saw women's influence as restricted to the home and therefore separate from the public/political world. The Chartist women used their 'moral superiority' differently, even calling for equal participation in the government of the country. The 'Real democrat' of Glasgow categorically states that, 'It is the right of every woman to have a role in the legislation of her country.'[57] Certainly the notion of woman as the 'better sex' must not be allowed to exclude women from the public world of politics. 'But are we, because we are women, to be excluded from the more rational enjoyments of life? If so, why then was woman gifted with a mind to which in point of delicacy of taste, depth of feeling, and devoted affection, even proud man himself must bow?'[58]

Other prominent radical discourses, such as that of religion, were called upon to sanction women's influence as a moral duty. Chartism was a 'holy Cause'.[59] Women's use of religion as a political discourse allowed them to inhabit 'approved' categories of discursive space, but to suit their own political objectives. It is certain that both Chartist women and men used religious languages in resistance to the dominant discourses of the Established Church, which they saw as promoting religion: 'for preaching passive obedience and non-resistance to persecute us if we offer to resist their tyranny'.[60] Through their use of a family discourse the Chartist women actively challenged dominant ideologies of family life. They did not see defending their families and their own future freedom and equality as mutually exclusive terms. Discourses which threatened to contain their political desires were manipulated and subverted by a Chartist politics which sought a complete transformation of society. Sophia of Birmingham outlined women's part in this transformative project like this:

> Let us as Chartist women and mothers, *instruct* and *encourage* each other, that our children shall be better informed of their *rights as citizens*, and that their morals be of a higher order, and that, when the time arrives when they should receive those rights, they shall be better prepared by the *training* received from their *mothers* to enjoy them.[61] [my emphasis]

This has been read by Thomis and Grimmett and other historians such as Jutta Schwarzkopf as a straightforward acceptance of woman's place. But in the context of radical rhetoric it can also be read as a public mapping out of women's *active* participation in, and formation of, a new moral world 'when the time arrives'. 'Family' was then an arena of struggle in which a private, economically oppressed and disrupted family was posed against the notion of the family of the people. Sophia's language sees the family as a collectivised unit, a training ground for future citizens of a better world. 'Family' could be used to articulate a vision of future equality, 'as members of one human family'.[62] The family was a complex territory over which bourgeois ideologies fought for dominance. Working-class women were caught in a double bind; they needed to earn money outside the home, yet their labour was undervalued in relation to their domestic role. At the same time working-class men saw their wages and employment opportunities undercut by cheaper women's and children's labour. The exclusion of women workers from underground labour in the mines illustrated the dominant need for certain restrictions on female employment. As Angela John has put it:

> Not only would her removal from work help resolve certain demographic imbalances, but it might help restore harmony to a country threatened by Chartism. At a time when Bronterre O'Brien was proclaiming that an entire transformation of society was essential it was felt important to re-affirm the value of familial control.[63]

## Conclusion

When Mary Ann Moore, representing the female radicals of Perth, addressed National Convention delegates Richardson, Bussey and Collins, she felt the need to apologise for the women's public intervention: 'Gentlemen we have no desire to appear conspicuous before the world, merely to gratify our own ambition, our present conduct ... has been, and is now, guided by the purest motives.'[64] This is a rhetorical apology as woman's place in political agitation appears to remain unsettled in the minds of the Chartist women themselves. There is a tension in the addresses where the language ricochets between the ritual bow to dominant notions of femininity in the form of continual apologies for their boldness, and a belief in their right to be out there agitating. The Chartist women all deny that women should have nothing to do with politics.

Females have everything to do with what concerns their own interests and the interests of their country. We further answer, that when it can be shown that females are not affected by unjust taxation, then will we confess that females have nothing to do with politics.[65]

Moreover, they offer their own definitions of politics itself, as the Bath women wrote, 'What are politics but an important branch of morals relating to our duty to our neighbours and to the interest and well-being of all about us?'[66] Discourses of femininity and moral duty have different resonance in the mouths of Chartist women, who had a distinct political agenda, from both middle-class radicals and often their fellow male Chartists.

The Chartist women's addresses have been judged as fatally flawed for their use of 'containing' discourses of domesticity. Yet there is a strong sense of the women using dominant discourses as an argument against the dominant. We do not know how these women saw themselves; what discussions they had in private, with each other or with their own selves. What we get in their public utterances is a sense of negotiation between apologetic, acceptable public rhetorics and radical calls to action. Often the apologies themselves sound like a sop for male audiences, particularly when considered against the women's real political effectiveness in raising funds, distributing newspapers and the Exclusive Dealing campaign.

The ideal held out by dominant discourses of domesticity was by definition out of the reach of most working-class women who already occupied public space and were anyway the object of scrutiny of the discourse. The bourgeois ideology was itself a collection of 'disparate discourse' which performed 'the function of enabling contradictions to be heard'.[67] Even middle-class female radicals in the abolition movement, 'implicitly tendered a challenge to patriarchal hegemony' in their own political agitations and writings.[68]

A female subject in the political realm is all too often an under-valued subject. She has been consigned by historiography to a place within the chronology of working-class radicalism. The Chartist women's place in this story is bounded on one side by her 'disabling' use of languages which correspond with prevailing notions of femininity, and on the other by her supposed 'disappearance' from the 'political' scene by mid-century. The women have been read sociologically, that is to say it has been assumed that their use of language reflects a straightforward 'internalisation of norms',[69] and that at some point they assumed the roles that bourgeois society had mapped out for them. When studied as rhetoric operating in a field of conflict it becomes clear that the addresses need to be read as structuring experience rather than as a reflection of it. There is always some gap between what discourse authorises and what people do, and history may never be able to disclose that gap precisely.

The Chartist women forced an entry into the political domain. Their inclusion in that sphere was predicated upon a rhetorical recognition that such a position was an *intrusion* into a world that desired to exclude unacceptable aspects of feminine subjectivity. The framing of their rhetoric in terms of family/personal relations serves to highlight the centrality of contemporary discourses of sexuality in relation to labour. Chartist politics left a discursive space for women as militant mothers and moral regenerators. The Chartist woman was not only involved in a continual process of conflict between conscious and unconscious life, but also with the political programmes she espoused. These conflicts are played out in the Chartist addresses, but are accompanied by a rhetorical confidence which demonstrates that an 'auxiliary' could be a powerful figure indeed.

## Notes

1  R. Samuel, B. Bloomfield and G. Boanas (eds), *The Enemy Within* (London, Routledge and Kegan Paul, 1986), p. 22.

2  I. Preston, 'A Strike Diary', in Samuel *et al.*, *The Enemy Within*, p. 100.

3  The NUM voted against the motion that Women Against Pit Closures become associate members of the union in July 1985. Since the closure of most British mines the WAPC has become a skeleton organisation. The financial devastation suffered by the mining communities has been the arena of concern for both women and men.

4  See, for example, D. Thompson, *The Chartists: Popular Politics in the Industrial Revolution* (London, Temple Smith, 1984), ch. 7; M. I. Thomis and J. Grimmett, *Women in Protest: 1800–1850* (London, Croom Helm, 1982). More recent studies, J. Schwarzkopf, *Women in the Chartist Movement* (London, Macmillan, 1991) and A. Clark, *The Struggle for the Breeches: Gender and the Making of the British Working Class* (London, Rivers Oram, 1995), both see the Chartist women as succumbing to the rhetoric of domesticity as political activists after 1848.

5  For example, Frances Morrison, writing as 'The Bondswoman', contributed

articles to the women's page of *The Pioneer*, initiated by her husband James.

6  Barbara Taylor, *Eve and the New Jerusalem: Socialism and Feminism in the Nineteenth Century* (London, Virago, 1983), p. 268.

7  D. Thompson, 'Women and Nineteenth Century Politics: A Lost Dimension', in J. Mitchell and A. Oakley (eds), *The Rights and Wrongs of Women* (Harmondsworth, Penguin, 1976), p. 138. She expands on this view in her chapter on 'The Women' in Thompson, *The Chartists*.

8  Thomis and Grimmett, *Women in Protest*, p. 114.

9  Schwarzkopf, *Women in the Chartist Movement*, p. 97.

10  *Ibid.*, p. 122.

11  Hannah More, quoted in C. Hall, 'The Early Formation of Victorian Domestic Ideology', in S. Burman (ed.), *Fit Work for Women* (London, Croom Helm, 1979), p. 31. For more on the redrawing of middle-class femininity and masculinity and its impact on women's economic roles, see L. Davidoff and C. Hall, *Family Fortunes: Men and Women of the English Middle Class 1780–1850* (London, Hutchinson, 1987); also C. Hall, *White, Male and Middle Class: Explorations in Feminism and History* (Cambridge, Polity, 1992), chs 4, 5, 8.

12  In particular the Poor Law Amendment Act 1834, and the Mines Regulations Act 1842, which Lord Shaftesbury introduced by claiming that, 'if you corrupt the woman you poison the waters of life at the very fountain': quoted in I. Pinchbeck, *Women Workers and the Industrial Revolution* (London, Virago, [1930] 1981), p. 267.

13  L. Davidoff, 'Class and Gender in Victorian England', in J. Newton (ed.), *Sex and Class in Women's History* (London, Routledge and Kegan Paul, 1983), p. 22. See chapter 3 in this volume for Sophie Hamilton's discussion of bourgeois fears of working women's 'dangerous' sexuality in the Royal Commissions on children's employment; also F. Mort, *Dangerous Sexualities* (London, Routledge and Kegan Paul, 1987).

14  See *Oxford English Dictionary*.

15  J. Walkowitz, *Prostitution and Victorian Society: Women, Class and the State* (Cambridge, Cambridge University Press, 1980).

16  *English Chartist Circular*, quoted in Thomis and Grimmett, *Women in Protest*, p. 118.

17  See C. Steedman, *Landscape for a Good Woman* (London, Virago, 1986), especially pp. 10–15, and L. Passerini, 'Work, Ideology and Consensus under Italian Fascism', *History Workshop*, 8 (1979), pp. 86–90.

18  J. W. Scott, 'Gender as a Category of Historical Analysis', *American Historical Review*, 91:5 (1986), p. 1063. See also her 'Deconstructing Equality-Versus-Difference: or, the Uses of Post-Structuralist Theory for Feminism', *Feminist Studies*, 14:1 (1988), pp. 34–8 and her *Only Paradoxes to Offer: French Feminists and the Rights of Man* (Cambridge, Mass., Harvard University Press, 1996).

19  S. Alexander, 'Women, Class and Sexual Difference in the 1830s and 1840s: Some Reflections on the Writing of Feminist History', *History Workshop*, 17 (1984), pp. 132–3; an extended version appears in her *Becoming a Woman and other Essays in Nineteenth and Twentieth-Century Feminist History* (London, Virago, 1994).

20  Scott, 'Gender as a Category', p. 1064.

**21** *Ibid.*

**22** Terry Eagleton, *Literary Theory, an Introduction* (Oxford, Blackwell, 1983), p. 117, referring to V. N. Volosinov's *Marxism and the Philosophy of Language* (New York, Seminar Press, [1929] 1973).

**23** Women would have to be educated out of their culturally induced inferiority.

**24** From Sheffield Ladies' Association for the Universal Abolition of Slavery, *Ladies Petition for the Abolition of Slavery*, 6 April 1838, John Rylands University Library of Manchester.

**25** See Clare Midgley, *Women Against Slavery: The British Campaigns, 1780–1870* (London, Routledge, 1992). She points out the caution with which ex-slave woman, Mary Prince, was treated and how the usefulness of Prince's autobiography for propaganda was tempered by the fact of her former 'moral degradation': pp. 88–91.

**26** Revd F. Close, *A Sermon addressed to the Female Chartists of Cheltenham, Sunday 25 August 1839, On the Occasion of their Attending the Parish Church in a Body* (London, Hamilton, Adams, 1839), pp. 3–4.

**27** Benjamin Wilson, *Struggles of an Old Chartist: What he Knows and the Part he has Taken in Various Movements* (Halifax, 1887), p. 1.

**28** James Watson (1799–1874), in D. Vincent (ed.), *Testaments of Radicalism: Memoirs of Working-Class Politicians, 1790–1885* (London, Europa, 1977), p. 10.

**29** On the Exclusive Dealing campaign, see for example the address to the *Northern Star* from the Nottingham women, 8 Dec. 1838, p. 6. Also reports in the *Northern Star*, 22 Dec. 1838, p. 8; 1 June 1839, p. 5; 27 July 1839, p. 5.

**30** Alexander, 'Women, Class and Sexual Difference', p. 140.

**31** *Ibid.*

**32** Scott, 'Gender as a Category', p. 1064.

**33** H. Cunningham, 'The Language of Patriotism 1750–1914', *History Workshop*, 12 (Autumn 1981), pp. 17–18.

**34** *Northern Star*, 8 Dec. 1838, 29 June 1839.

**35** E. P. Thompson, *The Making of the English Working Class* (Harmondsworth, Pelican, [1963] 1968), p. 86.

**36** M. Ferguson, 'Mary Wollstonecraft and the Problematic of Slavery', in E. J. Yeo (ed.), *Mary Wollstonecraft and 200 Years of Feminisms* (London, Rivers Oram, 1997), p. 94.

**37** *Northern Star*, 19 Feb. 1842.

**38** T. C. Salt, 'Address to the Women of Birmingham', *Northern Star*, 25 Aug. 1838.

**39** The successful slave revolt of 1791 in San Domingo showed that even colonial slaves had the power to resist: see Ferguson, 'Mary Wollstonecraft', p. 94; also her *Subject to Others: British Women Writers and Colonial Slavery, 1670–1834* (New York/London, Routledge, 1992), ch. 11.

**40** *Northern Star*, 8 Dec. 1838. The statement is a conflation of two biblical texts often coupled together: Lamentations iv. 9 and Luke xii. 36; see E. Yeo, 'Christianity and Chartist Struggle', *Past and Present*, 91 (1981), p. 113.

**41** *Northern Star*, 16 Nov. 1839, from the Female Universal Suffrage Association, Glasgow.

**42** More, quoted in Hall, 'Early Formation', pp. 22–3.

**43** *Northern Star*, 2 July 1842.

**44** Revd Close, *Sermon*, pp. 13–14.

**45** Thanks to Eileen Yeo and Alison Twells for this phrase.

**46** *Northern Star*, 8 Dec. 1838.

**47** I favour Jeffrey Weeks's description of discourse as 'a linguistic unity or group of statements which constitutes and delimits a specific area of concern, governed by its own rules of formation with its own modes of distinguishing truth from falsity ... The unity of a discourse ... does not derive from the fact that it describes a "real object", but from the social practices that actually form the object about which discourses speak. The "social" is constituted through these practices': J. Weeks, 'Foucault for Historians', *History Workshop*, 14 (1982), p. 111.

**48** *Northern Star*, 8 Dec. 1838.

**49** Quoted in Thompson, *The Chartists*, p. 119.

**50** *Northern Star*, 8 Dec. 1838.

**51** Address from the women of Upper Honley and Smallthorn: *Northern Star*, 29 Jan. 1842.

**52** *Ibid.*, 10 Dec. 1842.

**53** *Ibid.*

**54** Midgley, *Women Against Slavery*, pp. 103–14.

**55** *Northern Star*, 19 Feb. 1842.

**56** *Ibid.*, 8 Dec. 1838.

**57** *Ibid.*, 23 June 1838.

**58** *Ibid.*, 2 July 1842.

**59** See Yeo, 'Christianity and Chartist Struggle'.

**60** Bradford women, *Northern Star*, 19 Feb. 1842.

**61** English *Chartist Circular*, quoted in Thomis and Grimmett, *Women in Protest*, p. 117.

**62** *Northern Star*, 29 June 1839.

**63** A. V. John, *By The Sweat of Their Brow* (London, Routledge and Kegan Paul, 1984), p. 43.

**64** *Northern Star*, 29 June 1839.

**65** *Ibid.*, 16 Nov. 1839.

**66** *Ibid.*, 13 Oct. 1838.

**67** J. Barrell and H. Guest, quoted in Ferguson, *Subject to Others*, p. 304.

**68** *Ibid.*, p. 305.

**69** J. Rose, 'Femininity and its Discontents', *Feminist Review*, 14 (1983), p. 9.

# 5

# Protestant feminists and Catholic saints in Victorian Britain

EILEEN JANES YEO

In Victorian Britain, the tide of anti-Catholic feeling ran high. When Augustus Pugin, the eminent art critic, crossed himself on a train, a woman passenger screamed, 'you are a Catholic, sir! Guard, guard, let me out'. Intellectual men could be just as prejudiced. The Unitarian Revd Samuel Gaskell, perhaps better known as the husband of Mrs Gaskell, upon learning that their daughter was in danger of converting to Rome, subjected her for several days to re-education until she pulled back from the brink.[1] Why, in such an inflammatory atmosphere, did many Protestant feminists become interested in Catholicism from the 1850s onwards? Why, for instance, did Irish Protestant Anna Jameson give an influential lecture on 'The Sisters of Charity' in 1855? Why did Unitarian Bessie Rayner Parkes convert to Catholicism in 1864? Why did Evangelical Anglican Josephine Butler write a life of St Catherine of Siena in 1878?

This chapter will explore the religious elements that women drew upon to create their identities and to empower themselves for public activity. First, it will examine the three-fold attraction that Catholicism held for Protestant feminists, especially its resources for feminising divinity, its icons offering role models to single women and its provision of dignified public work through sisterhoods of various kinds. Then it will push beyond Catholicism to indicate other theological preoccupations of these Protestant feminists, particularly their concern with issues of authority and liberation. Finally, it will raise some general considerations about feminism and religion, and explore the psychological possibilities and dangers that follow from tapping into archetypal energy.

In the spotlight will be women active in the Langham Place group,[2] together with pioneers in the caring professions who were perhaps on the Langham fringe but contributed to the *English*

*Woman's Journal* and, last but certainly not least, Josephine Butler, an underrated theologian and the leader of the Ladies National Association Against the Contagious Diseases Acts, the most controversial women's campaign of the mid-century period because it was concerned with prostitution and sex. These women did not share a common religious position nor did they even always respect each other's positions: some Unitarians thought Evangelicals intellectually mushy while some Evangelicals thought Unitarian activists socially naive.[3] But all felt that some form of religious legitimation was absolutely necessary for a positive sense of self and to ratify their social action in the world.

## Madonnas, saints and sisters

The way in which feminists embraced the Madonna, despite some lingering distaste, indicated their desire to modify a Protestantism which had too excessively masculinised its gods. For them, as for many religious feminists now, this single-gendered godhead devalued not only the feminine dimension of life but constricted the development of real women. Art critic Anna Jameson (1794–1860), who played surrogate mother or attentive maiden aunt to the Langham Place circle, predictably lampooned an Italian statue dressed in a real blue silk gown 'spangled with tinsel stars'. But she also placed the Madonna in a line of 'mother Goddesses' who served as

> A mighty prophecy, sounded through all the generations of men, even from the beginning of time, of the coming moral regeneration and complete and harmonious development of the whole human race, by the establishment on a higher basis, of what has been called the 'feminine element' in society.[4]

Jameson argued that the Madonna was needed because earlier ideas of Christ both as masculine and feminine had split apart, necessitating a return of the repressed element.

Several feminists posited an androgynous deity. An exasperated Frances Power Cobbe (1822–1904), Evangelical Anglican turned theist, challenged the masculinisation of God and called for a parental (not paternal) deity:

> we have heard enough of man's thought of God – of God first as the King, the 'man of War', the demiurge, the Mover of All things

and then, at last, since Christian times, of God as the Father of the World ... But the woman's thought of God as the 'Parent of Good Almighty' unites in one the father's care and the mother's tenderness, that we have never yet heard.[5]

Josephine Butler too invoked 'the Great Father-Mother, God'. Both Jameson and Cobbe, in their different ways, insisted on restoring a feminine side to divinity which would, as a corollary, upgrade human femininity which they saw as nurturant tenderness. While God was androgynous, they still regarded human men and women as essentially different, although equivalent and complementary. None the less, they felt that God set the model for a 'communion of labour' between men and women in all spheres of public and private life: both the masculine and feminine elements being necessary to secure what Cobbe called a 'stereoscopic view' and effective social action. This version of the communion of labour subverted the Ruskinian idea of complementarity between the public man and the private woman. Now not only could women use the communion doctrine to justify their entrance into the public sphere but Butler reminded men that the family and home was equally their province too.[6]

Other mid-century theological strategies, which did not draw from Catholicism, did not so much feminise the Godhead as emphasise that the masculine Gods were on the side of the sexual equality of souls and authorised useful public lives for women as well as men. Unitarian then agnostic, Barbara Leigh Smith Bodichon (1827–91), who co-founded the Langham Place group, started her 1857 book on *Women and Work* with St Paul's words: 'For we are all children of God by faith in Christ Jesus; for there is neither Jew nor Greek, there is neither bond nor free, there is neither male nor female, for ye are all one in Christ Jesus.'[7] Emily Davies (1830–1921), an Evangelical who became a Christian Socialist, asserted a theological equality between the sexes precisely to counter the bogus 'dual theory' which kept women at home. 'Are women', she asked,

> to be regarded, and to regard themselves, primarily as children of God, members of Christ, and heirs of the kingdom of heaven, and, secondarily as wives, mothers, daughters, sisters? or are the family relationships to overshadow the divine and the social, and to be made the basis of a special moral code, applying to women only?[8]

The correct answer was obvious from the question. For Bodichon, since 'God sent all human beings into the world for the purpose of forwarding, to the utmost of their power, the progress of the world', women had a duty to perform useful work as well as men, a sentiment which Davies echoed in her campaign for women's university education on the basis of curricular equality.

Later, at the end of the century, some feminist theosophists went to the other extreme and totally feminised divinity. Theosophy, a hybrid faith which eschewed dogma but invited seekers ('without distinction of race, creed, sex, caste or colour') to distil the common essence from all the world's religions, which augmented Christianity with Eastern wisdom and a dash of evolutionary science, proved attractive to some suffrage activists. Most adherents, like Charlotte Despard (1844–1939) of the Women's Freedom League (who converted to Catholicism en route to Theosophy), carried on with the idea of a dual Godhead and of a humanity which was masculine and feminine. But Indian-born Frances Swiney (1847–1922), wife of a Tory major-general and a militant suffragette as well as founder of the League of Isis (1909), argued that the Elohim of Genesis was really the Supernal Mother ('from the womb of the I Am all things came') and that the Holy Ghost was also a feminine principle until, in the fourth century, the Church fathers pronounced the Trinity to be definitively masculine. For Swiney, even Christ the Son, the perfection of the male element of humanity, marked only a transitional phase, to be superseded by the reign of the feminine: 'in the consummation of all things the Father and the Son are reabsorbed, or return to the primal source. They enter into Zion, so that the Three may be One in the perfect fullness of the Divine Feminine.'[9]

If Catholicism provided materials for restoring a feminine dimension to the metaphysical realm, it also provided more mundane support. Frances Power Cobbe, who never married, who refused the protection of her landowner brother and who insisted on working to support herself, pointed to the second lesson that Catholicism could teach – to value the single woman. She protested that 'the Protestant "Old Maid" has been for centuries among the most wretched and useless of human beings'.[10] Whatever had been the spinster's fate for centuries, the mid-century in Britain marked a nadir in her status. The 1851 and 1861 censuses revealed a pool of unmarried women between the ages of twenty and forty, who were branded as 'surplus', 'superfluous' and 'redundant'.[11] Insult was the name of the game: the *Saturday Review* pronounced that 'married life is woman's profession', and that those who stayed single had 'failed in business'. Mid-century feminists worked hard to give single women positive value and to dignify their work. In a bourgeois culture which constructed femininity largely on Christian foundations, and prioritised married motherhood as true womanhood, respectable women who wanted to stretch conventional gender models needed also to use Christian materials, not only to convince others but to satisfy their own sense of self-esteem. In Catholicism, they found figures like the Madonna who provided an example of how moral motherhood was possible without full biological maternity. With the help of Catholic tradition, feminists could now place alongside the Protestant ideal of the married mother in the conjugal home, an icon of a virgin, moral or social mother doing self-sacrificial work with the poor and needy in the public world and introducing a home influence into it.

Unitarian minister's daughter Mary Carpenter (1807–77), after referring to a sermon on 'The Glory of the Virgin Mother', urged single women 'who are mothers in heart, though not by God's gift on earth' to work in the juvenile reformatory movement and thereby to 'bestow their maternal love' on 'those wretched moral orphans whose natural sweetness of filial love has been mingled with deadly poison'.[12] Carpenter had been trained by her father to become a teacher and closed her mind to marriage after a vision in which a composite of her father and Christ urged her to do social work instead; she became a pioneer in the analysis and treatment of juvenile crime.

Like any powerful symbol, the Madonna was available for differing interpretations. Even the version just discussed – the Virgin Mother as a role model for moving respectably into public work – can be placed midway on a spectrum of activist uses. A more conservative temperance activist, Clara Lucas Balfour (1808–78), while arguing that Protestantism had excessively underplayed the Virgin Mary, none the less reinstated the Madonna only to exemplify humility, meaning an intelligent submission to divine will, in this case of God-the-Father and Christ-the-son.[13] By contrast, American Margaret Fuller (1810–50), radical Unitarian and transcendentalist, embraced the Madonna as a powerful personal symbol who represented a balance between 'the independent and relational aspects of

female identity'.[14] The virginity of the Madonna signified not
spinsterhood or chastity but the self-reliance necessary for self-
development – her maternality represented woman in relationship
especially to husband and children. Fuller also invoked the more
powerful and uncontrolled goddesses like Isis but found the
socialised 'Christian Goddess', the Virgin Mary, to be a more relevant model for women grappling with seemingly contradictory
demands and desires.

In addition to the Madonna, female saints provided important
role models – but which saints were highlighted and which of their
characteristics received emphasis was illuminating. A divinely
sanctioned active public role for women was precisely what
Josephine Butler emphasised in her account of the life of St
Catherine of Siena. Butler, highly connected in gentry circles (the
niece of Earl Grey of 1832 Reform Bill fame), was a married mother
whose husband, the Revd George Butler, clearly thought her a
prophet or a saint. As a result, he gave her latitude unusual for a
bourgeois woman. He supported her public campaigning and
patiently sat in railway stations for hours waiting for her return
from speaking engagements. She headed the 'Great Crusade' for
the Repeal of the Contagious Diseases Acts, laws which gave police
in designated military towns powers to order women suspected of
being prostitutes to submit themselves to gynaecological examination but which did not interfere with their clients. Beautiful,
charismatic and flamboyant, her spirituality was deep and mystical: she saw visions and heard voices. Her effect on other people
was extraordinary. A member of a Royal Commission to which she
testified in 1871 said 'I am not accustomed to religious phraseology
but I cannot give you any idea of the effect produced except by
saying that the spirit of God was there'.[15]

Butler's life of *Catherine of Siena* extended and spiritualised all the
family roles in which respectable femininity was located, making
moral motherhood available to the single woman. Catherine was
'the Daughter of the Republic' and 'Daughter of the People' but
more importantly Daughter of God and the Church. She was sister
(receiving Friar Bartholomew 'with the tenderness of a sister
towards a brother'). She was mother 'of the great family for whom
she elected to live – humanity'.[16]

Spiritual relations overrode all duty to the biological family and
all social convention about the role of women. In an early dream,

Catherine pictured herself in her own home with a baby at her breast and felt great happiness. But over this scenario, 'the celestial wooer prevailed', and Christ married her instead. In another vision, God told her to go into the public world. When she objected that 'my sex is an obstacle', God assured her that 'I pour out the favour of my spirit on whom I will. With me there is neither male nor female, neither plebian nor noble but all are equal before me'.[17] Informing her parents that she would not marry in the conventional way, they built her a cell in the family home where she could live among them but remain a hermit.

When friction occurred, Catherine always asserted the pre-eminence of her Godly over her filial duties. She gently rebuked her mother Lappa, saying 'I must follow the path which God indicates to me by his providence; – you, my dear sweet mother – you ought to be content and not unwilling to suffer something for the honour of God'.[18] Catherine's life exemplified how the relations of family could be enlarged, allowing women to break beyond their conventional gender role. God became the father, Christ the husband, the whole family of humanity the children. Home was everywhere. On God's instruction, Catherine committed a cardinal sin against Victorian femininity by speaking in public. And she sinned in the most spectacular way by lecturing the chief cardinal on earth, the Pope.

The conventionally sanctified area of home also had to be re-defined, if gender possibilities were to expand. As usual it was Butler who proposed extensions and restructurings far beyond where most feminists would consider moving. In her 1869 introduction to *Woman's Work and Woman's Culture*, she responded to the majority of Englishmen who dreaded that women's claims would 'revolutionise our Homes'. Agreeing that Home was the source of all virtues, she argued that

> a great enlargement of hearts and a face opening out and giving forth of the influences of homes, as reservoirs of blessing for the common good, would ultimately result in the restored security of all the best elements in our present ideal of Home, and that saying would come true 'He that will lose his life for my sake' (for the sake of Him who taught that if a man have two coats he should give one to him that has none), 'the same shall find it'.[19]

She boldly asserted that the comfortable bourgeois home came 'near to selfishness' and urged that home be extended in a number of ways. She was on her own when she suggested that families should open their doors to poor lunatics and strangers: she continually absorbed dying prostitutes into her household.

But she was one with the rest of her feminist sisters when she pleaded that philanthropic mothering and the home influence be introduced into public institutions for the poor, particularly to soften the hard hand of the state. After the tragic death of her daughter, when she started obsessively to seek 'some pain keener than my own', one of her first ventures into public work was to visit young prostitutes in the workhouse.[20] Unlike many respectable feminists who kept their social distance at most times, she made an inspired display of solidarity by sitting on the floor, clad in her elegant silks, and ineptly picked oakum with them, to their great amusement, before she uttered a word.

A new way of extending the idea of home, mid-century feminists created a residential institution, often called a 'home', where virgin mothers could care for children and especially for young women in sexual danger. Mary Carpenter pioneered such homes for juvenile offenders who had tangled with the law. Cobbe became involved in providing homes for workhouse girls, for workhouse epileptics and for discharged female prisoners. Yet another way of extending home influence, richer women visited poorer women in their dwellings and helped to transform the people and the abodes into what the visitors considered to be families and homes.[21]

The Catholic monastic tradition provided another experience of family and home, but this time adapted by Protestant feminists for richer women alone. Communities for single women, even full-fledged sisterhoods, extended home beyond the limits of the marital or parental family. In her lecture on 'The Sisters of Charity', Anna Jameson praised Catholic women's efforts and pleaded for a Protestant equivalent, a nest from which single women could go out and do their sacrificial mothering to the poor:

> Let not the unremitting, self-denying efforts of 'Sisters of Charity' abroad, or devoted Catholic women at home, any longer cast reproach on English women and Protestants; let us emulate each other in works of Christian love.[22]

For the first time since the Reformation, British High Church Anglicans started forming full sisterhoods in the mid-century period, with abbesses as mother superiors although the orders were also kept subordinate to male hierarchies. These orders stirred up great controversy and fantasy about religious harems where women would fall prey to lascivious priestly advisers. Some Protestant feminists like Davies and Cobbe rejected female monasticism,[23] possibly partly to distance themselves from this rampant fear of women being both 'unmanned' and highly sexualised. More common were deaconess houses under the supervision of parish vicars, or secular homes for women working together in a branch of social work, for example nurses' homes and later social settlement houses.[24]

Bessie Rayner Parkes (1829–1925) insisted that it was chiefly this 'active ordered charity of the Catholic Church which made me captive'. The daughter of a Birmingham Liberal MP, raised in privileged Unitarian circles, she helped start the Langham Place group and edited their *English Woman's Journal*, the first feminist periodical. Continually having to explain her conversion, she admitted that the Catholic habit of faith was 'natural neither to my character ... nor to my education', that 'it was many months before I ceased to feel wretched in the new atmosphere', that she disliked 'the Catholic embroidery of words and phrases and extraneous devotions', that she did not 'take any personal interest in the emotional side of religion. Neither St. Teresa nor Mrs. Pearsall Smith touch me in my inner self'.[25]

As an intellectual seeker Parkes might have been happier as a sceptic or a freethinking Christian, at least this was what she sometimes said. She rejected charges of 'falling back on authority' and insisted that an historical argument, to which she gave a Whiggish touch, had convinced her that 'Catholicism is the Christian Nation, formed out of all peoples; its elective monarch is the Pope, who is obliged to rule according to the constitution'.[26] Within this historically continuous institution, the large-scale organisation of good works, the devising of systematic charity commensurate with social need, became possible. While admitting that the 'free Christian life produced admirable women', she felt that 'it is impossible to get a *regular supply*, disposable like soldiers or sailors, without some system ensuring strict discipline':

> I do not suppose that the Roman Church has any woman intellectually equal to Florence Nightingale; but it has 17,000 Sisters of Charity all over the world. I should never go to an Order to find a woman of wide and high cultivation and originality. But I should

find efficient and devoted workers by the hundred. Is the individual sacrifice worth the cost? Considering the deal of trouble the Devil makes in the world, I think it is; though I am quite aware that *it is* a sacrifice of a certain kind of individual growth and excellence.[27]

## Josephine Butler, authority and liberation

This chapter's cast of upright feminist characters seem almost promiscuous in the way that they borrowed from whatever Christian tradition suited their purposes. They took from Catholicism with one hand, from Quakerism with the other, particularly glorying in the doctrine of the inner light which opened the way into a public preaching role and into the practice of responsibility in Church government. Of course this did not mean that they were necessarily satisfied with the conduct of the institutional Churches from which the beliefs came. However much some Catholic doctrines appealed, relations with the Catholic Church itself remained deeply problematic for most Protestant women. Quaker feminists in Britain were embroiled in attempts from the 1870s onwards to undo the segregation of the Yearly Meeting and the Meeting for Sufferings, the highest assemblies for formulating belief and deciding organisational issues. The key women urging the reform, like Helen Priestman Bright Clark (daughter of Liberal politician John Bright) and Margaret Tanner, were also active in the Campaign against the Contagious Diseases Acts and more willing than the men to have the Meeting consider controversial issues, like vivisection. In 1896, some integration was achieved but not without a real sense of loss about Women's Yearly Meetings where Friends could 'speak to their sisters with greater freedom'.[28]

For Protestant feminists, the issue of authority was central. Who had the authority to identify true revelation from false or partial vision was the key question. As usual, Josephine Butler had the most daring answers. With 'hesitation and deep awe', knowing that she was stepping into an intellectual minefield, she asserted that the authority of the words and acts of Jesus 'must be higher than that of any man or society of men'. Higher certainly than that of St Paul, to whom most men appealed but who had applied 'the essential teaching of his Master to the accidents of the time and society in which he lived' so as not to stir up too much social conflict. While embracing Christ, other women, like Parkes, also repudiated Paul. 'My appeal', insisted Butler, 'is to Christ, and to Him alone, not to any Church, or traditions, or Councils, or catechism, not yet even to an Apostle.' If Christ was the only authority, who was most competent to expound his teaching? Butler's answer was the true Church: 'a company of faithful men and women who throughout all the ages have reflected the teaching of Christ himself in its integrity. These all asserted the equality of all men and women, and asserted it on Christ's teaching.' These interpreters would resonate with the prophetic message in the Bible about liberation for all human beings held in slavery, bondage or oppression, regardless of class or race or sex. As her life of Catherine had insisted, God was gender-blind when choosing prophets. Even St Paul acknowledged, according to Butler, that 'women as well as men were destined by God to be prophets', that is, people able 'to see as God sees' and 'judge of all things in the light of God'. God bestowed these gifts, 'without partiality, without recognition of sex or race or station in life'.[29]

Butler's own reading of the Bible convinced her that all of Christ's important dealings with women were 'accompanied by a distinct act of *Liberation*'. 'Search throughout Gospel history', she continued,

> and observe his conduct in regard to women, and it will be found that the word liberation, expresses above all others, the act which changed the whole life and character and position of the women dealt with and which ought to have changed the character of men's treatment of women from that time forward.[30]

Palpably, the true Church had not yet prevailed. None the less, Butler carved out an important role for women in bringing it into being.

For all the Victorian feminists 'the law of sacrifice' was a key conception which, although ambiguous, could be used to ratify women's robust resistance. In the least disruptive way, the doctrine of sacrifice was invoked to redeem single women from the charge of being selfish shirkers: 'not selfishness', Cobbe insisted, 'but self-sacrifice even more entire than belongs to the double life of marriage, is the true law of celibacy'.[31] Most feminists saw the law of sacrifice as the most extreme form of divine calls to love and service which justified all of their worldly work. Speaking of her conversion to Catholicism, Bessie Rayner Parkes felt that 'a profound faith in the Christian law of sacrifice is, I think, the main element which I have acquired'.[32] She confessed that she had never read the work of Christian Socialist Revd F. D. Maurice 'although one of my friends is perpetually referring to him'; Maurice also made sacrifice a central tenet and proposed an analogy between the clergy and women, as both being particularly expert in the knowledge of sacrifice.[33]

Butler's version of sacrifice developed an analogy between Christ and mothers which opened out in a different direction – to heroic sacrifice in holy battles, ideas which were later elaborated, in different ways, both by suffragettes and theosophists. Butler challenged the age-old dualism in Western religious thinking between woman as carnality and man as spirituality. Instead she proposed that women were the more spiritual of the sexes, by virtue of their very bodies. Like Christ who suffered and sacrificed himself on the cross for humankind, women were the epitome of altruism. Because they became pregnant, showed willingness to suffer pain and even to sacrifice their lives in childbirth, Butler observed that 'for Christ, and after him all the teachers, poets, and thinkers of the world, have used the travail and the joy of mother-hood, as the typical expression of all that is deepest and most terrible in spiritual anguish, and highest and purest in spiritual joy and fruition.'[34] But this was no simple invitation to submissive masochism.

'We are in times of battle', Butler insisted, when women must become 'rebels for God's Law' and use their spirituality to wage 'a consecrated rebellion against the rule of materialism and sensuality' made most manifest, she thought, in legal persecution of suspected prostitutes and in scientific cruelty to animals: 'embittering and deepening the groaning and travailing in pain alike of the animal creation and of the whole human family'.[35] Later, the militant suffragettes also made use of the idea of holy war and revitalised traditions of martyrdom, regarding hunger strikers as saints and featuring St Joan of Arc as a heroine, often dressed in armour and mounted on a horse, in their public pageants. Emily Wilding Davison mused on the significance of a sacrificial death, writing some time before she threw herself under the King's horse and died on Derby Day in 1913: 'To lay down life for friends, that is glorious, selfless, inspiring. But to re-enact the tragedy of Calvary for generations yet unborn, that is the last consummate sacrifice of the Militant!'[36] Echoing Butler's view, some feminist theosophists, like Charlotte Despard, leader of the Women's Freedom League, insisted that the woman's movement existed to reinstate a dual (masculine and feminine) humanity, but with a maternal side which resonated with the law driving the evolution of the vegetable, animal and human world: 'the law both of physical and spiritual life is sacrifice and that, in the higher spheres, manifests as love'.[37]

Butler extended the idea of spirituality in the sacrificial body to build a bridge to another powerful rhetoric. Her book, *The Constitution Violated* (1871), deliberately did not engage with the moral or the medical aspects of the Contagious Diseases Acts, but, instead, mobilised the dominant language of male reform agitation from the mid-eighteenth century onwards, from the middle-class Association Movement and the American Revolution to working-class Chartism, namely constitutional rhetoric. The book's title not only played upon the analogy between women's bodies and the body politic but insisted that the abuse of women violated the English Constitution. In a startling way, she absorbed prostitutes (the despised 'public women') into the citizenry by virtue of their bodies over which they had rights guaranteed by Magna Carta; she argued that no medical examination could be ordered without trial by jury for a crime designated by law. And she insisted that only votes for women could safeguard these rights. Depriving women of their constitutional rights not only introduced 'a species of villeinage or slavery' but gave them every justification to activate 'the right of the people to resistance'.[38]

Within the constitutional view, 'the People had the ultimate political and religious authority: *Vox populi, vox Dei*'.[39] Butler not only included women into the People but made use of the Chartist extension of the concept of the People to the working class. To this expanded People, she juxtaposed the oppressors or tyrants who included the usual radical targets, the aristocracy and their corrupt state, but also new additions to the rogues gallery of villains like medical doctors and the police. Continually she referred to the mass of the people having more true knowledge than educated men. 'Even where their education is but poor', she insisted, pointing up their similarity with the drafters of Magna Carta,

> the people nevertheless still know right from wrong; they are yet able to distinguish between truth and falsehood, between freedom

and slavery. It be said of our industrial classes generally as Lord
Chatham said of our forefathers who framed the Great Charter: –
'Their virtues were rude and uncultivated, but they were great
and sincere'.[40]

This true knowledge came partly from understanding the promise
of justice and then experiencing its denial: 'the poor are reminded
of what justice is, too often, by its absence ... Unlearned though
they may be, their actual experience of personal or social wrong is
a species of education'.[41]

Butler extended resonant old images of oppression in striking
new ways to mobilise a novel alliance between working people and
women. A powerful image of class exploitation much used by
working men was that of the rape of young innocent working girls
by aristocrats or bourgeois employers. Butler invoked this trope in
her sensational picture of medical rape by speculum which often
climaxed her talks: a pamphlet entitled *Vox Populi* contained letters
from working men expressing their rage over class rape condoned
by the law.[42] Unlike other repealers, she urged working-class self-
organisation in the traditional radical style: she insisted that
working people 'will feel much more interest in the movement and
much more committed to it if allowed to call their own meetings ...
and organize themselves'.[43]

As the century drew to its close, and as labour movements of
various kinds gathered strength, it became less unusual for radical
feminists to propose affinities between women and labour.
However, unlike Butler who discovered an equality in sacrificial
bodies, other radical feminists often placed women on top as the
superior force. Charlotte Despard saw a 'natural kinship between
two upheavals, the woman's movement and the labour movement'. She further fleshed out her meaning:

> with the great mass of the people at present the revolt is of the
> body – blind, vague, threatening – but neither fully conscious nor
> clearly reasoned out. Women of all classes, on whom these
> tremendous forces have been playing, have seen further. To the
> revolt of the senses and of the will is added a spiritual demand.
> They claim independence that they may serve.[44]

But however radical Butler was compared with other activist
women of her social background, it would be wrong to conceal the
contradictions which riddled her thought. 'Womanhood' was a key

category in her thinking and included women of all classes and all moral shades. Not only were the prostitute victims extending a hand and asking for help (like the Levite's concubine, pushed from the house and raped all night, stretching out her hand on the doorstep), but also the 'respectable' wives, 'the Sarahs are beginning to repent and stretch forth their hands to the Hagars and to bridge over the gulf which has so long separated them'.[45] While there was a radical thrust towards self-enacted liberation, there was also a contradictory story being told. I have argued elsewhere about her adopting the stance of the protective mother or stronger sister helping to rescue prostitutes (sometimes called daughters or 'enslaved sisters') and propel them into a new life as servants – not only of God but of middle-class households.[46]

## Feminism and religion

Feminists, by definition, are embroiled in the politics of sexual difference and usually commit themselves to enlarging the options for women. But the attempt to break beyond conventional gender limits involves some of the most difficult efforts at transformation that human beings can possibly make. Gender is such a basic part of the social and psychic bedrock of daily life that breaking up old conceptions involves nearly heroic efforts to imagine a situation beyond current common sense and to effect personal and wider re-formation. In these processes, religion can be helpful. Max Weber, in *The Protestant Ethic and the Spirit of Capitalism*, argued that only religion could stimulate desires and fears powerful enough to motivate people to try to make such profound psychological shifts.

Religious systems can offer, or can be interpreted in ways that offer, three key resources for liberation projects. First, on the intellectual level, religion can provide a belief system which is culturally powerful at a particular historical moment and yet which can be manipulated to shape gender identities different from the conventional models, legitimising them with transcendant authority. The way mid-century feminists reconfigured elements in 'patriarchal' Christian tradition, their attachment to the egalitarian and liberationist words and acts of Jesus, and their attempt to scrape away the historical encrustations of man-made institutions were examples of such a discovery of useful divinely sanctioned beliefs, as was their effort to add maternal and feminine elements to Protestant divinity. Second, religion can provide role models which women (and men) can emulate, and here again the mid-century Protestant women spotlighted virgin mothers, women saints and a feminised Jesus, all refashioned to fit their needs. Third, and this is to enter into the area of psychodynamics, religion can give tremendous power to belief by offering idealisations which can be internalised into the psyche and from there fortify the courage to be dissident or fuel a longing as intense as the passion of a lover for a new identity and a new life. Barbara Taylor, using Freudian theory, has written on the process of identification whereby 'as children we turn to our fathers and mothers with an idealising love which inscribes on our psyches imagos of masculinity and femininity which are the basis of our sexual self-identity', and has pointed to the way that Mary Wollstonecraft internalised, not so much her own inadequate parents as a fantasised and beloved father-God who ratified all her attempts to move beyond the merely human eroticising male gaze.[47]

Later on, in the mid-nineteenth century feminists seemed to be internalising a more feminised godhead. Or, looking at the process from a Jungian perspective, they seemed to be activating the feminine archetypes of the collective unconscious, not least the powerful archetype of the mother, which could give strong impetus to their desire to extend femininity and find a public place for women. For Jung it is not personal history alone which constellates the hugely powerful unconscious dimension of personality but there also exists a collective unconscious which is shared by human beings in different cultures and manifests itself in dreams, myths and, crucially, in the gods of the religions of the world.[48]

The mother archetype, according to Jung, has two quite opposite aspects which can be labelled the nurturing earth mother and the menacing witch mother or in his words 'the loving and the terrible mother'.[49] The mother archetype was obviously personified in the great goddesses who prevailed in many cultures before the advent of the father God religions of Judaism, Christianity and Islam.[50] Significant among them were goddesses who were virginal, in the sense of chaste and self-reliant, like the Greek Diana or Athena, or self-sufficient as in the case of Demeter and Persephone whose mother–daughter drama marked the recurring yearly cycle of springtime fertility to wintertime death. Also prominent, in the Bronze Age, were goddesses whose sons were sacrificed in order to bring about renewal of some kind – the story of Jesus was probably partly conceived in this mould.[51] Interestingly some Jungians are now encouraging their analysands to recover the goddess within and become that pregnant virgin, both self-sufficient and creative.[52] Feminist theologians and ecofeminists are also showing increasing interest in earth goddesses like Gaia and hypotheses about the entire planet as 'a living system, behaving as a unified organism'. Thus prominent theologian Rosemary Radford Reuther, who wrote on *Mary, The Feminine Face of the Church* in 1977, is now publishing works like *Gaia and God: An Ecofeminist Theology of Earth Healing*.[53]

To allow the archetypes to take over the conscious mind would be to take a quick trip to madness, but to access the power of the archetypes in a more limited way, according to Jungians, can be extremely energising and creative. And yet, tensions remain. If maternal and feminine archetypes were being mobilised by Victorian activists, then both the legacy of patriarchical religion and the inequality of social relations provided filters through which the energy passed and got refracted in complex ways. The dedication of Victorian feminists to the law of sacrifice which they also called the law of love moved in two directions. At one extreme, it led to heroinism, giving great courage to defy convention, sometimes in quite spectacular ways, as was the case with some of the suffragette women. But on the other side of the coin, it could reinforce already existing masochistic tendencies, a possibility both recognised and resisted by recent Christian feminist theologians like Karen Bloomquist:

> Jesus is not a model for women to imitate, in some kind of scapegoat, self-sacrificing role. To identify with him in that sense would only increase our victimization and mutilation. We are not to give ourselves up to be crucified for anyone's sake but are 'to struggle together against the injustice of all human sacrifice, including our own'.[54]

Interestingly, the inter-war Freudian analysts, like Helene Deutsch, succumbed to the masochistic undertow and argued that painful sexual fantasy and sacrificial motherhood formed an important part of femininity.[55]

Visions of social motherhood did enable women to stretch their public roles in Victorian Britain. Yet while trying to make these extensions acceptable to public men, there was always the danger of reinstalling subordination and even placing a glass ceiling over psychic as well as social life. Few, like Butler, tried to feminise men and conceive motherhood as a human quality of 'generous and cherishing helpfulness', present in many fathers 'with the hearts of mothers, who have shown the long-suffering patience and enduring love of a mother towards an erring child'.[56] Most activist women assigned maternality to the female sex alone, thus ratifying women's conventional monopoly over nurture and emotion, a division of human qualities inhibiting for the development both of women and men. Moreover, feminists often reconstituted subordination by translating metaphysical equality into mundane helpmeet status for women in the public communion of labour.

As problematic was the danger of using maternal archetypes in ways which cemented rather than transcended existing social divisions. To position yourself as a virgin mother in relation to adult women of other class, race or ethnic groups, who are seen as defenceless or deficient children, can produce authority relationships which can diminish the agency of the others and undermine the possibilities of more egalitarian sisterhood. Even Butler's rhetoric was loaded with the kind of imagery which conjured up prostitutes as defenceless victims and appealed on their behalf as 'a mother to mothers. Listen to me while I plead for the children'. Resistance to such well-meaning initiatives could then be misread as the unruly behaviour of undutiful daughters. The very sanctification of motherhood and sisterhood which Protestant feminists learned from Catholicism could then be turned into yet more strategies of domination, this time of women by other women.

This chapter has taken stock of the religious resources which Protestant women used to authorise their entry into public activity in the Victorian period. Starting with their surprising interest in Catholic doctrines and icons, which added a feminine dimension to divinity and dignified singlehood, it moved to consider some of the more radical beliefs, like those of Josephine Butler, about authority and liberation. It finally considered some of the possible psychodynamics of empowerment which were at work in the period and it speculated about the mobilisation of energy from the psychic unconscious. Coming back to everyday life, it spotlighted the social relations of power, whether of gender, class or race, through which such energised belief would pass and be refracted. Sadly these mundane relations of inequality were not always questioned, or seen to be in tension with spiritual equality in the Victorian period. As a result, Protestant feminists who embarked on a liberation journey for their sex as a whole, sometimes ended up stalling the progress of their less powerful sisters. These are the difficult contradictions which activists must navigate when they live within and against dominant discourses. The challenge is always to find ways of breaking the material, representational and psychic chains of subordination without reassembling them at the same time in a different form.

## Notes

1 E. Gaskell to C. Norton, 22 Apr., to W. Strong, 9 May [1862], *The Letters of Mrs Gaskell*, eds J. Chapple and A. Pollard (Manchester, Manchester University Press, 1966), pp. 682, 687. Pugin incident in K. Clark, *The Gothic Revival* (London, Constable, 1928), p. 158.

2 For Langham Place, see J. Rendall, '''A Moral Engine"? Feminism, Liberalism and the *English Woman's Journal'*, in her *Equal or Different: Women's Politics 1800–1914* (Oxford, Basil Blackwell, 1987); P. Levine, *Victorian Feminism, 1850–1900* (Tallahassee, Florida State University, 1987).

3 Bessie Rayner Parkes to B. Bodichon, 1863, Parkes Papers, box V, item 121; E. Davies to B. Bodichon, 17 Jan. 1863, Bodichon Papers, B.309, Girton College, Cambridge.

4 A. Jameson, *Legends of the Madonna as Represented in the Fine Arts*, new edn (London, Longmans, 1891), p. xlx; for Italian statue, G. Macpherson, *Memoirs of the Life of Anna Jameson* (London, Longmans, Green, 1878), p. 34.

5 F. Power Cobbe, 'Social Science Congresses and Women's Part in Them', *Macmillan's Magazine* (Dec. 1861), pp. 91–2. Jameson talked of a 'gentler power than that of the strong hand and the might that makes right': *Legends*, p. xlx. For current discussion, see E. Hampson, *After Christianity* (London, SCM Press, 1996), ch. 5.

6 I explore the 'communion of labour' in *The Contest for Social Science: Relations and Representations of Gender and Class* (London, Rivers Oram, 1996), pp. 127ff. See, too, Cobbe, 'Social Science Congresses', p. 62; A. Jameson, *Sisters of Charity and the Communion of Labour: Two Lectures on the Social Employment of Women* (London, Longman, Brown, Green, Longmans & Roberts, [1855] 1859); J. Butler (ed.), *Woman's Work and Woman's Culture* (London, Macmillan, 1869), p. xxvii.

7 B. Bodichon, *Women and Work* (London, Bosworth and Harrison, 1857), title page, and pp. 5–6 for God's purpose and the communion of labour; also, S. Herstein, *A Mid-Victorian Feminist: Barbara Leigh Smith Bodichon* (New Haven, Yale University Press, 1985).

8 E. Davies, *The Higher Education of Women* (New York, AMS reprint, [1866] 1973), pp. 36–7, 16, 22–3; see B. Caine, *Victorian Feminists* (Oxford, Oxford University Press, 1992) for more about her.

9 F. Swiney, *The Cosmic Procession: Or, the Feminine Principle in Evolution*

(London, Ernest Bell, 1906), pp. 126, 99–100, 117, xi for these beliefs. My thanks to David Doughan for sight of his *Dictionary of National Biography* entry on Swiney prior to publication. See, too, D. Burfield, 'Theosophy and Feminism: Some Explorations in Nineteenth-Century Biography', in P. Holden (ed.), *Women's Religious Experience* (London, Croom Helm, 1983); A. Linklater, *An Unhusbanded Life: Charlotte Despard, Suffragette, Socialist and Sinn Feiner* (London, Hutchinson, 1980).

10 Cobbe, 'Social Science Congresses', p. 90; *Life of Frances Power Cobbe by Herself*, 2 vols (Boston, Houghton Mifflin, 1894) and Caine, *Victorian Feminists*. J. Butler, *Lady of Shunem* (London, Horace Marshall, [1884]), p. 3.

11 See M. Vicinus, *Independent Women: Work and Community for Single Women, 1850–1920* (London, Virago, 1985), ch. 1 for an excellent discussion of the surplus woman 'problem'; also [W. R. Greg], 'Why are Women Redundant?', *National Review*, 14 (1862).

12 M. Carpenter, 'Woman's Work in the Reformatory Movement', *English Woman's Journal*, 1 (1858), pp. 219–??; J. E. Carpenter, *The Life and Work of Mary Carpenter* (Montclair, Patterson Smith reprint, [1879] 1974).

13 C. L. Balfour, *The Women of Scripture*, 2nd edn (London, Houlston and Stoneman, 1850), pp. 221, 230.

14 The words of K. V. Adams, 'The Madonna and Margaret Fuller', *Women's Studies*, 25:4 (1996), p. 390; Adams challenges the writing of feminist theologians and literary critics who see Mary as an enfeebling icon of submissive 'true womanhood', pp. 386, 389.

15 Mr Rylands quoted in G. and L. Johnson (eds), *Josephine Butler: An Autobiographical Memoir* (London, Hamilton Kent, 1909), p. 112.

16 J. Butler, *Catherine of Siena*, 3rd edn (London, Horace Marshall, [1878] 1894), pp. 36, 42, 182.

17 *Ibid.*, pp. 66, 36, 46.

18 *Ibid.*, p. 185.

19 Butler, *Woman's Work*, p. xxviii.

20 Johnsons, *Josephine Butler*, pp. 58–9.

21 For women and philanthropic visiting, see my *Contest for Social Science*, chs 1, 5, 9.

22 Jameson, *Sisters of Charity*, quoted in Carpenter, 'Women's Work', p. 295; Bodichon, *Women and Work*, p. 9.

23 Davies, *Higher Education*, p. 36; F. P. Cobbe, 'The Final Cause of Woman', in Butler, *Woman's Work*, p. 7.

24 For controversy over sisterhoods, *Englishwoman's Review*, 1 (Oct. 1866), pp. 99–103; for the range of religious communities, see Vicinus, *Independent Women*, ch. 2.

25 Parkes Papers, box X, items 34/1, 32, no dates; letter to Mr Byrne, 25 Mar. 1865, box IX, item 72; letter to M. Merrywhether [June 1865], box VI, item 89. Parkes's daughter wrote a biography: M. Lowndes, *I Too Have Lived in Arcadia* (London, Macmillan, 1941).

26 Parkes Papers, box V, item 112, 12 Jan. 1862.

27 *Ibid.*, box X, item 36, no date.

28 S. Holton and M. Allen, 'Offices and Services: Women's Pursuit of Sexual Equality Within the Society of Friends, 1873–1907', *Quaker Studies*, 2 (1997), pp. 20, 11–12, 22.

29 J. Butler, *Prophets and Prophetesses: Some Thoughts for the Present Times* (Newcastle, Mawson, Swan & Morgan, 1898), pp. 4–6.

30 Butler, *Woman's Work*, pp. lix, lviii, lii, liv; B. Parkes to B. Bodichon, 23 Apr. 1850, Parkes Papers, box V, item 47.

31 Cobbe, 'Social Science Congresses', p. 90.

32 Parkes Papers, box X, item 35; also an earlier letter to B. Bodichon, 4 June 1852, saying that she had learned from her 'The Religion of Entire Surrender to Duty', box V, item 63.

33 Revd F. D. Maurice, 'Plan of a Female College for the Help of the Rich and Poor', in his *Lectures to Ladies on Practical Subjects*, 3rd edn (Cambridge, Macmillan, 1857), p. 16: 'it is no novelty for women to make sacrifices; that is their ordinary business and vocation'; p. 24 for the clergy elucidating 'the whole mystery of sacrifice as involved in the least acts'.

34 Butler, *Lady of Shunem*, p. 5.

35 J. Butler, *The Hour Before the Dawn: An Appeal to Men* (London, Trübner, 1882), pp. 109–10.

36 E. W. Davison, 'The Price of Liberty', *Suffragette*, 5 (June 1914), p. 50, discussed in Vicinus, *Independent Women*, pp. 276–7, 259–62.

37 C. Despard, *Theosophy and the Woman's Movement* (London, Theosophy Publishing Society, 1913), pp. 48, 16, 45; on p. 46 she argues à la Butler: 'Woman, it should ever be remembered, is an example in herself of what the law of Duty and the deeper law of Sacrifice mean. Giving, often in pain and weariness, sometimes in danger: surrendering when the imperative summons calls, her life for the life of the coming world, which in her, as in a shrine, lives and moves! doing this generally as a natural thing, imposed upon her by her own mother – Nature – Woman, in the natural order of things, comes nearer to the Great Law and its observance than man.'

38 J. Butler, *The Constitution Violated* (Edinburgh, Edmonston and Douglas, 1871), pp. 27, 29, 144–6, 1. For predominance of constitutionality in male reform movements, see J. Epstein, *Radical Expression: Political Language, Ritual and Symbol in England, 1790–1850* (New York, Oxford University Press, 1994) and my 'Language and Contestation: The Case of "the People", 1832 to the Present', in J. Belchem and N. Kirk (eds), *Languages of Labour* (Aldershot, Scolar, 1997).

39 [J. Butler], *An Appeal to the People of England on the Regulation and Superintence of Prostitution … by an English Mother* (Nottingham, Frederick Banks, 1870), p. 31.

40 Butler, *Constitution Violated*, pp. 131, 2, 45, 126; J. Butler, *Truth Before Everything* (London, Dyer Brothers, 1897), p. 12.

41 *Ibid.*, p. 9.

42 J. Butler, *Vox Populi* (Liverpool, T. Brakell, 1871), for rape by speculum, see J. Walkowitz, *Prostitution and Victorian Society* (Cambridge, Cambridge University Press, 1980), pp. 108–9.

43 J. Butler to H. Wilson, 22 Apr. 1875, Josephine Butler Society Collection, Fawcett Library, London Guildhall University.

44 Despard, *Theosophy*, pp. 9, 54.

45 Butler, *Lady of Shunem*, p. 91; J. Butler, *The Duty of Women in Relation to Our Great Social Evil … 25 Nov. 1870* (Carlisle, Hudson Scott, 1870), pp. 5–6.

46 Yeo, *Contest for Social Science*, pp. 143–5.

47 B. Taylor, 'Religion, Radicalism and Fantasy', *History Workshop*, 39 (Spring 1995), pp. 109–10; also her 'For the Love of God: Religion and the Erotic Imagination in Wollstonecraft's Feminism', in E. Janes Yeo (ed.), *Mary Wollstonecraft and 200 Years of Feminisms* (London, Rivers Oram, 1997).

48 C. G. Jung, *The Archetypes and the Collective Unconscious* (London, Routledge, 1991), parts I and II; also his autobiography, *Memories, Dreams, Reflections* (London, Collins and Routledge and Kegan Paul, 1963).

49 C. G. Jung, 'Psychological Aspects of the Mother Archetype' ([1938] 1954), in *Archetypes*, p. 82.

50 A. Baring and J. Cashford, *The Myth of the Goddess. Evolution of an Image* (London, Viking Arkana, 1991) gives a good account of how the father-god religions absorbed or repudiated these powerful belief systems, pp. 155ff., 282ff., 302ff., 416ff.

51 *Ibid.*, ch. 4, 'The Bronze Age: The Mother Goddess and her Son-Lover'.

52 Especially Canadian analyst Marion Woodman, *The Pregnant Virgin* (Toronto, Inner City Books, 1985), pp. 78–81.

53 R. Radford Ruether, *Mary the Feminine Face of the Church* (Philadelphia, Westminster Press, 1977); *Gaia and God: An Ecofeminist Theology of Earth Healing* (San Francisco, Harper, 1992), p. 4 for quote about the Gaia hypothesis in biology; see also her *Women Healing Earth. Third World Women on Ecology, Feminism and Religion* (London, SCM Press, 1996).

54 Bloomquist, quoted in Hampson, *After Christianity*, p. 146, where Hampson rejects the whole doctrine of sacrifice.

55 See K. Millett, *Sexual Politics* (London, Virago, [1969] 1977), pp. 204–6; H. Deutsch, *The Psychology of Women. A Psychoanalytic Interpretation* (New York, Grune and Stratton, 1944), chs 6, 7.

56 Butler, *Lady of Shunem*, pp. 7–8.

## 6

# British freewomen: national identity, constitutionalism and languages of race in early suffragist histories

SANDRA STANLEY HOLTON

### 'Constitutionalism', the rhetoric of race and women's suffrage

The first accounts of the suffrage movement in Britain were written between the 1880s and the turn of the century, at the zenith of imperialism, and by women with impeccable middle-class-radical credentials. All sought to legitimate their cause through appeals to notions of national identity, or by a 'constitutionalist' claim to women's supposed heritage as 'freeborn Britons'.[1] This was a radical rhetoric of some long standing, but it was one that these suffragist historians also increasingly adapted so as to incorporate vocabularies of race and of racial difference. Jane Rendall has drawn our attention to how the early suffragists emphasised a sense of national heritage sometimes designated 'Anglo-Saxon', other times 'Germanic' or 'Teuton', using language which might be adopted equally by radical and by Tory suffragists. Through such a national identification, for example, Frances Power Cobbe, of Tory, Anglo-Irish gentry descent, presented British women as the inheritors of a political and legal culture that allowed their sex 'a freedom and respect unknown to their sisters of the south'. She celebrated also belonging to a people 'whose moral nature has been in more equipoise with their passions'.[2]

Jane Rendall suggests that such remarks reflect 'that particular preoccupation with socio-cultural evolution' that marked intellectual endeavours in the latter part of the nineteenth century, and which sought to distinguish British society and institutions from the '"savage" brutality' and despotism of less enlightened cultures elsewhere.[3] Such cultural racism shaped and informed the earliest accounts of the history of the suffrage movement and its place in Britain's development as a nation.[4] We find here an extension of the language of the radical 'patriot' so as to incorporate discourses

of empire as national destiny, as a process of spreading the 'civilisation' of Britain to the far-flung, dark and 'barbarous' quarters of
the world.[5]

The following discussion will focus on a set of histories written
from within the women's movement, each of which adopted in
varying ways a rhetoric of national identity, heritage and destiny
that may be characterised as 'constitutionalist': Millicent Garrett
Fawcett, 'England' (1884), Caroline Ashurst Biggs, 'Great Britain'
(1886), Charlotte Carmichael Stopes, *British Freewomen* (1894), and a
work written very much under its influence, the first book-length
history of the British suffrage movement, Helen Blackburn's
*Women's Suffrage* (1902).[6] The adjective 'constitutional' and the
noun 'constitutionalist' subsequently became terms applied in the
early decades of the twentieth century to the members of the older
and more moderate wing of the movement, organised by the
National Union of Women's Suffrage Societies and led by Millicent
Garrett Fawcett. They were meant to characterise and distinguish
the National Union from the very different approach adopted by
the 'militant' suffrage societies, notably the Women's Social and
Political Union formed in 1903 by Emmeline Pankhurst. My designation of these early suffrage histories as 'constitutional' looks
forward, then, to the early twentieth-century characterisation of the
long-established suffrage societies. It is also intended to reflect
their distinctiveness from the counter-histories subsequently
produced by two 'militant' suffragists, and to be examined here:
Emmeline Pankhurst, *My Own Story* (1914); Sylvia Pankhurst, *The
Suffragette* (1911) and her later *The Suffragette Movement* (1931).[7] But
my use of these terms also harks back to earlier radical representations of British history, so as to suggest certain previously
neglected continuities between the suffrage movement and the
popular radicalism of an earlier era.

As Eric Hobsbawm has emphasised: 'Even revolutionary movements backed their innovations by reference to a "people's past"',
so that history itself may not merely record, but serve also to form
'part of ... the ideal of nation, state or movement'.[8] The earliest
suffrage historians shared a largely celebratory view of British
history, society and culture, a perspective from which they sought
legitimacy for their own cause. Hence, the first suffrage histories
might variously characterise their cause in terms of an appeal to
national character, or of the heritage of the 'freeborn Briton', locat-

ing their demand as one for the *restitution* to women of supposedly lost ancient rights. Appeals to a radical 'patriot' understanding of the British past have been traced back to responses to the French Revolution, and more particularly to the campaigns that preceded the first Reform Act of 1832. Suffragist histories redeployed such radical 'constitutionalist' rhetoric, adopting and adapting it to the cause of women's rights, most elaborately in Charlotte Carmichael Stopes, *British Freewomen*. It was a rhetoric that was, significantly, largely abandoned in the later 'militant' histories produced by a subsequent generation of suffragists, which in both its polemic and its practice largely displaced the 'constitutionalist' perspective of the older, more moderate mainstream.

In examining the constitutionalist rhetoric of British radicalism in the age of revolutions, James Epstein has concluded that claims for women's rights 'were more problematically situated within radical popular discourse and were not easily legitimated through an appeal to England's past'. He also suggests the gendered nature of the constitutionalist account of citizenship, one where 'the virtues of manly independence were among the key terms of constitutionalist reference', and which drew on 'traditions of Anglo-American thought in which civic virtue was armed and male'. Hence claims for women's rights by British Jacobins were more usually grounded on Enlightenment premises, on appeals to 'rational fellowship' between the sexes, and a vision of 'a rationally ordered, non competitive new moral world'. After the anarchy of the Terror, however, James Epstein finds among British radicals a turning away from the language of the Enlightenment and of republicanism. Radical constitutionalism now centred on a supposed libertarian heritage, and more particularly on claims to the right of the (male) British subject to bear arms. Equally, citizenship was increasingly conceived of in terms of the right and duty to resist tyranny, through a repertoire of peaceful methods of protest and 'rituals of solidarity' wherever possible, and through a resort to armed insurrection where such avenues had been exhausted.[9]

However problematic the rhetoric of constitutionalism for the pursuit of women's rights, its practice, especially in terms of peaceful protest, did leave a place for the participation of women. Linda Colley has argued that it was the popular 'patriotic activism' of the Napoleonic wars which first allowed women to share some sense of citizenship, in providing 'a *public* role of a kind'. The processions and marches that followed Napoleon's defeat at Waterloo saw the emergence of female patriot symbols, while female societies marched in civic demonstrations in their own right, leading Linda Colley to conclude: 'Consciously or not, these female patriots were staking out a civic role for themselves'.[10] But it was not until the end of the nineteenth century, and almost thirty years into the suffrage campaigns, that women's claim to share in the heritage of the 'freeborn Briton' received its fullest and clearest articulation, in Charlotte Carmichael Stopes's *British Freewomen*.

## Suffrage history and identities of nation and race

In the meantime suffragist historians appealed as best they might to versions of a national identity, adopting also a 'constitutionalist' voice to express resistance to the tyrannies under which the women of their country suffered. Within this shared rhetorical strategy, however, there are to be noted some subtle and suggestive differences between the four early histories discussed here. In the case of Millicent Garrett Fawcett, her essay is marked by an immoderate celebration of the character of *English* institutions and culture. She herself appeared to one admirer as 'English through and through', a characteristic explained in terms of her East Anglian family origins.[11] Wife of Henry Fawcett, a minister in Gladstone's reforming government, and like her husband a Radical-Liberal disciple of John Stuart Mill, Millicent Garrett Fawcett had grown up in the company of older sisters and friends who helped found the women's rights movement in the mid-1860s. By 1884 she was herself to the fore among its leadership, and in 1897 was chosen to head the newly formed National Union of Women's Suffrage Societies. This body organised what became known as the 'constitutionalist' wing of the movement after the emergence of a 'militant' section in the early years of the twentieth century.[12] It was surely no accident that she entitled her essay on the early suffrage movement 'England', a title that in no way reflected the recognition general among present-day historians that suffragist efforts elsewhere in Britain and its colonies might each deserve separate and particular attention. This strong sense of her English identity, together with a celebration of her English heritage, inflected all Millicent Garrett Fawcett's writings, as well as her political activism on behalf of women's rights.

She failed entirely, for example, to examine the ideas of the Enlightenment and the French Revolution as possible origins for a wider concern with women's rights. She managed no more than a nod towards the 'upheaval of the human mind' which Jacobins like Mary Wollstonecraft had helped foster in 'the awakening of the democratic spirit, the rebellion against authority, the proclamation of the rights of man'. She chose instead to emphasise the 'adaptation' of such influences in Britain to 'the practical spirit of the nineteenth century'. This she identified especially with the attack on 'the fortress of old-world custom and prejudice' that had been undertaken by John Stuart Mill, both in his writings and as the Member of Parliament who had helped revive the claim for votes for women in the mid-1860s.[13]

Millicent Garrett Fawcett celebrated Mill's contribution to the British suffrage movement in terms of 'the character of practical good sense and moderation which has been its distinguishing feature'. More particularly she sought to distinguish Mill's emphasis on grounding the claim for women's enfranchisement on its expediency, and especially that 'important branch of expediency called justice', as against any 'abstract and inalienable right' deriving from the ideas of the Enlightenment. She argued that it was Mill's influence that explained the 'character of practical moderation and rather humdrum common sense' that in her eyes marked out the British suffrage movement from others around the world. In particular she believed this national particularity had 'prevented a good deal of what strikes one as rather comic about the movement in other countries. We talk about "women" and "women's suffrage", we do not talk about Woman with a capital W. We leave that to our enemies.'[14]

There is an ill-disguised dismissiveness about her counterparts in the United States movement here. Both the volume to which she was contributing, and a subsequent multi-volume history put together by United States suffragists, adhered to the principally North American English usage of 'Woman Question' and 'Woman Suffrage'. This was a usage that had been frowned upon in the very earliest years of the British movement by leading figures like John Stuart Mill. In this otherwise gratuitous aside, Millicent Garrett Fawcett was making clear her unequivocal determination to distinguish what she held to be the special character of suffragists in Britain. In particular, she celebrated her own movement as an expression of the phlegmatic, patient, commonsensical national character of the English: 'The studious moderation of the societies, the absence of tall talk, is one great secret of the progress the women's movement has made in England.' She continued in similar vein: 'The words Man, Woman, Humanity, etc., send a cold shudder through the average Briton, but talk to him of John and Elizabeth and he is ready to be interested and, up to his lights, just.'[15] Here the 'English' and the 'Briton' are one, and simply absorb suffrage activity in other parts of the British Isles, or within the empire, into a celebration of the prosaic, practical nature of English reformers and radicals.

In order to reinforce this presentation of the history of the British movement, Millicent Garrett Fawcett had to play around to some extent with its chronology, and omit from her account those pioneers who had failed to conform with her ideal of the measured, patient, reasonable Englishwoman. She was writing her history just as the tensions within middle-class radicalism more generally were becoming increasingly evident, and bringing in turn divisions and splits within the suffragist movement. Within a few years British suffragists were to find it impossible for a time to continue to work together within a single national body. Millicent Garrett Fawcett was among the leadership of moderate opinion that became increasingly at odds with its ultra-Radical wing, and her view of the movement's history is necessarily informed by this partial perspective.[16] Hence she identifies Lydia Becker as the secretary of the influential Manchester Society from its outset, although Elizabeth Wolstenholme Elmy might more properly have deserved this recognition.[17] Neither the latter's unconventional personal life, nor her ultraist position that included married women in the claim for the vote, fitted the character of 'studious moderation' that Millicent Garrett Fawcett sought to establish for the British movement.[18] It was left to Theodore Stanton, the editor of *The Woman Question in Europe*, to extend some recognition to the contribution of the ultra-Radical suffragists in Britain, in footnotes that he subsequently added to Fawcett's essay.[19]

In similar vein, Millicent Garrett Fawcett identified 1868 as the year in which 'ladies', among whom she herself was included, began to speak from public platforms. It seems most likely, however, that one of the first, if not the first, women to address mixed, middle-class audiences publicly in Britain was the Afro-

American abolitionist, Sarah Parker Remond.[20] Here again, Millicent Garrett Fawcett must be one of the few historians, either in her own time or since, who chose to ignore completely the links between the anti-slavery and the suffrage movements. Abolitionists like Sarah Parker Remond, be they of Afro-American or English descent, found *no* place whatever on the canvas on which in 1884 Millicent Garrett Fawcett chose to paint her version of suffrage history.[21]

One further aim emerges in this account of British suffragists – a determined effort to place them in the vanguard of suffrage movements around the world. Hence Millicent Garrett Fawcett paid considerable attention to the enfranchisement of women in 1881 in the Isle of Man, and claimed that women had voted in large numbers in the elections for the House of Keys that same year. She directly compared this advance with the granting of the vote to women in Wyoming in 1883, claiming far greater significance for the first event on the grounds of the 'very great antiquity' of the Manx Constitution, its legislative independence from the House of Commons, and the much larger population of that island than the United States territory. The enfranchisement of women in the Isle of Man, she insisted, was 'even more important as a political experiment' than that in Wyoming, 'the youngest and smallest' of the components of the United States. She concluded: 'it may be claimed that when a similar experiment is tried with success in a place that is rigidly conservative of its ancient institutions, the history of which may be traced back to the sixth century, the example is one that is entitled to even greater respect than that set by the good people of Wyoming'.[22] Her pride of race was subsequently to inform Millicent Garrett Fawcett's support for Britain's part in the Boer War, and in her jingoistic stance against suffragist internationalists and pacifists during the First World War. Her history-writing was, then, quite of a piece with her sense of 'English' political and cultural pre-eminence.

Leaving aside their respective places at its top, a hierarchy of race was one about which most British and United States suffragists would have had little difficulty agreeing. Indeed, it dictated the overall organisation of *The Woman Question in Europe* by its United States editor, Theodore Stanton, whose radical credentials were no less impressive than those of Millicent Garrett Fawcett. Son of one of the founders of the women's rights movement in the United

States, Elizabeth Cady Stanton, he had a wide acquaintance with
Radical suffragists in Britain through his mother's international
networks. He himself married and settled in France while his sister
Harriot Stanton Blatch married and settled in England, consolidat-
ing her family's links with Radical suffragist circles there, and
extending them also to socialist circles through her membership of
the Fabian Society.

In the European context, at least, Theodore Stanton was able to
accede to Millicent Garrett Fawcett's claim to England's international leadership of the suffrage cause. He placed her essay at the
beginning of his collection as reflecting the society in which 'the
most marked progress' had been made, especially in terms of the
political rights gained for women in local government in Britain.
England was, as he put it, 'the Mother Country' for suffragists
throughout Europe. He placed the subsequent contributions to his
collection in what he called 'an ethnological order'. The account of
the women's movement in 'Anglo-Saxon' England was thus
followed in this order: the 'Teutonic' countries, then Scandinavia,
the 'Latin' nations, 'the Latin-Teutonic' nations (signalling that
ethnic purity was also a factor in this ethnological ordering) and
the 'Slavonic states', with 'the Orient' coming last of all. This final
contribution in turn concentrated on the women of independent
Greece alongside Christian Greek women still under Muslim domination within the Ottoman empire. The effective exclusion of
Armenian, Jewish and Bulgarian women from the discussion of the
situation in 'the Orient' was excused in terms of their 'state of
lamentable inactivity'.[23]

Frances Power Cobbe used her 'Introduction' to this same
volume to give further voice to her sense of racial supremacy. She
declared, for example, her anxiety about the inappropriateness to
'other nations with different tendencies and untrained in self-
government' of 'The system of Representation, with Trial by Jury
and the whole scheme of civil and political liberty' that had 'grown
up through a thousand years ... among our law-abiding Anglo-
Saxon race'. Frances Power Cobbe especially had in mind here
Ireland, Greece, Italy, France and Spain, but she used this occasion
to regret the admission to the franchise in Britain of 'a rabble of
"illiterates"', and in the United States of the 'aliens' that comprised
the 'hordes of immigrants', and of 'the emancipated negroes'
(though here her fears were quieted by the knowledge that they

formed a minority among a large white population). She antici-
pated that 'not even American democracy will contemplate for
many a year to come following up this heroic act by enfranchising
Chinese immigrants; nor English radicalism ask for the admission
of Hindoos' to a share in the government of India.[24]

This insistence on the 'English' origins of modern democracy,
especially in terms of Saxon law and institutions, continued to
mark subsequent histories of the British suffrage movement. It is
also evident, for example, in the essay that Caroline Ashurst Biggs
contributed to the *History of Woman Suffrage* put together by
suffragists in the United States. Caroline Ashurst Biggs, editor of
*The Englishwoman's Review*, was a suffragist with a particularly
impressive middle-class radical pedigree, going back to her grand-
father, the radical lawyer, abolitionist and Corn Law-repealer,
William Ashurst. Her aunts, Caroline Stansfeld and Emilie
Venturi, were also at the forefront of the movement for women's
rights. Perhaps these extensive and long-standing radical connections account for her altogether less compromised references back
to the earlier 'patriot' identity of former generations of radical
'Britons'. Her title, as we have already seen, was the more inclu-
sive 'Great Britain'. Her account also charts the links between the
early suffrage movement and other radical causes in some of
which her own immediate forebears had played a part: the Anti-
Corn Law League, Chartism and the anti-slavery movement.
Caroline Ashurst Biggs's account was also the first to introduce
another aspect of British history that was to recur in subsequent
histories: the argument that what British suffragists sought
was *a restitution* to women of the ancient constitutional rights
accorded them in the past, and the access to public office
enjoyed by certain elite women in previous centuries. Such rights
had gradually fallen into disuse and had only been finally
removed by nineteenth-century statutes, most notoriously in the
1832 Reform Act, which for the first time had expressly limited the
parliamentary franchise to men.[25] Such invocations of an earlier
golden age of freedom for female Britons remained a constant
theme in chronicles of the British suffrage movement for
some decades more, and it was one that was eventually taken
up by suffragists in the United States who, in looking into their
own history, found that some women had also voted there in
colonial times.[26]

## British freewomen and imperial destiny

Though women in England might continue to participate in
debates over nationhood and adopt the stance of the radical
patriot, Jane Mackay and Pat Thane have also concluded that as a
sex they were by this time being 'identified not with nation but
with race'.[27] This view is confirmed by the line of argument
pursued in what is otherwise the most extensive and the most clas-
sically 'constitutionalist' account of women's claim to the vote,
*British Freewomen*, by Charlotte Carmichael Stopes.[28] Its author is
perhaps best remembered now as the austere and puritanical
mother of Marie Stopes, the campaigner for a woman's right to
control her fertility. In her own day, however, Charlotte
Carmichael Stopes was herself a scholar and writer of some standing, and one of the first women to study at the University of
Edinburgh. Perhaps it is not so surprising, then, that her 'constitutionalist' history is more fully inflected by the new 'scientific'
discourses of racial difference than any of its earlier versions. She
organised her study of the 'British freewomen' on what she, like
Theodore Stanton, called an 'ethnological' basis, so as to establish
'the racial characteristics' of past exemplars for the new British
freewomen whom she hoped were soon to be re-created by the
possession of a vote.

Hence Charlotte Carmichael Stopes posed her argument in the
form of 'an authentic history of British traditions' going back to
Roman times. She drew on Roman accounts to establish 'the equality of the sexes among the Northern nations' during the period of
the Roman conquest of Britain. Here the origins of the rights of the
British freewoman are traced back to the social organisation of the
Ancient Britons, and the related Belgic and Celtic peoples. The
moral codes, sexual equality in physical height, the participation of
women in public debate and in warfare, the worship of 'Mother-
Goddesses' are all presented as evidence that these ancient peoples
had already 'advanced out of barbarism' before the coming of the
Romans. Indeed, the 'Romanisation' of a rival British Queen,
Cartismandua, is argued to account for the defeat of Boadicea, a
defeat which 'rang the death-knell of the freedom of British
womanhood, and of the spirit of British manhood'. The significance of this historical heritage for Charlotte Carmichael Stopes
was once more as a past golden age for women, which might still

be regained for the present. She emphasised she '*has lived* the typal woman of the British past'.[29]

She argued, too, that Britain had been fortunate in that the subsequent Roman retreat had been followed by 'an infusion of new blood into the land, fortunately not of the Latin race, but of good northern stock, that reverenced women still'. The Saxons, in Stopes's account, shared many of the 'racial peculiarities' of the Ancient Britons, especially in allowing women to hold high office and to own land in their own right. Even after the 'whirlwind' of the Norman conquest, the 'records of Saxon liberties and the customs of Saxon times' had survived in church and cloister: 'The conquest was not one of extermination but of superposition. The great mass of the people remained Saxon in heart. The Normans were, too, of a kindred race', having inhabited a 'Latinised' land only in more recent times. So, according to Charlotte Carmichael Stopes, while the feudal system put women's rights second to men's, it did not entirely extinguish them. Here her narrative diverged significantly from earlier radical 'patriot' accounts of British heritage, in which 'the Norman yoke', in the form of the feudal system that followed the conquest, destroyed the freedoms allowed under the Saxon system of government.[30]

According to Charlotte Carmichael Stopes it was not the Norman conquest which had taken away the rights of British freewomen. These had only gradually been lost over the following centuries as the feudal system went into decay and 'service payments' were translated into 'money payments'. What she designated the 'Long Ebb' in the social position of women only began in her view in the seventeenth century, most especially with the work of the jurist Sir Edward Coke. It culminated in his enunciation of the legal doctrine of coverture, whereby the legal personality of a married woman became submerged under that of her husband, so that she could no longer hold property in her own right. In such a way, Charlotte Carmichael Stopes argued, 'women have been ousted by degrees from the building up of the superstructure of the English constitution, in whose foundations they had been considered', a process that culminated in the 1832 Reform Act, when 'the privilege of abstention was converted into the penalty of exclusion'.[31]

Charlotte Carmichael Stopes argued that such an account of British institutions might offer encouragement to the women's rights movement in two ways. First, she wrote: 'in the Light of the modern doctrine of Heredity, we see that our far-away ancestors held opinions to which we may hope that our successors may yet *revert'*, a questionable reading of Darwin that was not unusual at this time, and one that suggests an additional reason for her close attention to the Ancient Britons, the Saxons and the Normans. Second, she argued British history demonstrated that 'a recognition of the existence of women in the State, far from being novel or revolutionary would only be fulfilling the principles of the English constitution!'.[32]

Charlotte Carmichael Stopes had initially been encouraged in her researches into the ancient rights of women by Helen Blackburn, one-time secretary of the Central Committee of the National Society for Women's Suffrage, and following the death of Caroline Ashurst Biggs, editor of *The Englishwoman's Review*. Given to 'marked antiquarian tastes', Helen Blackburn had originally planned to undertake a similar project herself.[33] Instead, she was able to provide research notes of her own to help forward the work of Charlotte Carmichael Stopes, who insisted in her Preface that in consequence 'this little book may be taken as her voice as well as mine'.[34] It is not surprising, therefore, to find that when Helen Blackburn came to write the first book-length account of the British suffrage movement, she began by reiterating the argument that votes for women were sought as a restitution of ancient rights deriving from the origins of the British constitution, and most especially 'the pervading influence' of the Anglo-Saxon heritage as the basis of governance.[35]

Once again the position of women under Roman law was contrasted with that recorded under Anglo-Saxon government: while the former involved the 'absorption of the will and the possession of the wife' by her husband, Anglo-Saxon women had been accorded 'a share of personal independence'. Blackburn also took up Charlotte Carmichael Stopes's periodisation of 'the Long Ebb' in the affairs of women which became evident in the seventeenth century, and culminated in a series of attacks on women's rights in the 1830s: their express exclusion from the Reform Act of 1832, and the Municipal Corporation Act of 1835, alongside the ending of dower rights in 1833. Again, it is Britain's ancient cultural, constitutional and legal heritage which is invoked to explain why since then 'the movement towards recognizing the public duties of women should have made most progress amongst the English-speaking race, the founders of the Constitutional form of government'.[36]

Helen Blackburn also extended to some degree Charlotte Carmichael Stopes's vocabulary of race when she claimed that the Anglo-Saxons were the closest of 'all the Indo-German races ... to the free and open life of the early Aryans'. Women of British stock carried in consequence a particular historical burden, for in seeking to regain their ancient rights they also found a role as 'part of the continuity of historical development'.[37] Such a perspective on the suffrage movement allowed Helen Blackburn, like her predecessor Caroline Ashurst Biggs, more readily to acknowledge some of the origins of the women's suffrage movement in earlier radical campaigns – against the Corn Laws and slavery, for example. Such origins fitted well with the overarching framework of the progressive nature of the historical process, and of the particular place for Britons in that process. It was a role to be fulfilled also by British women in the outposts of empire, women who themselves might claim the vote on grounds of their racial 'superiority' to the indigenous peoples. Hence, her 'record of the women's suffrage movement in the British Isles' (as this history was subtitled) also included a roll-call of suffragist endeavour far beyond those isles – in place of honour, New Zealand, the first nation to pass a law enfranchising women, followed by Australia which had not been far behind. In comparison to these prime examples, Canada and South Africa appeared to need some explanation, for the demand for women's suffrage had so far been altogether less successful there. Once again theories of racial difference were invoked to explain such a lack of comparability between these far-flung colonies – more specifically, Helen Blackburn suggested that it was the particular mix and ratio of white and indigenous races in these two countries which explained their relative slowness in realising the historical mission of the British woman.

Such accounts of the suffrage movement chose for the most part to ignore contemporary scholarly works that would have served to cast serious doubt on their pursuit of the ancient legacy of British freewomen. The English translation of Ostrogorski's comparative study of the rights of women under different legal and political systems had been published the year before Charlotte Carmichael Stopes's work. She claimed that it had appeared too late for her to respond to it in her own work, but she also failed to take the opportunity in further editions of *British Freewomen* to rebut his very different analysis. Ostrogorski opened his account by insisting, 'From the very beginning of history woman appears everywhere in a state of complete subordination', a position he maintained was equally the case under 'barbarian', feudal and Roman law.[38] Similarly, Ostrogorski insisted on an external impetus to the demand for women's emancipation in Britain, which he saw as 'the rebound of the French Revolution', and a consequence of 'the new gospel of liberty, preached on the banks of the Seine'.

Nor did the celebration of British character and heritage in the movement's earliest chronicles sit well with all suffragists, of course. Millicent Garrett Fawcett, Caroline Ashurst Biggs and Helen Blackburn each gradually moved away from their early association with Radical-Liberal circles, and became part of the moderate section of the movement's leadership that had gathered around Lydia Becker. Ultra-Radical suffragists might justly feel that they had been unscrupulously written out of these first efforts in writing the history of their movement.[39] They might also feel a greater ambivalence towards any celebration of the British past. From their perspective the legacy of ancient constitutional glories was overshadowed by the more recent history of British repression of subject peoples, and of imperial conquest. Such ultraist opinion was also likely to see the demand for women's enfranchisement as a further aspect of more general radical movements against established powers and authorities, and on behalf of subject peoples.

Ultra-Radical suffragists not uncommonly expressed a sense of the wrongs promulgated under British rule. Hence they might declare a decided sympathy, for example, with Irish or Indian or Boer ambitions for freedom from that rule. Ursula Bright, otherwise one of the most intransigent among the ultraist leadership, explained how she and other suffragists of like mind 'quietly resigned long-cherished hopes' for their own cause, so as to work for the Liberals in 1892, as 'the party pledged to do justice to the sister island'.[40] Similarly, Josephine Butler, who had found her firmest and closest allies among the ultraist suffragists, challenged imperialist domination when she extended to India her crusade against the Contagious Diseases legislation. Viewing Indian women as victims of the British male elite, and to a lesser extent of their own culture, she expressed a special sense of responsibility towards them as 'Britannia's other daughters'. Her version of imperial feminism combined Christian beliefs and ethics with a sense of metropolitan responsibility for the welfare of imperial subjects, and a clear consciousness of gender solidarity among women.[41] Ultraist and moderate suffragists were also at odds in their stance towards the monarchy. This was evident in their contrasting memorials to Queen Victoria during the celebration of her sixtieth Jubilee in 1897, for example. While the Radicals trucu- lently demanded of the monarch some sign of support for the cause of women's rights, a counter-memorial rapidly organised by Millicent Garrett Fawcett issued only fulsome praise of the queen as an exemplar of British womanhood.[42]

There was, however, no outright rejection of the rhetoric of race by ultra-Radical suffragists, for they too might identify with the earlier notion of the radical patriot, and make appeals to the ideal of the freeborn Briton. This ideal in itself provided a sense of common ground with their closest allies within the United States suffrage movement, most notably Elizabeth Cady Stanton and Susan B. Anthony. The record of these two suffragists was marred by their antagonism to the extension of civil rights to freed male slaves when such rights were being denied white women. They also acquiesced in the racially discriminatory practices of suffrage organisations in the states of the old South. It was an aspect of the United States suffrage campaigns to which British colleagues, both moderates and ultraists, generally chose to turn a blind eye.

## Counter-histories of the suffrage movement

Either from lack of opportunity or lack of interest, no extensive alternative narrative was offered in the nineteenth century to the 'constitutionalist' histories so far examined. The ultraist Elizabeth Wolstenholme Elmy had apparently, over the course of her long suffrage career, collected a mass of documentary material in order to write an account from her own perspective. All she left, in the event, was a short article that appeared in one of the leading radical quarterlies in the late 1890s. But in the years that followed she became closely associated with a new current among those she identified as 'the insurgent women', one that shortly helped form the 'militant' wing of the twentieth-century movement. She was an old friend of the Pankhurst family, from the time she became founding secretary in 1865 of the influential Manchester suffrage committee, in which the young Radical lawyer, Richard Pankhurst, played an active part. For a time, Emmeline and Richard Pankhurst had also been her close colleagues in the Women's Franchise League, which she had helped form in 1889 to challenge the moderate national leadership of the movement. She welcomed Emmeline Pankhurst's formation of the Women's Social and Political Union in 1903, and continued into her mid-seventies to participate in its major demonstrations. She also made her papers and her memories available to Sylvia Pankhurst when her old friend's daughter came to write the first counter-history of the movement in *The Suffragette* (1911).[43]

Here at last an assertively oppositional, 'militant' narrative is offered to challenge the long-standing conventions of 'constitutionalist' history. The designation 'militant' is suggested not simply by its organisational origins, but also by the view of historical processes to which it provided expression.[44] Sylvia Pankhurst's *The Suffragette* and Emmeline Pankhurst's autobiographical *My Own Story* were equally important in this respect. Each work was largely written as an apologia for the new methods and strategies introduced by militant suffragists in the early years of the twentieth century, but this fresh interpretation of the suffrage movement provided a very different account of its origins, and of women's claim to the vote. It emphasised rupture and conflict in the place of the putative historical continuities and gradual, orderly, organic processes of social change that marked 'constitutionalist' history. It also displaced cultural heritage, racial memory and national character as the potential motors of social change, and gave far greater prominence to courageous, daring acts of will on the part of heroic individuals intent on wresting such change.[45] Militant histories told their story very much by reference to relatively recent events, and in terms of the actions of 'fine-souled' individuals. The furthest they looked backwards was to the parents of Emmeline and Richard Pankhurst, as participants in early nineteenth-century popular radicalism.[46]

There is far greater recognition, also, of foreign importations of emancipatory potential, most especially in terms of the movement of ideas associated with the French Revolution. Like Ostrogorski, then, this new 'militant' interpretation found some of the origins of the British suffrage movement on the banks of the Seine, in ideas mediated through the writings of Mary Wollstonecraft who from now on begins to find an increasingly routine place in twentieth-century histories of the British suffrage movement. Equally, from this time Jeanne d'Arc was more likely than Boadicea or Britannia to figure in the iconography of the suffrage movement, at least in the years before the outbreak of war. And Emmeline Pankhurst's identification with France became a constant refrain: her birth on Bastille Day; her Paris finishing school; her long-standing friendship with the daughter of a communard, Neomie de Rochefort; the impact made upon her as a young girl of reading Carlyle's history of the French Revolution, one of the first accounts to celebrate, and not to decry, the Terror. Here was a view of history as something directed by the indomitable will of great individuals, of social change as accomplished in fire, ferment and the fracturing of established institutions.[47]

Not surprisingly, given its emphasis on rupture and rejection of the past, there is no place for Ancient Britons or Celts or Teutons or Anglo-Saxons or Aryans in the counter-narrative of the militant account of suffrage history. The pride of race that characterised much of the constitutionalist histories of the movement is thus largely displaced. There is no radical-patriot identification with the 'British freewomen' of the past in such accounts (though, of course, Emmeline and her oldest daughter Christabel came later to adopt a super-patriot identity both during and after the First World War, one now focused on 'the Hun' as representing the other). And to the roll-call of middle-class radical causes with which the suffrage movement was earlier identified were now added references to the popular radicalism of the early nineteenth century. Emmeline Pankhurst, as well as working-class militants like Hannah Mitchell, could claim an ancestor at Peterloo, for example. And though militant suffragists became the most effective proponents of this version of the history of their movement, its influence was also increasingly evident in the work of 'constitutionalist' historians, including Millicent Garrett Fawcett.[48]

Yet the heritage of radical constitutionalism also remained evident in the twentieth-century campaigns, most especially in the 'rituals of solidarity' and past models for challenging but non-violent forms of protest. Many of these well-established radical practices, not surprisingly, had long proved suitable to 'constitutionalist' protest. From its beginnings in the 1860s the suffrage movement had made extensive use, for example, of petitions and

the staging of orderly demonstrations in major public halls, especially at key points in parliamentary politics. In the early twentieth
century, however, the militants also adopted less restrained 'constitutionalist' practice, including the heckling and the harassing at
public meetings of those politicians opposed to their cause. The re-
invigorated 'constitutionalist' societies, for their part, were the first
to adopt the processionary march, with banners and symbols, to
publish their demand. It was a practice at which the militants soon
excelled through their superb use of pageantry and street theatre.
The constitutionalists also harked back to radical feasting rituals to
celebrate heroes or mark events of significance to their demand,
when they organised the first suffrage banquet to welcome
released prisoners with a breakfast at the Savoy in November 1906.
Such events thereafter became a routine part of the Women's Social
and Political Union (WSPU) activities. In addition, the WSPU
revived the practice of holding conventions as alternative 'parliaments' for the voicing of the popular will. From 1907, it organised a
series of 'Women's Parliaments' where resolutions were formu-
lated prior to a march on the House of Commons to deliver the
demands of the meeting. These were all practices within which
'constitutionalist' as well as 'militant' might, and did, join and
share some part.[49]

The ethos of 'militancy' continually threatened a breaking out
from the boundaries of 'constitutionalist' protest, however, most
especially because it validated authentic and spontaneous acts of
will on the part of great individuals who had rendered themselves
forces of history. However, the 'militancy' of the WSPU was also
clearly gendered, articulating a female heroic, celebrating the
'symbolic' violence of the 'suffragette', and contrasting it with the
violence of the existing all-male government, as well as the male-
dominated popular radicalism of previous conflicts over the right
to vote.[50] It was a heroic designed to move previously passive and
respectable women to pursuit of personal martyrdom in
confronting mob violence, imprisonment, the hunger strike and
forcible feeding. It was also a heroic designed to move previously
uncommitted or opposing men to a chivalrous defence of the militant in her pursuit of martyrdom.[51]

And finally, there are contrasts in the kinds of stories that constitutionalist and militant historians chose to tell in their alternative
. accounts of the suffrage movement, as a comparison of Helen

Blackburn's *Women's Suffrage* with Sylvia Pankhurst's *The Suffragette* demonstrates. The parliamentary and election timetable tended to dominate the chronology of both narratives, though this is finally and firmly displaced in Sylvia Pankhurst's longer and more free-ranging *The Suffragette Movement* (1931). But much of the action in Helen Blackburn's history takes place within the drawing room, the public hall and the House of Commons, whereas most of that in Sylvia Pankhurst's accounts occurs on the street corner, at the hustings or in the prison house. Similarly, Helen Blackburn's chronicle emphasises the impersonal, time-consuming deliberations of committees and societies and the considered acts that from time to time followed from them. Sylvia Pankhurst's narrative, in contrast, is organised around the depiction of inspirational figures, their rapid movement from one assertive act of public protest to the next, and the martyrdoms endured for the cause.

## Conclusion

The influence of the counter-histories produced by the 'militant' wing of the suffrage movement continues on to some extent in the 1990s, despite the extensive work of revision undertaken by historians of the suffrage movement since the 1970s. Moreover, earlier neglect of the nineteenth-century beginnings of the movement has only recently begun to be addressed. Further revisions of this history now require also a more extensive recognition of how suffrage campaigning from the beginning drew on an earlier radical rhetoric and practice of 'constitutionalism'. Equally, to legitimise their cause, the early histories produced by the movement incorporated appeals to a range of national and 'patriot' identities, and increasingly adopted the new languages of race and the seeming imperatives of the imperial mission. Nineteenth-century demands for female enfranchisement often argued from a particular narrative of the legal and constitutional heritage of 'British freewomen', reaching back into the mists of ancient (and dubious) history; and such history in its turn served to adapt the rhetoric of women's suffrage to incorporate the language of racism, in claiming for female 'Britons' a special place in humanity's march forward from barbarism to civilisation.

## Notes

1 My discussion draws especially on the analyses of radical languages of race, constitutionalism and patriotism, in Jane Rendall, 'Citizenship, Culture and Civilisation: The Languages of British Suffragists, 1866–1874', in Caroline Daley and Melanie Nolan (eds), *Suffrage and Beyond: International Feminist Perspectives* (Auckland, University of Auckland Press, 1994), pp. 127–50; James A. Epstein, *Radical Expression. Political Language, Ritual, and Symbol in England, 1790–1850* (Oxford, Oxford University Press, 1994), especially ch. 1, 'The Constitutionalist Idiom'; Hugh Cunningham, 'The Language of Patriotism', in Raphael Samuel (ed.), *Patriotism: The Making and Unmaking of the British National Identity* (London, Routledge, 1989, 3 vols) 1, pp. 57–89.

2 Quoted in Rendall, 'Citizenship, Culture and Civilisation', p. 140. For two recent re-evaluations of Frances Power Cobbe, see Eileen Janes Yeo, 'Social Motherhood and the Sexual Communion of Labour in British Social Science, 1850–1950', *Women's History Review*, 1 (1992), pp. 63–88; Barbara Caine, *Victorian Feminists* (Oxford, Oxford University Press, 1992), especially pp. 103–49.

3 *Ibid.*, p. 141.

4 Compare the account of British missionaries and national identity in Catherine Hall, *White, Male and Middle Class. Explorations in Feminism and History* (Oxford, Polity Press, 1992), pp. 205–14, especially p. 208.

5 The incorporation of the women's movement into the imperial mission has recently come under increasing scrutiny; see, for example, the special issue 'Feminism, Imperialism and Race. A Dialogue between India and Britain', *Women's History Review*, 3:4 (1994); Antoinette Burton, *Burdens of History. British Feminists, Indian Women and Imperial Culture, 1865–1915* (Chapel Hill, University of North Carolina Press, 1994); Vron Ware, *Beyond the Pale. White Women, Racism and History* (London, Verso, 1992).

6 Millicent Garrett Fawcett, 'England', in Theodore Stanton (ed.), *The Woman Question in Europe. A Series of Original Essays* (London, G. Putnam's Sons, 1884), pp. 1–29; Caroline Ashurst Biggs, 'Great Britain', in Elizabeth Cady Stanton, Susan B. Anthony and Matilda Joslyn Gage (eds), *History of Woman Suffrage* (New York, Source Books, [1886] 1970, 6 vols), 3, pp. 833–94, a work primarily concerned with the history of the suffrage movement in the United States; Charlotte Carmichael Stopes, *British Freewomen. Their Historical Privilege*, 4th edn (London, Swan Sonnenschein, [1894] 1909); Helen Blackburn, *Women's Suffrage: A Record of the Women's Suffrage Movement in the British Isles, with Biographical Sketches of Miss Becker* (London, Williams and Norgate, 1902).

7 Emmeline Pankhurst, *My Own Story* (London, Nash, 1914); E. Sylvia Pankhurst, *The Suffragette* (London, Gay and Hancock, 1911), and her *The Suffragette Movement. An Intimate Account of Persons and Ideals* (London, Virago, [1931] 1977 reprint).

8 Eric Hobsbawm, 'The Invention of Tradition', in Eric Hobsbawm and Terence Ranger (eds), *The Invention of Tradition* (Cambridge, Cambridge University Press, 1983), pp. 12, 13; and see also his *Nations and Nationalism since 1780: Programme, Myth, Reality* (Cambridge, Cambridge University Press, 1990), especially pp. 120–5.

**9** Epstein, *Radical Expression*, pp. 3, 12–19, 25–7, 147.

**10** See Linda Colley, *Britons. Forging the Nation 1707–1837* (London, Pimlico, 1992), pp. 260–1, 236, and see also 336–47, especially p. 340. See also Jane Mackay and Pat Thane, 'The Englishwoman', in Robert Colls and Philip Dodd (eds), *Englishness: Politics and Culture 1880–1920* (London, Croom Helm, c. 1986), pp. 191–229.

**11** Ray Strachey, *Millicent Garrett Fawcett* (London, John Murray, 1931), p. 1, which goes on to describe the East Anglian community as one that had 'clung obstinately to their ancient liberties and preserved their civic rights', and which in an earlier century had produced Oliver Cromwell. Robert Young, *Colonial Desire. Hybridity in Theory, Culture and Race* (London, Routledge, 1995), especially pp. 62–82 examines the tensions within mid- to late-nineteenth century thought on the nature of the English as either varying regionally as to 'purity' of racial origin (when East Anglians were often seen as among the 'most pure'), or increasingly as a celebration of the 'hybridity' of the English as compared, for example, to the 'Aryan' purity of the German people.

**12** Ann Oakley, 'Millicent Fawcett and her 73 Reasons Why', in her *Telling the Truth about Jerusalem. A Collection of Essays and Poems* (Oxford, Basil Blackwell, 1986), pp. 18–35, provides an especially stimulating discussion of the character of her political leadership. See also David Rubinstein, *A Different World for Women: The Life of Millicent Garrett Fawcett* (Brighton, Harvester Press, 1991); Caine, *Victorian Feminists*, especially pp. 196–238.

**13** Fawcett, 'England', pp. 2–3.

**14** *Ibid.*, pp. 4, 5, 6.

**15** *Ibid.*, pp. 6–7.

**16** Tensions between moderates and ultra-Radical suffragists had centred on the sexual politics of the women's movement, most especially on whether to include or exclude married women from the demand, and on whether to associate the suffrage cause with that of repeal of the Contagious Diseases Acts. When the Liberal Party split over home rule for Ireland in 1886, Millicent Garrett Fawcett departed to join the ranks of the Liberal Unionists. For a concise account of these divisions, see Sandra Stanley Holton, 'Women and the Vote', in June Purvis (ed.), *Women's History. Britain, 1850–1945* (London, UCL Press, 1995), pp. 277–305.

**17** Fawcett, 'England', p. 9, and contrast to the account of the formation of the Manchester Society, in Pankhurst, *The Suffragette Movement*, p. 30.

**18** Fawcett, 'England', p. 9. On Elizabeth Wolstenholme Elmy's unorthodox private life, see Sandra Stanley Holton, *Suffrage Days. Stories from the Women's Suffrage Movement* (London, Routledge, 1996), especially chs 1, 2.

**19** Stanton's notes are clearly distinguished from the author's own, and recount something of the activities of the ultra-Radical suffragists. See, for example, his additions in Fawcett, 'England', pp. 8–9, 10, 14, 16, 22–4, 29.

**20** Clare Midgley, *Women Against Slavery. The British Campaign, 1780–1870* (London, Routledge, 1992), p. 170.

**21** In contrast, Fawcett gives prominence to events that have otherwise gone generally unremarked by suffrage historians, for example, when she praises the two-minute speech of an otherwise little-known Conservative MP, J. W. Henley, as a 'characteristically English and common-sense declaration': Fawcett, 'England', p. 20.

22 *Ibid.*, pp. 27–8.
23 Stanton, Editor's Preface, *The Woman Question*, p. vi.
24 Frances Power Cobbe, 'Introduction', to Stanton (ed.), *The Woman Question*, pp. xv, xvi.
25 Biggs, 'Great Britain', pp. 833–5.
26 See, for example, in 'Ignota' (pseudonym of Elizabeth Wolstenholme Elmy), 'Women's Suffrage', *The Westminster Review*, CXLVIII (1897), pp. 357–72; Bertha Mason, *The History of the Women's Suffrage Movement* (London, Sherratt & Hughes, 1912); Stanton *et al.*, *History of Woman Suffrage*, 3, p. v.
27 Mackay and Thane, 'The Englishwoman', p. 192.
28 Stopes acknowledged Sidney Smith's 'Enfranchisement of Women. The Law of the Land' (1879) and T. Chisholm Anstey's book and papers on the 1867 Reform Act as her main authorities, both works concerned with the legal and constitutional origins of the franchise.
29 Stopes, *British Freewomen*, pp. 3, 4, 7.
30 See Christopher Hill, 'The Norman Yoke' in his *Puritans and Revolution. Studies in Interpretation of the English Revolution of the Seventeenth Century* (London, Panther History, 1969 reprint), pp. 58–125, especially pp. 64–80.
31 Stopes, *British Freewomen*, pp. 20, 21, 23, 163.
32 *Ibid.*, pp. 29, 30 (her exclamation mark).
33 Millicent Garrett Fawcett, 'Helen Blackburn. In Memoriam', *The Englishwoman's Review*, 256 (15 Jan. 1903), pp. 1–3, especially p. 2.
34 Stopes, *British Freewomen*, p. vi.
35 Blackburn, *Women's Suffrage*, p. 1. Helen Blackburn also acknowledged the research of Florence Griswold Backstaff in the United States and Sara Entrican, in *The Englishwoman's Review* of October 1896 and April 1897.
36 Blackburn, *Women's Suffrage*, pp. 4, 1–2.
37 *Ibid.*, pp. 1–2.
38 Moisei J. Ostrogorski, *The Rights of Women. A Comparative Study in History and Legislation* (London, Swan Sonnenschein, 1893), pp. 1–2. Subsequently, he moderated this emphatic statement somewhat, declaring that the evidence as to women's right to vote under the feudal system was 'not very clear'; *ibid.*, p. 38.
39 Contrast the accounts of Fawcett and Blackburn, for example, with 'Ignota', 'Women's Suffrage', which attempts to put Radical suffragists back into the history of the movement. Mason, *Women's Suffrage Movement*, also attempts a more even-handed recognition of the activities of Radical and moderate suffragists.
40 Mrs Jacob Bright, 'The Origin and Objects of the Women's Franchise League of Great Britain and Ireland', in M. W. Sewall (ed.), *The World Congress of Representative Women* (Chicago, Rand McNally, 1894), pp. 415–20, especially p. 420.
41 See the discussions in Ware, *Beyond the Pale*, pp. 150–64; Burton, *Burdens of History*, pp. 130–55.
42 See Holton, *Suffrage Days*, p. 101.
43 *Ibid.*, ch. 5, especially p. 109; Sandra Stanley Holton, 'Now You See It, Now You Don't: The Place of the Women's Franchise League in Contending Narratives of the Women's Suffrage Movement', in Maroula Joannou and

June Purvis (eds), *The Women's Suffrage Movement: New Feminist Perspectives* (Manchester, Manchester University Press, 1998), pp. 15–36.

44  The term 'militant' was adopted in the early twentieth century by suffragists committed to more sensational modes of campaigning, and more aggressive political tactics. In practice 'militant' and 'constitutional' suffragists were not always easy to distinguish from each other, for many belonged to both wings of the movement.

45  I explore some of these issues more extensively in Sandra Stanley Holton, '"In Sorrowful Wrath". The Romantic Feminism of Emmeline Pankhurst and Suffrage Militancy', in Harold L. Smith (ed.), *British Feminism in the Twentieth Century* (Aldershot, Edward Elgar, 1990), pp. 7–24.

46  E. S. Pankhurst, *The Suffragette*, preface (n.p.), pp. 3–4; E. Pankhurst, *My Own Story*, pp. 1–2.

47  *Ibid.*, p. 3. E. S. Pankhurst, *The Suffragette*, p. 3. See also the discussion in Holton, '"In Sorrowful Wrath"'.

48  See, for example, Millicent Garrett Fawcett, *Women's Suffrage. A Short History of a Great Movement* (London, T. C. and E. C. Jack, 1912), pp. 5–6, which makes a less compromised acknowledgement of the contribution of Mary Wollstonecraft than previously.

49  Here I draw especially on Epstein, *Radical Expression*, pp. 147–60.

50  See, for example, Mary E. Gawthorpe, *Votes for Men* (London, Women's Press, 1907).

51  I examine this point at greater length in Sandra Stanley Holton, 'Manliness and Militancy. The Political Protest of Male Suffragists and the Gendering of the "Suffragette" Identity', in Angela V. John and Clare Eustance (eds), *The Men's Share. Masculinities, Male Support and Women's Suffrage in Britain, 1890–1920* (London, Routledge, 1997), pp. 110–34.

# 7

# 'Let the women be alive!':[1] the construction of the married working woman in the Industrial Women's Movement, 1890–1914

## GERRY HOLLOWAY

One of the most enduring images of women is that of homemaker and mother. Before industrialisation this image was only part of women's role and women usually formed part of the family work team. During the nineteenth century married women became increasingly isolated from the workplace.[2] By the end of the century, the bourgeois domestic ideology of the male breadwinner with dependent wife and children even came to dominate the ideas of radicals and feminists. Most feminists assumed that when a woman married she would give up any paid work to become a full-time housewife and, eventually, a mother. This assumption ignored two, not necessarily discrete, groups of women. First, working-class women who, although they might aspire to the position of full-time housewife, in reality often found it impossible to give up paid work entirely. Whatever paid work women did – factory work, homework, laundering or charring – for many it was essential and they had an ambivalent attitude towards it. For some, it gave a degree of financial independence which they were loath to lose. For many, it was a tedious necessity. Second, this assumption ignored married women who, despite their husbands' reasonable income, enjoyed the financial independence paid work gave them.

Embedded in the assumption that a married woman's place was in the home was the inference that working married women were a problem and various proposals were propounded to solve it. In this chapter, I want to explore how the normative ideal of the married woman influenced the ways in which the married working woman was constructed in the writings of activist women involved in the Industrial Women's Movement (IWM). By the IWM, I mean that part of the women's movement concerned with the lives of women and girls working in industry, whether it was in the factory, workshop or the home. The organisations that it encompassed were the women's trade unions affiliated to the Women's Trade Union League (WTUL) under its various names, and the Women's Trade Union Association (WTUA); the Women's Industrial Council (WIC), which dealt mainly with industrial questions, and its daughter organisation the Clubs Industrial Association, which organised Working Girls' Clubs; the Women's Labour League (WLL) and the working-class suffrage groups which were political organisations; and the Women's Co-operative Guild (WCG), which dealt with all these issues from a working-class point of view. Generally, middle-class women ran these organisations for the benefit of working-class women, with the exception of the WCG, which operated through the mechanism of locally determined policy-making (see chapter 8).

In the first part, I shall discuss the way the problem of the married working woman was constructed in public discourse. I will then focus on the writings of some middle-class activists identified with the IWM which demonstrate that their general acceptance of the dictum that a 'married woman's place was in the home' undermined the challenges which many of these women made to other dominant ideas of women in Victorian and Edwardian society. I shall then examine the ideas of some women who wanted to reconstruct domestic work to free women to do paid work. Linked to these ideas I want to explore the ideas of one working-class feminist, Ada Nield Chew, whose radical views on married working women were influenced by personal experience as well as feminist ideology and offered an alternative vision of the married working woman. I will conclude by analysing the limitations of all the ideas forwarded in the debate and suggest that the problematising of married women's work is an issue that is still with us today.

## The married working woman debate

In an age when knowledge and availability of contraception were still limited, it was difficult to separate the married working woman from motherhood. Although, of course, some married working women had no children or had grown-up children, all married working women were perceived in terms of their reproductive functions. From the 1890s onwards, the married working woman became increasingly the focus of social reformers.[3] There were two interconnected reasons for this. First, the *Report of the Lady Assistant Commissioners* to the Royal Commission on Labour had firmly placed women's industrial role on the agenda. Amy Bulley, herself a writer on women's work, noted:

> It is certain, too, whatever direction social progress may take, the position of women in the industrial world, bound up as it is with the question of the home and the welfare of the coming generations, must receive much closer attention in the future, both from social reformers and from legislators than it has done in the past.[4]

Although married working women were the subject of debate before the *Report*, it spotlighted women's employment as an important issue, especially concerning high infant mortality rates.[5] Second, this high infant mortality rate and the poor physique of the recruits to the Boer War caused alarm and brought the debate sharply into focus by the beginning of the twentieth century.[6]

Anna Davin argues that in the latter half of the nineteenth century, economic competition from more populous nations, such as America and Germany, added to Britain's increasing imperial responsibilities and this meant that population was increasingly regarded as an important index of power.[7] This together with the prevalence of the eugenics discourse translated into a simple argument that the more white and, what was more important, more British children there were in the world the better it would be for Britain's position as an imperial and industrial power.[8] Unfortunately, the demand for more healthy British children was not being met by working-class women. Carol Dyhouse has shown that infant mortality rates in Britain were high throughout the century, about 149 per 1,000 on average, but as death rates among the total population fell towards the end of the century, the consistently high infant mortality rates looked even worse. Coupled with this, there was a decrease in the birth rate. This meant that despite fewer babies being born, just as many were dying.[9] Given that population was increasingly fixed upon as an indicator of power, it is no wonder that the rhetoric of 'race suicide' was gaining currency and ways of preventing it were anxiously being sought.

Although the size of the population was seen as an economic issue, increasing infant survival rates was regarded as a social one.

Politicians, health and medical practitioners and social reformers all sought to improve infants' chances of survival and looked to mothering as the key to the problem. Consequently, women played a vital role in the movement to improve the 'race' both as mothers and as advisers to mothers, and these roles were largely divided on class lines. It was assumed that the mothers who needed advice were working class and the women who should provide it were middle class. A whole army of doctors, health visitors, district nurses, sanitary inspectors, teachers, social workers and investigators mobilised to combat the assumed ignorance and apathy that undermined working-class women's ability to keep their children alive. Often, these advisers were not biological mothers themselves.[10]

Many of these workers were members of the National Union of Women Workers (NUWW), an organisation that had close connections with the IWM, especially the WIC, WLL and WCG.[11] These workers introduced Mothers' Meetings, clinics and feeding programmes to working-class women. However, working-class mothers often resented vehemently the patronising attitude and obvious lack of knowledge of working-class life of the women who organised these initiatives. Mrs Layton, a member of the WCG, described her experience of Mothers' Meetings:

> I had attended Mothers' Meetings, where Ladies came and lectured on the domestic affairs in the workers' homes that it was impossible for them to understand. I have boiled over many times at some of the things I have been obliged to listen to, without the chance of asking a question. In the Guild we always had the chance of discussing a subject. The Guild was more to my mind than the Mothers' Meetings, so I gave up the Mothers' Meetings and attended the Guild.[12]

For many social reformers, household management not poverty was considered the important factor in infant mortality and morbidity. The advice given reflected middle-class notions of childhood and childcare, all other practices being measured against middle-class norms and inevitably found lacking. Working-class mothers were accused of neglect because they did not breastfeed, although many were unable to because of their own poor nutrition; because they fed babies from their own plates; took infants out in public; or left them with other people while they did paid work.[13] In other words, they did not live up to middle-class notions of good childcare practice. Therefore, there was an assumption that working-class women needed instruction in how to be 'good mothers'. The calls to middle-class women to take on this work were expressed not only in an appeal to their sense of moral duty, but as a way of transcending class difference. Mrs Sumner, a leading light in the Girls' Friendly Society and a member of the NUWW, in an essentialist plea to middle-class mothers to unite all women as mothers wrote:

> The Mothers' Union includes all classes of mothers ... in as much as the duties of mothers are the same to a certain extent in every rank. We feel strongly that if mothers in the upper classes will lead the way by joining this movement, we may be able to win all sorts and conditions of mothers to see their responsibility, ... May we not as mothers, combine and unite together, for the good of our homes and for the glory of God, to try to put a stop to the moral plague which abounds, and to undermine the kingdom of evil by laying as far as we can, the foundation of strong principle and good habits in the hearts and lives of our children?[14]

The clear message was that working-class women needed instruction in the physical care of their children, but, above all, the middle-class values of their instructors were of utmost importance and offered them and their children appropriate role models. Others were even more harsh in their opinions and their language was far more judgemental and punitive. Mrs Molesworth, who worked for various charities concerning the social welfare of poor children, thought she knew exactly where the responsibility for child ill-health and neglect lay:

> Let it be proclaimed on the housetops that want and degradation are the lawful results of thriftlessness and intemperance, that wherever there is abnormal suffering, it has been *somebody's* fault, that till starvation stares them in the face in the shape of their half-naked and half-dying children, vicious and improvident parents will never take heed to their ways ....
>
> Let us punish with the sternest severity not only tangible cruelty on the part of the parents and guardians of our poor children, but the neglect or indifference almost as fearful in the consequences; let us instruct and enlighten by every means in our power the dense and stupid ignorance of their elders; which is often the cause of childish misery; let us get at the parents whenever and as much as we can, pointing out and emphasizing in every conceivable way the results of their misdoing.[15]

Some, while still believing that bad mothering was the problem, wanted further restrictions on married women's work and an adequate family wage for men. John Burns, a Member of Parliament who had worked with the feminist social investigator, Clementina Black, organising women in the WTUA during the 1880s and 1890s, regarded married women's employment as the real evil. In addressing two national conferences on infant mortality in 1906 and 1908, he blamed women's paid work for infant deaths, rickets, broken homes, low wages and idle husbands. He wanted married women in the home. Paid work was for men in the first instance and unmarried women who were obliged to work in the last instance. There was no room for the married woman worker in his ideal.[16] At the 1906 conference, resolutions were passed to introduce further restrictions on married women's work through extending the provision of the 1891 Factories and Workshop Act to prohibit women from returning to work until three months after childbirth. At this time there was no provision for maternity benefit so women would have no income for this period. All the benefits of having a stay-at-home mother would be negated by the lack of income. Further, there was no real evidence to support Burns's claims. In 1908, the Medical Officer of Health in Birmingham made an investigation that demonstrated that in the poorest wards infant mortality was lower among working mothers than those who only carried out domestic work.[17] Obviously, ideology concerning women's role in society rather than solid medical evidence was dominant in Burns's assertion.

Not all reformers had such conservative views of motherhood. Social investigation began to demonstrate the stark reality of working-class life and some activists began to turn their attention to the problem of poverty. For example, the Fabian Women's Group (FWG) was particularly concerned with women's economic independence and their work took them beyond the plight of the single woman to investigate the economic independence of married women.[18] Increasingly, they highlighted the lack of control women had over the means at their disposal to care for their families.[19] Their solution was to transpose the notion of state intervention in the industrial workplace to the working-class home. Consequently, as well as health visitors and district nurses instructing working-class mothers on sanitation and childcare, there were social investigators asking questions about working-class budgets

and household management. By doing this, they elided the notion
of privacy which was the mainstay of the middle-class home, with
public scrutiny for the working-class home. This meant that
nothing escaped the prying eyes of the servants of the state and
social reformers.[20] The focus was on low and irregular pay, lack of
rights to the family wage, bad housing and homework. All these
factors were regarded as contributory to working-class women's
inadequate care of their children and added to the debate on
married women's work. Various solutions were propounded.

Some believed that low pay and irregular employment were the
root of the problem and that paying men a decent wage would
mean that women would be less likely to have to work and would
have more resources to feed their children properly. Many trade
unionists and Labour Party men took this position and were more
concerned with gaining a larger wage for the male breadwinner
through the exclusion of cheap female labour than campaigning for
the endowment of mothers or pressing for equal pay or minimum
wages for married women. Michèle Barrett and Mary McIntosh
argue that men in the labour movement defended the campaign for
a family wage as a way to increase incomes, but in practice it only
led to the subordination of women and divisions between the sexes
in the labour movement. This, they insist, was a choice of the
labour movement and not something foisted on them by the 'needs
of capitalism'.[21] The attitudes of men in the Labour Party and trade
unions made it especially difficult for women's organisations affiliated to them to argue against them. As with the protective
legislation debate, feminists who wanted economic independence
for women, whether through endowment of motherhood or wage-
earning, were accused of putting gender interests before class
interests, whereas it is equally valid to argue that working-class
men, despite their protestations, put gender interests before class
interests. Caroline Rowan extends this argument by adding that
although working-class men, or the bulk of them, tended to hand
over their wages to their wives to manage, they defended 'the
status quo in which men were *structurally* in a position of power
over women'.[22]

As Rowan has indicated, the more autonomous WCG was in a
better position to fight for the economic rights of women than the
WLL or, indeed, the WTUL.[23] Consequently, Labour and trade
union supporters stood in an uneasy alliance with certain middle-

class liberal reformers, such as Millicent Fawcett, who believed that the endowment of mothers would undermine the man's role in the family and those who believed that working-class married women should not work at all. Further, some of the middle-class leaders in the IWM did not regard working-class women in the same light as themselves. Mary MacArthur, a leading figure in the IWM who was a member of the Committees of the WTUL, NFWW and WIC and married to a Labour MP, argued

> We are familiar with the old ideal that woman's place is the home, and I am sufficiently old-fashioned to agree that there is something to be said for it. In the ideal world as I conceive it a woman would not be driven by economic necessity, and her home would be a home in every sense of the word, and not a mere shelter from which she might quite justifiably desire to escape on every possible occasion.[24]

For MacArthur, men and women were not equally entitled to economic independence and she regarded the man's role of provider as paramount. This attitude contributed to her signing away the rights of women munitions workers in the National Federation of Women Workers without too much of a struggle during the First World War, as she did not regard working women's claim to be as legitimate as men's. Similarly, Margaret MacDonald, wife of the Labour leader Ramsay MacDonald, leader of the WLL and an active committee member of the WIC, argued that a 'Right to Work' Act for men would be a charter of the 'Right to Leisure and Home Comfort' for their wives[25] and was horrified to discover that some women preferred to leave their children with their own mothers and work for a pittance rather than stay at home and be a 'good mother'.[26] Both these women were extremely active within their organisations, travelling widely and working long hours despite being married with children. No one ever criticised them for leaving their children in the care of other people and they never seemed aware of the contradiction of what they were preaching and their own position.

Other activists neither condemned married women for working nor constructed them entirely through their marital status. In 1911, Anna Martin, a district visitor in south-east London and a committed suffragist, wrote an article, 'The Married Working Woman: A Study' that appeared first in *The Nineteenth Century and After* and then was reprinted as a booklet by the National Union of Women's

Suffrage Societies (NUWSS). From the outset, she saw her role as a defender of the married woman worker against her detractors. She noted perceptively that commentators on the working mother regarded her as 'a creature of limited intelligence and capacity, who neither has, nor ought to have, any desires outside her own four walls. She is not so much an individual with interests and opinions and a will of her own, as a humble appanage of husband and children.'[27] This image she went on to refute strenuously. She also defended the women against the charge that they neglected their domestic duties. Drawing on an evolutionary paradigm, she argued that it was wrong to judge working-class women by middle-class standards:

> Of course, the homemakers of the mean streets are not to be judged by middle-class standards. Theoretically, most people acknowledge the evolutionary nature of manners and morals; practically, they fail to see that a code which works well enough in the household of a prosperous professional man would often prove disastrous in the household of a dock labourer.[28]

She went on to detail at length the practicalities of combining homework with domestic work and the problems of rearing healthy children on an inadequate and irregular income. In doing so, she constructed the working mother as pragmatic and flexible, able to assess the amount of work she needed to do in order to survive and prioritise the tasks she had to complete in her conflicting roles. This was a very different construct to the wilfully neglectful or ignorant monster in most writings. Further, she argued that 'a very common reason for a wife's going out to work, perhaps the most common is that the man's wages alone are too small and too irregular for the family to live upon'.[29]

For Martin, the measures that Burns and others were advocating would not solve the problem. In fact it was

> The proposal ... which strikes most terror to the hearts of the working women of the district ... They did not realise the political danger of such a prohibition, which would inflict a serious disability on their class and come perilously near repealing, as far as they are concerned the Married Women's Property Act, but they know from their own life experience the wholesale ruin that would result, under the present industrial system, from the passing of such a law ... the women are appalled at the idea of their liberty of action in this matter being forcibly taken from them. To do this,

and to leave untouched the causes which drive them into the labour market seems to them about as wise a proceeding as trying to cure a broken leg by removing the splints.[30]

However, she joined ranks with the Labour Party when she argued that the problem would only be solved by paying the husband a 'Living Wage' through minimum wage legislation supported by state insurance against unemployment and the establishment of Fair Rents courts.[31] She argued from an economic perspective:

> In order to ensure a supply of future workers that man's wage must enable him to maintain his family, and this expenditure should be the first charge on the cost of all production. If the sum paid as wages is insufficient to maintain the labourer and his family in physical and moral health, the employer, or sometimes the ground landlord, benefits at the expense of the general community, which has to make up the deficiency at immense expense by school meals, infirmaries, workhouses, asylums and so forth.[32]

This argument was based on two suppositions: first, that working-class men would use the extra money to benefit the family and second, that working-class women did not object to being totally dependent on men. Despite her insights into the lives of the working class, Martin was still using the middle class as a model on which to base the working-class family.

Not all feminists were convinced that men would hand over extra money to their wives. Investigations into working-class life showed that men always kept back a certain part of their wage for their own use and a family wage offered no guarantee that extra money would be handed over.[33] Many activists advocated some form of endowment of motherhood.[34] Mabel Atkinson of the FWG regarded it as the ultimate ideal, envisaging such an endowment as allowing women respite from paid labour during the early months of a child's life and then a return to her previous job. Forestalling any argument that might be forwarded by 'equal rights' feminists that endowment would give men the excuse to expel women from the labour force, she argued that only in a socialist system where women were guaranteed certain rights to return to the labour force would this be possible.[35] This argument assumed that under socialism patriarchal power structures would dissolve and women would be treated equally with men. Helena Swanwick, a leading suffragist, drew attention to Lady Aberconway's proposal 'that men should be obliged by law to give their wives a fixed proportion of their incomes, and there appear to be in England more followers of this idea than of endowment of motherhood'.[36] However, Swanwick rightly argued that this would be difficult to enforce, particularly as so many men did not earn adequate amounts in the first place. Further, this again assumed that married women should be dependent on their husbands for their income. Margaret Llewellyn Davies, the general secretary of the WCG, like Atkinson, also argued for maternity rights, but thought low pay was just one of the problems and supported a more radical analysis of the marital relationship in which medical knowledge of reproduction and the relationship between husband and wife were taken into account.[37]

## Married women's work

As the debate continued between conservatives and progressives, the voice of the married working woman was conspicuously silent. Her fate was in the hands of activists whose experience at best was second-hand. In 1908, these debates around the effects of married women's work prompted the Investigation Committee of the WIC to instigate a nationwide investigation into married women's and widows' paid work. In a letter circulated to both national and local newspapers in their search for help, the WIC claimed that

> This subject is of immense interest at the present time, the more so because the driving of these people into the labour market has done so much to create the demand for women's suffrage. The lack of authoritative and exact statistics and general information, such as is to be collected, is always commented upon whenever anything related to working women is publicly discussed.[38]

The investigation was the first of its kind. For the first time, working-class married women workers' lives were systematically investigated. This call aroused great interest amongst social reformers throughout the country. WIC members collaborated with members from the WLL, FWG and NUWW, many of whom were also members of the WIC. Potential investigators were given a list of questions to ask and a case study and hints on carrying out an interview. Significantly, there was no attempt to discover what working-class women wanted. All the questions were aimed at discovering *how* working-class women lived and not at giving working-class women a voice. These investigators, by the very nature of the investigation – there was no pay, and the work required a large input of time and a relatively high degree of literacy – were mainly middle class. Dissension and splits in the WIC meant that the book *Married Women's Work* was seven years in the making and was not published until 1915. The war radically altered the lives of many people and the legislation that Black, as president of the WIC, had been seeking, the Trades Board Acts, had long been implemented. However, despite the possible limitations imposed by the class of the investigators on the findings of the report, the interpretation of those findings by the editor, Clementina Black, are interesting and indicate some of the reasons for dissension amongst the WIC Committee members, especially Margaret MacDonald.[39]

In the introduction to the book the editor, Black, a middle-class woman with many years' experience working in the IWM and suffrage movement, like Martin, rounded on those who criticised working-class women for the way they conducted their lives. She divided the women interviewed into four categories: Group A were women who did no work even when they did not have an adequate family income. They were often sickly or lazy, she argued. They neglected their homes and children and were probably the women that Mrs Molesworth was attacking. However, Black did not condemn them completely. She argued that they lacked the material means to keep their homes clean and would idle their time away as 'gossipers at doorways and frequenters of public houses'.[40] She did concede that this was a generalisation and like all other groups there were exceptions to the rule. Therefore, although these women were keeping to their place, that is their home, their extreme poverty prevented them from fulfilling their domestic duties. These women were grist to the mill of both the family wage and endowment of mothers campaigners who argued over the best way to help them.

Class B, 'a very numerous group', were the women who worked because their family income was inadequate. These, she claimed, were 'the most overworked, the hardest pressed, and probably the unhappiest of working women'.[41] However, she continued, the very act of earning money, no matter how little, gave them 'the sense of partial freedom and independence by which their hearts are thus warmed'.[42] She agreed that the children of these women often suffered, but argued that they would suffer more if their mothers did not work and that it 'would be rash' to prevent the women from working. She called for the establishment of more nurseries and referred to Ada Nield Chew's articles in the *Common Cause* as an example of working women seeking their own solutions to their childcare problems.[43]

Class C were not included in the study because these were the working-class women who did not work because their family income was adequate. However, she combined them with women in class D who did work even though they had an adequate income and commented that these classes 'belong [to] that great body of intelligent, able and efficient mothers, examples of whom may be seen at the meetings, large and small, of the Women's Co-operative Guild'.[44] Black could relate more readily to these women and they won her admiration rather than sympathy. Class D were, she wrote ironically but fondly, 'those reprehensible women who could if they chose afford to live upon their husband's earnings but devote many of their hours to paid work'.[45]

None of the women, she argued, wanted any restriction on married women's labour and she believed that wage-earning was beneficial to women. The thrust of her argument was against low pay for both men and women and the primitive conditions in which they lived. She quoted Mabel Atkinson on the contemporary household:

> A modern Rip van Winkle coming back to life now, after a sleep of a century or so, would be totally lost in a big modern hospital or up-to-date weaving shed. He simply would not know the use or the significance of most of the objects around him. But put him in an ordinary kitchen, with its dirty coal-burning cooking stove, its always unpleasant and often insanitary sink, its pots and pans, brooms and brushes, and he would feel that after all the world had not in every direction moved with such strides while he was still asleep.[46]

The issue of the reorganisation of domestic life was not a new idea. Dyhouse has shown that as early as the 1880s Jane Hume Clapperton was writing about co-operative ways of living and was influenced by the ideas of the Owenites.[47] The American feminist, Charlotte Perkins Gilman, also wanted to reorganise domestic work and like Atkinson, who was probably influenced by her, looked towards new technology to revolutionise women's domestic duties.[48] Further, in 1918, Black herself wrote *A New Way of Housekeeping*, her last major work which was based on further research instigated by the WIC at the beginning of the war, the experience of the war itself, i.e. canteens, nurseries and hostel living, her own experience as a working woman with limited resources, and her insights of thirty years of studying working women's lives.[49]

Again, this work was carried out by middle-class investigators and the solutions offered by Black in her book were aimed largely at middle-class incomes and were too expensive for working-class families. So what did married working women want? It is not easy to answer the questions as they were never asked. Some probably would be content to have a husband in a regular reasonably paid job. However, as Black had discovered, there were women who enjoyed the economic independence, however small, paid work gave them and would not be content to rely on their husbands. There was one such woman who did write about her experience and desires and those of women she knew. That woman was Ada Nield Chew.

### Ada Nield Chew and the married working woman

Ada Nield Chew was a vociferous supporter of the right of the working-class mother to financial independence. Unlike Anna Martin, she was no advocate of the minimum family wage for women, which she suspected would not help women and children; neither did she support the campaign for the endowment of mothers as the way to secure women's financial independence. This she regarded as a retrograde step and would fix more firmly women's role as domestic workers. In an article in the *Common Cause* she put forward her inevitably iconoclastic views in her own inimitable way:

> It is desirable that married women should be economically independent, and free to develop their humanity on lines best suited to that object. The bondage of the married working woman is two-fold: the dependence of her young children, and the primitive stage in which domestic industry still remains. In other words, her babies and her domestic jobs are the chains which bind her; and it

is these chains which must be broken before talk of human development for her ever becomes more than talk.[50]

Common to many feminist discourses, she compared the married woman to a slave. For example, John Stuart Mill used this metaphor when arguing for the legal rights of married women in the debate around the Married Women's Property Act.[51] In an atmosphere in which women were portrayed as a civilising force and the moral guardians of the empire, the imagery of the married woman, the highest goal of womanhood, as a slave was very powerful and revealed the contradictory nature of the prevailing domestic ideology. Chew insisted that, in reality, domestic responsibilities were too great a burden for one individual to bear, especially if the family income and housing were inadequate, as they were in so many cases, and prevented women from participating in 'human development' and 'progress'. She made two radical suggestions. First, state-run nurseries should offer places to all children so that all women were free to work and be economically independent of their husbands. To pre-empt the riposte that babies need their mothers, she added that middle-class mothers did not spend all their time with their babies but left them with nurses and no one would dare accuse them of being worse mothers than working-class women. Second, she refuted the essentialist argument that domestic work was innately women's work and that all women shared this 'vocation'. Like childcare, domestic work would become a paid job.

Chew wanted women to rebel against prescribed femininity and to become 'human'. Domestic slavery was less than civilised: 'Rebellion, refusal to do and submit, are the first steps to progress; and if we consciously discourage the domestic ideal in our girls, domestic work will of necessity have to step out of the painfully primitive stage into line with progress generally.'[52] This rebellion, she asserted, should take the form of married women 'demanding the right to paid work and refusing to do domestic work simply because they are wives'.[53] The *Common Cause*, being less radical than Chew, attached a disclaimer to the article stating that 'IN NO CASE does the NUWSS take responsibility for the views set forward in signed articles. Our object is to provide a platform for free discussion'.[54] In her views Chew was more in line with the Social Democratic Federation, which advocated communal childcare as part of their socialist vision, rather than the largely liberal middle-class readership of the *Common Cause* who wanted to mould working-class women into an ideal they were rejecting for themselves, or the Labour Party who were more concerned with gaining a larger wage for the male breadwinner through the exclusion of cheap female labour.

So how was it that Chew's construction of the married working woman was so at variance with other activists in the IWM? Chew's feminism was a direct result of her personal experience.[55] Ada Nield was the second child and eldest daughter in a family of thirteen children, nine of whom survived. Her only sister was an epileptic who was eventually institutionalised, so the whole brunt of mother's help fell to Ada who hated to see the drudgery of her mother's life even more than she hated housework. Her father was a small farmer whose fortunes declined during the 1880s and eventually the family moved to Crewe. Consequently, Ada did not have the rosy view of domesticity promoted by so many middle-class reformers. Her mother's constant childbearing, as well as the difficulties of rearing a large family on an uncertain income and in poor housing are reflected in her later fictional and polemical writing. In 'The Mother's Story' which appeared in the *Common Cause* in 1913, Chew described the constant battle against dirt that working-class women living in industrial areas faced:

> The vision of their lives of which they had given me a glimpse, remained. I knew that colliery village in which they live as one knows vitally only one spot – that in which one's own life took root. I know the houses where their daily battle with dirt is waged. The 'house-place' about four yards square, door opening onto the village street, a little kitchen beyond, with absurdly inadequate cooking apparatus; back door opening, maybe, onto a tiny tiled yard, or, quite as likely, onto an open waste, exposed to the bleak countryside and pit brows. Imagine the wind sweeping through, leaving in its trail clouds of dirt and coal-slag, covering the beds, the table, the clothes, the cupboard shelves, the food! No, verily, a woman could not cope adequately with housing conditions such as these, though she were a ministering angel from heaven, and not a mere human woman of the earth.[56]

Chew did not need surveys to inform her about the realities of working-class women's lives because it was her reality too. Her use of the image of the 'angel from heaven' parodies the middle-class idea of women as the 'angel in the house'. For the working-class woman this ideal was an absurdity.

Chew's childhood experiences were reinforced by her work as an organiser first for the Clarion Van where she toured with Charlotte Perkins Gilman, the WTUL and later the NUWSS.[57] Her work involved organising working-class women in trade unions and suffrage groups. It also gave her insight into the lack of understanding her employers had about working-class life and she used her writing skills to 'explain' working-class experience to those middle-class women prepared to listen. Chew realised that it was essential for middle-class activists to understand and appreciate that the differences and commonalities between women had to be recognised if women's lives were to improve. In this she was again at variance with other activists who unquestioningly thought they could speak on behalf of working-class women and were constantly dismayed or shocked by working-class indifference or rejection of their help.

Chew was a working mother and used part of her wages to pay other women to do her domestic work, just like MacArthur and MacDonald.[58] However, unlike them, she wanted to extend this privilege to more women as she argued that not until 'women see that it is within *their* province not only to bear and nurse, but to provide for their young' will 'women recognise their glorious duty to the race and act to end starvation of the minds and bodies of themselves and their children'.[59] However, like the other women discussed here she did not challenge the gendering of domestic work. Although working-class men did help their wives with domestic duties it was always regarded as just that – help. The main responsibility was always seen as the woman's. Even when new technology such as electric irons, gas cookers and vacuum cleaners was introduced to assist in the home after the First World War, the advertisements were always aimed at women readers and showed women using the equipment.[60] Although the domestic role of married women was being challenged by some women before the war, the dominance of the domestic role of women prevented feminists from challenging the non-domestic role of men.

## Conclusion

As I have shown, the debate around the married working woman was a contentious one whether working mothers were blamed, problematised, praised or seen as a progressive force. There was no agreed solution and the desires and hopes of working-class women themselves were largely absent from the debate. However, the married working woman debate was of tremendous importance for the women's movement, although the reasons why I think it was important are different from the reasons why it was usually considered important at the time.

Middle-class feminists at the turn of the century had been engaged in a long but fairly successful struggle to open up education and work for themselves and legal and civil rights for women generally. Their ability to devote large portions of their time to this work rested on the support they received from working-class women who looked after their homes and children, washed and made their clothes and bought and prepared their food. Even those activists who did not have much in the way of paid domestic help often lived with a friend who took care of the domestic side of their lives. Consequently, the domestic side of life was submerged for many feminists and they did not question the domestic status quo because, like most men, they were not adversely affected by it unless they had problems in obtaining servants.[61]

When these activists considered the question of married women's work they assumed, very much as men assumed, that domestic work was working-class married women's primary responsibility and did not question their assumption. Consequently, they sought to solve the problem of the double burden of domestic and paid work by eliminating the paid work rather than challenging the prescribed role for working-class women. The question of economic independence for working-class women, if considered at all, was resolved by calls for the endowment of motherhood or increased pay for men. A few more radical feminists, such as Clementina Black and Ada Nield Chew, who had personal experience of combining domestic duties with paid work, did look towards challenging these assumptions but they, too, overlooked the possibility of men participating in domestic work, seeking to revolutionise domestic organisation or the professionalisation of housework instead.[62]

Black felt that the whole question of married women's work was complex and that there was not one simple solution to family poverty. She summed up the situation succinctly:

> In one direction lies the effort towards the establishment of a minimum wage, in another the tendency to introduce improved methods of child nurture and saving of domestic labour, in yet a

third the demand for endowment of mothers and the rights of wives to a fixed share of their husbands' incomes.[63]

She then outlined her own preferred vision of the future family, a vision she shared with Chew:

> It is possible that society is evolving in the direction of a family supported by the earnings of both parents, the children being cared for meanwhile and the work of the house being performed by trained experts. To me personally that solution seems more in harmony with the general lines of our social development than does any which would relegate all women to the care of children combined with the care of households.[64]

Chew concurred with this, but took the argument one step further and wanted to attack the socialisation of women. For her, women needed to be freed psychologically from domestic duties and she argued there could be no freedom for the nation if the mothers were not free. Criticising the call for endowment of motherhood she declared, 'You can not breed a free people from slave mothers, and husband-kept or State-kept women can never know the meaning of liberty'.[65]

The ideas of state nurseries and reorganisation of domestic arrangements were rejected by most feminists and Black and Chew were ignored or marginalised. The failure to challenge conventional views of women's domestic roles had important implications for women after the war. Increasingly, working-class women were encouraged and cajoled into believing that their place was in the home. Little was done to encourage young women to pursue economic independence.

Feminists had played their part in relegating working-class women to the home. By concentrating on entrance into male worlds on male terms for some or insisting on the importance of homemaking and motherhood for the majority, without discussing with those women their own views on the matter, the impetus of a 'common cause' for all women which had found expression in the suffrage movement was lost. The few radical voices who challenged conventional constructions of married working-class working women disappeared for many years. The married working woman was increasingly regarded as an anomaly only to be encouraged in times of national emergency.

Today the debate is as alive and as contentious as ever although it concerns working mothers rather than married working women as the two are no longer regarded as synonymous. Challenging the assumption of the pre-eminence of women's domestic role and the assumption in the workplace that there is someone, usually the woman, servicing the family is still a matter of urgency and vital to women's economic independence. New technology and new work patterns could challenge the gender divisions of paid and domestic work.[66] However, ideological assumptions around women's economic independence and domestic responsibilities need to be challenged constantly. The debates around responsibilities for caring, new working patterns and locations and the continuing issue of economic independence should be of vital importance to all feminists if we are to avoid the mistakes made by activists involved in the Married Working Woman debate before the First World War. Central to these debates is the need to ensure that a wide range of views are heard so that those of us who are in more privileged positions do not assume that we know what is best for all women. As Ada Nield Chew so shrewdly observed about the emancipation of working-class women, 'Tis a long row to hoe!'[67]

## Notes

1  Ada Nield Chew, 'Let the Women be Alive!', *Freewoman*, 13, 18 Apr. 1912.
2  This has been discussed by many historians but for recent analyses see J. Rendall, *Women in an Industrializing Society: England 1750–1880* (Oxford, Basil Blackwell, 1990) and C. Hall, *White, Male and Middle Class: Explorations in Feminism and History* (Cambridge, Polity Press, 1992).
3  Many articles were written concerning different aspects of the lives of married working women. For example, between 1908 and 1912 they included: 'Married Women's Work', *Women's Industrial News* (Dec. 1908, Oct. 1901); M. Bondfield, 'Human Documents', *Women's Industrial News* (July 1909); B. L. Hutchins, 'Some Aspects of Women's Life and Work', *Women's Trade Union Review* (July 1909); J. Haslam, 'The Burden of Factory Mothers', *The Englishwoman* (Oct. 1909); Lady MacLaren, 'Wage Earning Women', *The Englishwoman* (Nov. 1909); A. S., 'The Case of the Working Mother', *The Nineteenth Century* (Apr. 1910); A. Martin, 'The Married Working Woman' *The Nineteenth Century* (Dec. 1910, Jan. 1911); T. Billington-Greig, 'The Taxation of Married Women', *Contemporary Review* (Feb. 1911); J. Haslam, 'Factory Mothers and State Insurance', *The Englishwoman* (Aug. 1911); M. MacDonald, *Wage Earning Mothers* (London, 1911) and A. Nield Chew's articles in the *Common Cause*: 'The Charwoman' (Sept. 1911); 'The Pottery Worker' (Jan. 1912) and in *The Englishwoman*, 'All in a Day's Work – Mrs Bolt' (July 1912).

**4** A. A. Bulley, 'The Lady Assistant Commissioners' Report', *Fortnightly Review*, 55 (Jan. 1894), p. 39.

**5** See, for example, in the *Transactions of the National Association for the Promotion of Social Science*, R. W. Cooke Taylor, 'The Employment of Married Women in Manufactures' (1873); R. W. Cooke Taylor, 'What Influence has the Employment of Mothers in Manufactures on Infant Mortality; and Ought any, and what, Restrictions be placed on such Employment?' (1874); T. M. Dolan, 'How does the Employment of Mothers in Mills and Manufactures Influence Infant Mortality?' (1882).

**6** For an in-depth examination of this issue see A. Davin, 'Imperialism and Motherhood', *History Workshop*, 5 (Spring 1978), pp. 9–65.

**7** *Ibid.*, pp. 9–12.

**8** For a discussion on the prevalence of a eugenics discourse at this time see E. Janes Yeo, *The Contest for Social Science: Relations and Representations of Gender and Class* (London, Rivers Oram, 1996), chs. 7, 8.

**9** C. Dyhouse, 'Working-Class Mothers and Infant Mortality in England, 1895–1914', in C. Webster (ed.), *Biology, Medicine and Society, 1840–1940* (Cambridge, Cambridge University Press, 1981), p. 73.

**10** For a discussion of social maternalism see Yeo, *Contest for Social Science*, ch. 9.

**11** For example, local branches of the NUWW became involved in the WIC's research into married women's work: see *Women's Industrial News* (Dec. 1908). Further, Margaret MacDonald is an example of a woman who belonged to the NUWW, WIC and WLL.

**12** M. Llewellyn Davies, *Life As We Have Known It: By Co-operative Working Women* (London,Virago, [1931] 1984), p. 40.

**13** Davin, 'Imperialism and Motherhood', pp. 34–5.

**14** Mrs Sumner, 'The Responsibilities of Mothers', in Baroness Burdett-Coutts (ed.), *Woman's Mission* (London, Sampson Low, Marston, 1893), pp. 68–9.

**15** Mrs Molesworth, 'For the Little Ones – Food, Fun and Fresh Air', in *Woman's Mission*, pp. 11–12.

**16** *Report of the Proceedings of the National Conference on Infantile Mortality … with Address by the Right Honourable John Burns, MP* (London, 1906); and *Report of the Proceedings of the Second National Conference on Infantile Mortality* (Westminster, 1908).

**17** C. Dyhouse, *Feminism and the Family, 1880–1939* (Oxford, Basil Blackwell, 1989), pp. 85–6.

**18** FWG pamphlet, 'Three Years Work of the Women's Group 1908–1911', in S. Alexander (ed.), *Women's Fabian Tracts* (London, Routledge and Kegan Paul, 1988), pp. 145–63.

**19** For example, see M. Pember Reeves, *Round About a Pound a Week* (London, Virago, [1913] 1979). Maud Pember Reeves is an example of how women in the IWM were concerned with other social reform work and suffrage. Apart from being a prominent member of the FWG, she was on the Executive Committees of the WTUL and National Anti-Sweating League and the Central Committee of the NUWSS.

**20** J. Lewis, 'The Working-Class Wife and Mother and State Intervention, 1870–1918', in J. Lewis (ed.), *Labour and Love: Women's Experience of Home and Family, 1850–1940* (Oxford, Blackwell, 1986); Yeo, *Contest for Social Science*, ch. 9, and G. Holloway, 'A Common Cause? Class Dynamics in the

Industrial Women's Movement, 1888–1918' (University of Sussex Ph.D. thesis, 1995), chs 3, 5.

21 M. Barrett and M. McIntosh, 'The "Family Wage" – Some Problems for Socialists and Feminists', *Capital and Class*, 2 (1980), pp. 51–72.

22 C. Rowan, 'Mothers, Vote Labour! The State, the Labour Party and Working-Class Mothers', in R. Brunt and C. Rowan (eds), *Feminism, Culture and Politics* (London, Lawrence and Wishart, 1982), p. 66.

23 Rowan, 'Mothers, Vote Labour', p. 79 and C. Rowan, 'Women in the Labour Party, 1906–1920', *Feminist Review*, 12 (Autumn 1982), p. 75.

24 M. MacArthur, 'The Woman Trade-Unionist's Point of View', in M. Phillips (ed.), *Women and the Labour Party* (London, Headley Bros, 1918), p. 18.

25 Mrs Player and Mrs J. R. MacDonald, 'Wage-Earning Mothers', *The League Leaflet*, 3 (Mar. 1911), p. 3.

26 *Ibid.*, p. 2.

27 A. Martin, 'The Married Working Woman', *The Nineteenth Century and After* (Dec. 1910, Jan. 1911), p. 3.

28 *Ibid.*, p. 10.

29 *Ibid.*, p. 43.

30 *Ibid.*, pp. 40–1.

31 *Ibid.*, p. 45.

32 *Ibid.*, p. 46.

33 For discussions concerning the concept of the family wage see, for example, J. Humphries, 'The Working-Class Family, Women's Liberation and Class Struggle: The Case of Nineteenth Century British History', *Review of Radical Economics*, 9:3 (1977), pp. 25–41; Barrett and McIntosh, 'The "Family Wage"', and H. Land, 'The Family Wage', *Feminist Review*, 6 (Autumn 1979), pp. 55–77.

34 For discussions on the endowment of motherhood question see, for example, E. Mahler, *The Social Effects of Separation Allowances: An Experiment in the Endowment of Motherhood* (London, no publisher given, 1918); E. Rathbone, *The Disinherited Family* (London, Edward Arnold, 1924); M. Stocks, *Eleanor Rathbone* (London, Victor Gollancz, 1949); M. Stocks, *My Commonplace Book* (London, Davies, 1970), pp. 120–2; H. Land, 'Eleanor Rathbone and the Economy of the Family', in H. L. Smith (ed.), *British Feminism in the Twentieth Century* (Amherst, University of Massachusetts, 1990), pp. 104–23; and Dyhouse, *Feminism and the Family*, pp. 88–104.

35 M. A. (M. Atkinson), 'The Economic Foundations of the Women's Movement', Fabian Tract No. 175, June 1914, in Alexander, *Women's Fabian Tracts*, pp. 278–9.

36 H. Swanwick, *The Future of the Women's Movement* (London, G. Bell and Son, 1913), pp. 86–7.

37 M. Llewellyn Davies, 'Introduction', in M. Llewellyn Davies (ed.), *Maternity: Letters from Working Women* (London, Virago, [1915] 1978), p. 6.

38 *Sussex Daily News*, 21 July 1908.

39 The reasons for dissension in the WIC are discussed in E. Mappen's Introduction to the Virago reprint of C. Black (ed.), *Married Women's Work* (London, Virago, [1915] 1983), pp. viii–ix and her essay 'Strategies for

Change: Social Feminist Approaches to the Problems of Women's Work',
in A. V. John (ed.), *Unequal Opportunities: Women's Employment in England
1880–1918* (Oxford, Blackwell, 1986).

40 Black, *Married Woman's Work*, p. 2.

41 *Ibid.*

42 *Ibid.*, p. 4.

43 *Ibid.*, p. 6.

44 *Ibid.*

45 *Ibid.*, p. 7.

46 *Ibid.*, pp. 8–9, quoted from M. Atkinson, *The Housewife as Bursar* (n.d. or
publ.).

47 For a fuller discussion of domestic reorganisation, see Dyhouse, *Feminism
and the Family*, ch. 3.

48 See also S. Rowbotham, 'Consumer Power: Women's Contribution to
Alternatives and Resistance to the Market in the United States 1880–1940',
in B. Einhorn and E. Janes Yeo (eds), *Women and Market Societies: Crisis and
Opportunity* (Aldershot, Edward Elgar, 1995).

49 C. Black, *A New Way of Housekeeping* (London, G. Bell & Sons, 1918) and
C. V. Butler, *Domestic Service: An Enquiry by the Women's Industrial Council*
(London, Bell and Sons, 1916).

50 A. Nield Chew, 'The Problem of the Married Working Woman', *Common
Cause*, 6 Mar. 1914.

51 J. S. Mill, *The Subjection of Women* (London,Virago, [1869] 1983), p. 147.

52 Chew, 'The Problem of the Married Working Woman'.

53 *Ibid.*

54 *Ibid.*

55 For Ada Nield Chew's biography and writings, see D. Nield Chew, *Ada
Nield Chew: The Life and Writings of a Working Woman* (London, Virago,
1982) and D. Nield Chew and M. 'Epinasse, 'Ada Nield Chew, Women's
Labour, Trade Union and Suffrage Worker (1870–1945)', *Dictionary of
Labour Biography*, vol. 5, pp. 57–64.

56 A. Nield Chew, 'The Mother's Story', *Common Cause*, 1913.

57 For the meeting of Charlotte Perkins Gilman and Chew, see Dyhouse,
*Feminism and the Family*, p. 117.

58 'The Married Working Woman: A True Story', *Common Cause*, 21 Sept.
1911.

59 A. Nield Chew, 'The Mother-Interest and Child Training', *Common Cause*, 6
Mar. 1914.

60 D. Beddoes, *Back to Home and Duty: Women Between the Wars, 1918–1939*
(London, Pandora, 1989), chs 1, 4.

61 For a discussion of this, see 'The Servant Problem', in Dyhouse, *Feminism
and the Family*, pp. 107–11.

62 Following the death of her brother and his wife, Clementina Black took on
the responsibility of raising her four-year-old niece on the small amount of
money she earned by translation and journalism. See L. Glage, *Clementina
Black: A Study in Social History and Literature* (Heidelberg, Carl Winter,
1981).

63 Black, *Married Women's Work*, p. 14.

64 *Ibid.*

65  Chew, 'The Problem of the Married Working Woman'.
66  See E. Janes Yeo, 'Conflicts Between the Domestic and Market Economy in Britain: Past and Present', in Einhorn and Yeo, *Women and Market Societies*, for a discussion of this challenge.
67  Chew, 'Let the Women be Alive!'.

# 8

# 'As a war-horse to the beat of drums': representations of working-class femininity in the Women's Co-operative Guild, 1880s to the Second World War

GILLIAN SCOTT

## A widening vision

When Mrs Bury of Darwen, guildswoman, housewife and former millworker, described her attendance at the first Guild Congress of 1893, she sought to convey the sense of liberation which she experienced there. It was, she wrote, 'a revelation'. On each of the three days of the gathering,

> my vision seemed to be widening, and my spirit felt that here was the very opportunity I had always been seeking, but never put into words. I had longings and aspirations and a vague sense of power within myself which had never had an opportunity for realisation. At the close of the meetings I felt as I imagine a war-horse must feel when he hears the beat of the drum.[1]

This metaphor of a war-horse called by the beat of drums seems an appropriate title for this piece because it is hard to think of an image more at odds with the Victorian ideal of femininity – the 'angel in the house' – which was as pervasive among the skilled working class, to which Mrs Bury belonged, as it was in the higher echelons of society in which it originated.[2] It is clear that by the late nineteenth century, the middle-class model of a housebound wife, along with a sentimental idealisation of homelife, had become hallmarks of the respectable working class,[3] not the least effect of which was to impede the access of those women to the public sphere. Yet little work has been done on the attempts of working-class women's organisations to contest or rework the feminine ideal to create new opportunities for themselves. Indeed, it has even been suggested that the ideology of domesticity was not contested by working-class women, who were fully occupied with more practical issues such as wages and working conditions.[4]

This chapter is intended as a corrective to such assumptions. Its focus is the Women's Co-operative Guild (WCG), an auxiliary body of the English consumers' co-operative movement, from its inception in the 1880s to the Second World War.[5] It sets out, first, to explore the language and concepts mobilised by guildswomen in the period up to 1920 to redefine working-class femininity in ways that would empower them in both the public and the private sphere and, second, to consider the decline of this radical project against a background of major political change in the inter-war years.

The WCG was founded in 1883 to provide opportunities for association and learning for co-operative women but, it was stressed, 'without departing from our own sphere', or taking up the 'vex'd question of women's rights'.[6] In the 1890s, however, this relatively modest programme, and the concern to respect the orthodox sexual hierarchy, were superseded by a far more political agenda which aimed to launch co-operative women as a progressive but autonomous section of the working-class movement. Writing in the 1920s, Margaret Llewelyn Davies, General Secretary from 1889 to 1921, was able to pinpoint the 'outstanding fact about the Guild movement' as 'the emergence of the married working-woman from national obscurity into a position of national importance'.[7] In contrast to their traditional role, hidden from sight within the working-class family, the Guild's development as 'a sort of trade union for married women'[8] had made them visible and vocal in the co-operative movement, in the local and in the national state; working-class wives, as a collective entity, with views, needs and interests had entered the public domain. To highlight the Guild's achievement in representing, and re-presenting, working-class women, it is instructive to compare two snapshots of the organisation: in its infancy in the 1880s and fully mature on the eve of the First World War.

In the 1880s the Guild held a 'fringe meeting' each year for members present at the annual Co-operative Union Congress; the occasion merited a one-page account in the massive tome of the Co-operative Union *Annual Report*.[9] In 1885 the meeting was attended by about '80 ladies'. The General Secretary, Miss Allen, reported a membership of 376, and ten branches whose activities had included 'three scientific dress-cutting classes, five plain and fancy needlework classes, one choral society, one self-improvement class for young people from 14 to 20, two children's classes, one writing and one dress-making class'. Mrs Lawrenson (Woolwich) 'gave a most interesting address on the way in which the Guild might be made of the greatest use and help to young people'. Miss Webb (Vice-President) spoke rather despondently of the difficulties in establishing Guild branches:

> some of the most unjust criticism comes from co-operators, or so-called co-operators. We are told by some of them that 'we should do more good staying at home and educating our children'. My answer is, a woman who has no feelings of humanity, or does nothing to help her fellow women, cannot educate her children, for children are educated by your words and deeds. Some of us have no children to educate; we have taken upon ourselves a higher education, that of humanity.

A mildly discordant note came from Mrs Ben Jones, who bravely suggested that, when accompanying their husbands to meetings connected with the movement, women might, if invited to do so, speak from the platform; however, no resolution was passed on this subject and subsequent correspondence in the 'Women's Corner' of Co-operative News made it plain that some members did not think that it would be proper for a woman to speak in public on behalf of the Guild.[10]

The 1885 meeting was characterised by a concern to maintain a respectable reputation, deference to convention, and an acceptance that women's proper place in the movement and in society was defined by their sex. While it was accepted that co-operative women should have greater opportunities for education and association, it was envisaged that the beneficiaries of such activities should be others; thus their cautious forays beyond the home were justified in terms of possible gains for the movement, young people, children or husbands. In the main, these early guildswomen conceived of their potential public role in terms of a philanthropic model of service, which confirmed, as the price of widening, an essentially maternal identity.

In contrast, the 1914 Guild Congress revealed the organisation in fighting form. Now a three-day, independent event and the high point of the Guild's calendar, this notable public occasion was attended by hundreds of delegates, funded by the Guild. They were primed to represent their branches on matters that had previously been the subject of education and debate, and to approve the

Guild's own lengthy *Annual Report*.[11] Also present were guests from labour and women's organisations, and a sizeable press corps. 'In the large hall at Birmingham,' reported the *Manchester Guardian*, 'under the banners of their branches, sat some 600 delegates. They are women of the working classes ... worthy representatives not only of 30,000 co-operative women, but of all the women who have borne children and lived laborious lives since Eve.'[12]

The most pressing item on their agenda was the ultimatum from the Co-operative Union Central Board that the Guild either abandon its campaign for divorce law reform, or lose its £400 annual grant. In near unanimity, delegates voted to stand firm against the Board. The tone and the content of their speeches expressed determination, confidence and the conviction that guildswomen had every right to speak out on one of the most controversial social issues of the day, in defiance of the male bureaucrats of the movement and the pious injunctions of the Catholic lobby that had initiated the dispute. Mrs Daymond (St Budeaux) stressed that 'she knew what the proposed reforms meant for downtrodden women, and she could not help but raise her voice in protest of the action taken by the Co-operative Union ... It was to be regretted that there were such men in the co-operative movement but she hoped that they would repent of their ways and apologise' (laughter and loud applause) Mrs Holdness (Derby) pointed out that it 'was repeatedly said that the women were the backbone of the movement; was it not time they showed the strength of that backbone?' and Mrs Baldwin (Clapton Park) exclaimed 'at the ignorance of the Union. Did they think that they were the only ones who knew what was good for the women? Then they forgot that the women could think for themselves.'[13]

The 1914 Congress highlighted the strength and vitality of the WCG after thirty years of development. Far from being careful not to stray from their proper place, guildswomen now took it for granted that they could and should intervene in public debates on any and every subject and, if necessary, criticise officials, institutions or politicians who were responsible for unjust and discriminatory policies. There was, too, an explicit recognition that the Guild's role was not only to contribute to the social good, but to tackle wrongs in the lives of working women. The delegates manifested a strong sense of collective agency, of speaking not for themselves as individuals but as representatives of a wider constituency – tens of thousands of co-operative women who were themselves the organised expression of the interests of the millions of working-class housewives so long denied any public voice.

To build an effective movement from what was virtually a zero base required organisational, political and ideological innovation. One of the greatest obstacles which the Guild faced was the rigid belief – as prevalent in the co-operative movement as it was in the wider society – that nature and custom dictated that women belonged in the domestic sphere. The arguments which the Guild developed to refute this presumption, and to demonstrate that women were both entitled to and capable of public work, consti- tute a new and emancipatory account of working-class femininity. Three new and distinctive claims about working-class women took shape. First, that they possessed a great capacity for public service that had previously had no opportunity for expression; second, that as citizens they had rights and duties far beyond the confines of the home; and third, that far from being a safe haven, the private sphere often contained forms of sexual oppression which were only now being exposed and challenged as a result of the self- organisation of working women. In each of these the Guild was effectively turning the ideology of separate spheres on its head. To propose that housewives possessed an aptitude for public life subverted the notion that their social role as wives and mothers was dictated by their biology; to propose that citizenship tran- scended biological difference problematised the sexual division of society into separate spheres of activity; to propose that the domes- tic sphere was the location of hidden suffering undermined the idealised conception of the domestic sphere as the font of all virtue.

## A culture of affirmation

Separate sphere ideology presupposed that while women were naturally equipped for domestic life, as men were for public activity, women were no more capable of functioning in the world outside the home than men were of bearing children. Thus, an essential part of the Guild's efforts to open the public sphere to women was to prove their fitness for the tasks involved, not least to the women themselves, many of whom had long internalised an understanding of their limitations derived from mainstream attitudes and enforced by their own lack of experience and formal education. In response to this need the Guild developed practical training methods for co-operative women, but also a 'culture of affirmation' whose central message was that guildswomen possessed a vast but hitherto untapped capacity for public work that only needed the right organisational setting to become manifest.

At the most basic level, there was a need to convince women that they could combine Guild membership with their very considerable burden of domestic labour. The first step was to recognise just how limited their time was. As an article in *Co-operative News* pointed out: 'Women are, as a rule, so hemmed in by their domestic surroundings that they have far fewer chances of becoming interested in the national affairs than men'.[14] While wealthier women employed servants, the majority of co-operative women did their own housework, and running a home, and caring for children and a husband left them very little time to spare. The 1904 Guild history described members' homes as 'the workshops of many trades, where overtime abounds, and where an eight hours' day would be a very welcome reform ... Few men can realise how much drudgery and lonely effort there is in the everyday work of a housewife'.[15]

Housework and childcare could not be abolished, but it could be rationalised and minimised to free time for other activities. The Guild advocated the collectivisation of domestic labour and the introduction of labour-saving technology: 'Modern methods of production, namely machinery and association, should be applied to women's domestic work, and with that view co-operative societies are urged to use a portion of their capital in the establishment of co-operative washhouses, bakeries, laundries and kitchens.'[16] More immediately, the Guild encouraged greater proficiency and more effective time management as a means rather than an end. Thus even the domestic craft classes that dominated branch programmes in the 1880s could be turned to good account. Cookery lectures, clear starch classes, and so forth, noted Sarah Reddish in 1891, 'could teach them to make their homes brighter and happier. These things being done well left more time for mutual help.'[17] 'One of the things the Guild teaches, is system', explained one member. 'To be able to attend branch meetings and conferences, and do your household duties, you must have a system in your home work. You can't loiter over it. The Guild

really gives a zest to it.'[18] An 'elderly Guild member' confessed that
'I let it (housework) keep to a more convenient season, when it
means a little more time to rid a little more dirt and dust and a few
more microbes to kill'. Yet she also admitted that she carried out
most of her Guild work 'in the small hours of the morning, when
otherwise I should be in bed'.[19]

The Guild's approach, then, was not to devalue the occupation of
most of its members, and certainly not to suggest that the organisation was founded on neglect of the home. Lancashire members
were said to be 'as "house proud" as any'; and one guildswoman
took pleasure in the claim that in twenty-one years of married life
she had never bought bread.[20] The Guild's aim was rather to
dignify the work of women in the home as highly skilled but nevertheless hard and often thankless, while urging that housewives
could and should be able to develop wider interests. 'Many
economies of time, labour, and temper could be made', pointed out
the 1892 *Annual Report*, 'so as to give women more leisure and
freedom for other work. Much is done by our lectures in making
women more efficient housewives. But the main object of the Guild
is to give women a knowledge of labour questions, and make them
take an active part in ... the labour movement.'[21]

Guild training started from the assumption that new members
had no previous experience of public life. Talks on such subjects as
'Women's Duties outside the Home' and 'Practical helps to would
be Speakers',[22] were supplemented by articles in the 'Women's
Corner' of *Co-operative News*.[23] The acquisition of new skills, particularly speaking in public, received special attention. In April 1897,
the General Secretary congratulated the North Western Section on
its work: 'Great progress had been made in bringing out new
speakers.' A discussion on the subject of factory 'Accidents and
Compensation' had 'brought out a first speech from Miss Oldfield'
(West Bowling, Bradford) on her experience as a weaver.[24] Leaflets
were distributed to assist new branches, for example, *Outline of
Work with Model Branch Rules* (1891), and *How to Start and Work a
Branch* (1897).[25] In 1899, after several years of such practical effort,
the General Secretary requested that reports for the 'Women's
Pages' should concentrate on discussions rather than procedures.

> The meetings are now generally so well managed that it is hardly
> necessary ... to mention such things as: – That the arrangements

for the meeting were very satisfactory. That the members did full justice to the tea. That the music was rendered in very good style. And that the meeting passed votes of thanks.[26]

As the Guild developed, it projected a strong sense of the distinctive qualities of its members. 'The Guild certainly ought to grow into a structure which is good to look on, as the material from which it is being shaped is so full of beauty', wrote the General Secretary in 1899.[27] Guildswomen were presented as capable and hard-working women; if they could balance household budgets and carry out the range of tasks involved in housework, why should they not be fit to take on wider social questions and participate in public life? As Sarah Reddish was quick to point out to Mr Rae, Co-operative Education Committee chairman, guildswomen were keen to learn more about all aspects of the movement, 'and to study the economic questions which many people supposed that women would not be interested in at all'.[28] 'What is so remarkable about so many of the Guild members', wrote Davies in 1904, 'is that, although no longer young in years, and having had little or no early advantages, they possess a most youthful spirit; taking up new ideas, attending lectures, writing papers, and throwing themselves into a wider life with enthusiasm.'[29]

The idea that the Guild had, as one member put it, 'brought us out'[30] was amplified in its literature. In 1899 Davies referred to 'the great capacity – the practical wisdom and public spirit – which the Guild is bringing out and turning to valuable account'.[31] 'The women say', she reported in 1904, 'that the Guild has broadened their minds, enlarged their ideas, and taught them to think on social questions they would at one time have passed over as outside their capacity.'[32] New delegates to sectional conferences were reported often to be struck by the quality of the debates, making such comments as: 'My word, I never thought that women could speak on such subjects.'[33] As the preface to the 1927 Guild history explained:

> It might well have been thought a hopeless task for a class of women who 'never know when their day's work's done', and on whom personal claims are insistent, ceaseless, and irresistible, to organise and educate themselves and undertake public work and responsibilities. But the miracle has been accomplished, and who can say that the Guild has not justified its existence and that a great and hitherto untapped source of strength has not been added to national life.[34]

## Citizenship

Another priority for Guild leaders was the need to establish strong grounds for women's entry into the public sphere. During the 1890s an uncompromising insistence on citizenship, or comradeship, as having no sex and bestowing responsibilities as well as rights on men and women alike became a central tenet of Guild philosophy. Members were increasingly encouraged to take their public role more seriously and not to be deterred by the opposition that they might encounter. Sarah Reddish in her organiser's report of 1894 offered a powerful argument for sex equality in the public sphere. 'We are told by some', she acknowledged, 'that women are wives and mothers, and that the duties therein involved are enough for them. We reply,' she continued briskly,

> that men are husbands and fathers, and that they, as such, have duties not to be neglected, but we join in the general opinion that men should also be interested in the science of government, taking a share in the larger family of the store, the municipality and the State. The WCG has done much towards impressing the fact that women as citizens should take their share in this work also.[35]

Reddish thus neatly demolished the conceptual divide of separate spheres – private-female/public-male – and with it the presumption that it reflected sexual difference, asserting instead that men and women had equal responsibilities in the interlocking spaces of the national and local state, the co-operative movement and the home. Rather than being a private and atomised unit imprisoning women, 'the family' is used here as a generic term for human association; the affective role of men as husbands and fathers, complementing that of women as wives and mothers, is highlighted alongside the contribution that both have to make as citizens and co-operators.

As the suffrage campaign gained momentum at the turn of the century, it became an important focus for Guild arguments about citizenship. The vote, declared the General Secretary in 1897, was 'part of the great movement for the freedom of women, which will give them their true status in society and lead to a trustful and respectful comradeship between men and women'. 'We are tired', she continued, in a pointed attack on the feminine ideal,

> of being flattered, of being told of our wonderful 'influence' – of hearing that 'the hand that rocks the cradle rules the world' –

when a moment afterwards our brains are compared with rabbits, and we are told that men do all the work of the world, and that wives 'should stay at home to wash their husbands' moleskin trousers.' We do not believe that the home is our only 'sphere', and we are suspicious when we are told we are 'the angels in the house'.[36]

The Guild was not, Davies insisted, trying to 'turn women into men', but to enable both to achieve their full potential. Whatever 'peculiar insight, knowledge, and sympathy' women might offer *qua* women, it was their common humanity rather than their sexual specificity that should define their role: 'below all differences of sex there is the great bond-likeness of human nature, and it is the complete human being, whether man or woman, whom we have in view'. The proper place for women was 'side by side with men', in complete possession of 'the power we claim for them in shaping our ideal society'.[37]

As well as establishing the justice and good sense of women's claim to political rights, Guild writers were also quick to expose the unfairness and absurdity of the opposing arguments. A 'Women's Pages' report of the Second Reading of the 1897 Suffrage Bill, for example, drily observed that one MP, 'Mr Labouchere, in an amusing speech, poured ridicule on the proposal. It had always been held since the world began that it was most undesirable that women should take an active part in public affairs as men did.'[38] A commentary the following week added: 'It is difficult to take seriously the contention that women are not fit to vote. The same could be said of many classes of male voters.'[39] Furthermore, as J. Green (Canning Town Branch) pointed out in a letter, the fact that women had been excluded from public affairs 'since the world began' was no reason not to include them in the nineteenth century.[40]

The conviction that what men and women had in common outweighed the sexual differences that were continually invoked to justify women's exclusion from public life became a basic principle of Guild organisation. Arguments about 'Women's Sphere', Davies insisted in a 1904 article, 'Women and Citizenship', had no bearing on women as citizens. 'Citizenship is above sex, party, class and sect ... A citizen is a human being, belonging to a community, with rights and duties arising out of a common life.'[41] Discrimination on the grounds of sex was nothing other than a glaring injustice. As Mrs Mellor pointed out: 'No right should be taken from us simply because of sex.'[42] There was 'a great need', urged Sarah Reddish, 'for all women to join together to work for the removal of the sex disability. This was a sex question and no matter what their position in life, they ought to join together in order to remove all disability.'[43]

As the Guild gained in strength and size, and more of its members entered public life, it began to embody its own claims about citizenship. As a 1913 pamphlet stated: 'Our Guild is an example of what is going on among married women. It is the reply of the married women of today to those who have told them that "the woman's place is at home", meaning, of course, by this that woman's only place is at home.' No longer accepting what they were told, women were now 'inquiring for themselves what their place is', and 'answering the question for themselves'.[44] The guildswoman's answer was: 'My place is in the Co-operative Movement, because I am the wage spender; my place is in my Town and country, because I am a wife and mother; my place is in my Home because I am a joint maker of the family life; and I find I cannot do my work properly in any one of the three places without doing it in all.'[45] In twenty years, Sarah Reddish's polemic about men and women's shared responsibilities in the different areas of social existence had evolved into a model of female citizenship in an organisation which now consisted of some 30,000 working women.

## Parity begins at home

In the 1890s the Guild's priority was to legitimise co-operative women's entry into the public sphere as part of the working-class movement; as Davies later wrote, at that stage its 'unique position' as 'the only organisation whose interests are specially those of married working women ... was only dimly seen'. But 'by degrees', as the organisation gained strength and developed its own momentum, 'it became apparent that the need for reforms in the lives of the married women themselves was urgent'. This growing awareness of the wrongs of working women in the private sphere meant that in addition to being an organisation *of* working women, the Guild became also an organisation *for* working women, and it was in this capacity that it made 'its chief contribution to national life'.[46]

Guild organisation thus provided the means by which aspects of married life that had previously been regarded as private matters for the individuals concerned were presented in the public domain as social problems with social solutions. This entailed a major assault on a pillar of Victorian domestic ideology: that the home was the source of all that was virtuous in society, a place of harmony in which the wife nurtured and replenished her children and husband, morally as well as physically, protected from the harsh reality outside. Davies was well aware of both the resonance and the falsity of this idealised image of home life. As she wrote in 1911:

> It seemed as if in the past, when women married, they retired behind a dark curtain on which was embroidered all sorts of beautiful sentiments about the beauty of motherhood and the sanctity of the home; but now the curtain was being withdrawn, and from the discussions that had taken place they had learned much of the sufferings of married women, the pain and misery that were going on behind the curtain.[47]

Davies began to learn of this suffering soon after she became General Secretary. In contrast to her own privileged and enlightened background, Guild work opened up to her 'a new world, practically unknown to the well to do classes'.[48] On tour, staying in the homes of guildswomen, she witnessed 'hard battles being waged against heavy odds, or the marks which such fights have left behind them ... struggles with want, concealed under thick coverings of pride; daily work done under the weight of constant ill-health; unselfish devotion rewarded by lack of consideration'.[49]

One of Davies's most important contributions as General Secretary was to begin to document and publish information about the lives of working women. In its two most significant campaigns, for divorce law reform and state care of maternity, the Guild elicited written statements from members giving details of marriage and childbirth. Guildswomen's letters, presented as part of the Guild's evidence to the Royal Commission on Divorce in 1910, and published in the book *Maternity Letters from Working Women*, in 1915,[50] described instances of sexual, physical and psychological abuse and hardship that exploded the ideal of the wife-nurturer/husband-protector. Members told of 'cases where a woman, ill-used and kicked, has taken her husband back five times; of a diseased husband compelling co-habitation, resulting in deficient children; of excessive co-habitation, regardless of the wife's health; of a man frightening his wife during pregnancy in order to bring on a miscarriage'.[51] Frequent references were made to attempted abortions, while phrases such as 'A Time of Horror', 'Mother Last', 'I am a Ruined Woman' and 'Men need Education' used in relation to childbearing signalled self-sacrifice, physical and mental distress, and the selfishness of husbands.[52]

Material of this kind made a great impact on public opinion. Herbert Samuel, MP, in his preface to *Maternity*, referred to 'the miseries, sometimes the agonies' afflicting millions of people as 'a consequence of normal functions', adding that 'an unwise public reticence' had prevented the 'public mind' from realising that such matters presented 'urgent social problems'.[53] As Dr Ethel Bentham of the Women's Labour League commented, the Guild's divorce material left readers in no doubt 'that some of the very foundations of society are rotten beneath their feet'.[54] The Guild's publication of shocking information about the lives of married women clearly strengthened its case for reform. Yet there is also a sense in which it was a double-edged weapon. Potentially, the images thus evoked, of women as passive victims, patiently suffering hardship, were thoroughly subversive of the strong, capable and assertive version of working-class womanhood that the Guild had wanted to project. Thus the price of proving need could be the surrender of agency: these women obviously needed help, but equally obviously were incapable of helping themselves. It is important, therefore, to notice that the Guild inflected this material in ways that buttressed both its demands for women's rights, its claims about women's aptitude for public life, and its insistence on the value of autonomous women's organisations.

In its discussions of domestic abuse the Guild skilfully used both its own dignified, fully human conception of womanhood, and the mainstream ideal of domesticity, to point up the severity of the degradation that was occurring. The 'hidden suffering amongst working women', Davies pointed out at a Manchester Guild District Conference in 1911, meant that 'home-life was degraded'. The current divorce laws upheld an 'unequal standard of morality' which 'did not conduce to the dignity of womanhood nor to the sanctity of home life'.[55] Even some of the most shocking information thrown up by the Guild enquiries – the extent of illegal abortion – could be used to highlight the gap between the ideal and reality and as evidence that women were rebelling against such prevalent stereotypes of femininity as maternal self-sacrifice. As an article in the 'Women's Pages' on 'The Declining Birthrate' pointed out, the 'sacrifice' expected from married women was too great: 'Many a woman, as soon as she has reason to expect another child, tries to escape by taking drugs.' In Lancashire alone there were reputed to be 1,000 people making a living from carrying out abortions. If, as the various critics of small families maintained, 'married women owe a duty to society to bear children, society must see to it that the conditions of child bearing and rearing are made more attractive to the average mother.'[56]

The Guild was also able to make much of the fact that the context in which this 'hidden suffering' had come to light was the self-organisation of working women, and that were it not for such organisation it would still be hidden. As the introduction to *Maternity* stated, the situation of the mother had previously been overlooked 'for the isolation of women in married life has, up to now, prevented any common expression of their needs'. Now that married women had an organisation of their own, the curtain that had previously fallen on marriage was being lifted by the women themselves.[57] In the maternity benefit and divorce law reform campaigns, the Guild made claims about the rights and wrongs of working-class women with a confidence that reflected both conviction about the proven justice of its case, and the collective strength of tens of thousands of women. Lloyd George's exclusion of 'non-working' women from the terms of his National Insurance proposals in 1911 was denounced as 'a most serious blot on this scheme' and a massive undervaluing of their work.[58] In her report to Congress that year, the General Secretary pointed out that

> in the Bill Mr Lloyd George spoke of married women who were not wage earners as non-workers. ('Oh', and laughter.) Mr Lloyd George needed a little reminder of the fact that they were workers. (Hear, hear.) They had to make a great stir, and show the Chancellor of the Exchequer that women who remained at home were workers, and that their work was as arduous as any other kind of work and just as valuable. (Hear, hear.)[59]

The confrontation between the WCG and the Central Board of the Co-operative Union brought out the same potent mixture of a deep sense of grievance and a firm belief in collective agency. The Central Board's ultimatum that the Guild drop divorce law reform or lose its £400 annual grant demonstrated that 'a body practically composed of men, does not understand or give due consideration to the views of women, and that therefore it is most undesirable that the Guild's freedom of action should be limited by such a body'.[60] Its effect was to crystallise the organisation's understanding of its own identity and purpose. 'We reached our highest point at [the] Birmingham [Congress]', Davies wrote to Leonard Woolf.

> I had no idea the strength and unity of feeling would be so great and that the determination to keep our Independence should be connected with divorce was all the more remarkable. There was never any doubt in the women's minds about the way the Independence vote would go – nor had they any doubts during the Divorce debate. I feel the women have now 'arrived' and they will never go back.[61]

By the second decade of the century, the Guild had constructed a version of working-class womanhood which set norms within the organisation and projected empowering images outwards. The ideal guildswoman was a housewife, a co-operator and a citizen, signifying, respectively, her place in the community, the co-operative movement and the state; in all these roles, she was also what might be described as a 'feminist-comrade', active on behalf of her class but with a developed consciousness of the distinct interests of her sex. Thus in 1913 we find 'the Guildswoman', fully aware 'of what helps to shape her home life', and 'her inseparable connection with the Store, the Town Council and Parliament', but simultaneously reflecting

> on her own position in her home, and all that in her relations with her husband and children go to make the best family life. She understands that the first need is equal comradeship of husband and wife, of brothers and sisters, and how destructive of this is the subordination which we always know is expected when we hear 'A woman's place is at home'.

She thus appreciated the need for 'parity to begin at home', and she was alert to the extent to which social, rather than biological, characteristics determined the sexual hierarchy:

> Mistakes have been made from the beginning: boys have been given more chances than girls, and allowed to nourish a sense of superiority; and wives have been taught to be obedient to their husbands; while the fact that no money value is attached to the

services of a woman in her home is also responsible for the position of so many women. Guildswomen are now facing the problems of marriage and divorce, of economic independence, of the moral training of their boys and girls. It is only by men and women alike studying these problems that true companionship in the home can be arrived at, and the best atmosphere created for children to be brought up in.[62]

## Reverses and retreats

The model of militant proletarian femininity, evolved as part of the Guild's development over more than a quarter of a century, appeared by the time of the First World War as an integral part of its culture, identity and politics; during the inter-war period, however, while the organisation continued to grow in size, to a membership peak of 88,000 in 1938, the radical cutting edge of the Guild project was rubbed smooth. It retained a visceral loyalty to the principle of women's rights and continued to sponsor a public role for women, but a diminishing proportion of its energies was committed to women's issues as such and, critically, the key question of sexual inequality in the private sphere disappeared not simply from its policy but from its conceptual apparatus.

In a limited sense, the Guild's activities in the 1920s and 1930s provided roles for guildswomen that were consistent with its earlier drive to establish women's aptitude for and right of access to the public sphere. It maintained links with the residual feminist organisations and the principle of equal rights was frequently ventilated in *Co-operative News*. One piece, following the 1928 franchise reform, stressed that 'we are still far from complete emancipation' and pointed to low wages and opposition to the employment of married women as major obstacles to economic independence.[63] Early in 1933, against a background of rising unemployment, a 'Women's Pages' leader noted a tendency of the press 'to emphasise the old and outworn dictum, "Woman's place is at home"'. This must be watched carefully 'lest our daughters have to fight for recognition as responsible citizens and workers worthy of a "living" wage. The theory still exists that the woman in the home is not a wage-earner, but dependent upon the man wage-earner, and therefore can have no standard remuneration for her work except in the love and gratitude of her family.' The Guild, the piece continued, was the 'champion of the *Woman* in the Home, while at the same time striving to give her a wider outlook and openings for service OUTSIDE her home'.[64]

To some extent the texture of the Guild organisation ensured that it practised what it preached. As well as recruiting large numbers of new members, it continued to operate as a 'base camp' from which many working-class women became more widely active in public life; branches educated women in the principles of co-operation and the working of local government, and gave them experience of public speaking and organisational and committee work. In terms of being the housewife's 'champion', however, its record was not impressive; indeed it is possible to argue that many of the Guild's policies during this period confirmed rather than contested women's primary identity as wives and mothers in a shift which marked a significant departure from the Guild's earlier and more substantial commitment to the emancipation of working-class wives.

The main reason for this reversal was the Guild's growing attachment to party politics following the enfranchisement of women and the formation of the Co-operative Party, organisationally separate from, but operating negotiated electoral alliances with, the Labour Party. The new generation of Guild leaders increasingly understood their role to be the deliverance of the female vote at election times, with no awkward questions asked about policy. This commitment to parliamentarism meant that Guild policy, indeed its whole conception of the 'woman question', was effectively limited to what the leadership of the labour movement would find acceptable. This resulted in a steady retreat from an analysis of working-class women's situation capable of recognising that their needs were determined by their gender as well as their class relations.

This trend is apparent in the Guild's attitude towards the campaigns for birth control advice and family allowances. In many ways a logical extension of the Guild's pre-war activity on maternity and divorce law reform, these demands were taken up by left-wing feminists in the 1920s to enable married women to control their fertility and to achieve a degree of economic independence. They were, however, unpopular with the leadership of the labour movement, and by the end of the decade had been scotched as a matter of policy. 'We do plead', ran an editorial on birth control in *The Labour Woman* in 1924, 'that this subject of the relations of husband and wife should not be treated as a political issue at all.'[65] The Guild leadership was clearly reluctant to take a lead on this controversial matter. In the early 1920s, after a Congress decision calling for birth control information to be made more widely available, the Central Committee (CC) received a warning letter from the same Catholic body that had precipitated the controversy over divorce law reform a decade earlier. This time the CC was more careful; it decided not to make birth control a Guild special subject but to leave it to branches to take local action if they so chose.[66] The following year the national Standing Joint Committee of Working Women's Organisations, on which the Guild was represented, and which effectively controlled the policy of the working-class women's organisations, found itself unable to recommend that birth control advice be given out at maternity clinics.[67] While the Guild leaders seem to have recognised that this was a pressing matter for working women, they shied away from initiating a prominent national campaign that was seen as potentially divisive for labour politics, in stark contrast to the bold stand taken on divorce law reform in 1914.[68]

The demand for family allowances touched a raw nerve in dominant trade union circles on the grounds that any such cash payment would undermine their members' defence of the 'family wage' and thus weaken their position in collective bargaining.[69] For this reason, proposals for a scheme of family allowances were rejected, in favour of services in kind, by the Trades Union Congress (TUC) General Council in 1930, and then shelved by the Labour Party for over a decade. So, too, at a national meeting of Guild officials in 1931, CC members explained that the earlier plans for a 'State Bonus Scheme' had been abandoned because 'the trade unions and the Labour Party had rejected it'.[70] At the 1937 Congress a resolution in favour of family allowances was defeated because the official line was to support the TUC, 'who at the present time thought it more advisable to press for social services to be established'.[71] Yet two decades earlier the Guild had supported the principle of cash payments direct to the mother, in the form of maternity benefit, despite the concerted opposition of Labour MPs, precisely because it did not accept that women always got their proper share of the 'family wage'.[72]

In the late 1920s the Guild revived maternity as part of its citizenship work. By now many women were using arguments about maternal mortality rates to press for access to birth control and the provision of family allowances,[73] but the Guild was careful to present the issue in ways that were compatible with Labour's demands for better housing, wages and health care for the workers, avoiding such contentious issues as contraception or the economic position of married women, and instead collapsing the specific needs of women into a general concern for the welfare of the working-class family. [74]

The same tendency is apparent in the vision of the ideal co-operative community sketched out in a 1928 pamphlet, *Woman – in the Home, the Store and the State*, written by the Guild General Secretary, Eleanor Barton, for the Co-operative Party:

> Where the health and welfare of the people is the first law.
> Where old age is tended and honoured.
> Where childhood is cherished and made lovely.
> Where young people are trained to useful and capable social service in those things for which they are best fitted.
> Where men have employment at reasonable human wages and
> Where the woman can survey her family and her home, and be happy that the State in which she lives is a home of homes, holding out the hand of affection and friendship to her homes in all parts of the world.[75]

Right at the bottom of the list, it is striking that the adult woman is promised no more in this utopia than marriage and motherhood. She will have the satisfaction of seeing others – children, young people, men, the elderly – enjoy full and rewarding lives, largely, one assumes, as a result of her services. Furthermore, it is made clear that her entry into the state, as a full citizen, can only take place via her domestic role. In 1893 Sarah Reddish had proposed a two-way movement – of women into the public sphere, and men into the private; thirty-five years later Eleanor Barton is to be found endorsing women's place in the home by advocating an extension of its boundaries:

> Now that women have full political power it rests with them to see that the affairs of the nation are adjusted and carried on with that same earnestness and desire for the good of all as is to be found in the vast majority of cottage homes in this country ... What women have to realise is that the State is nothing but a larger home, and that its problems, duties, and responsibilities should be considered in the same spirit of mutual helpfulness as in the home.[76]

What had vanished was the sensitivity to inequality between working-class men and women that characterised the earlier work on divorce and maternity care. Instead the Guild's literature tacitly endorsed the position held by senior Labour women which deprecated 'any Party interfering in the intimate relationships between husbands and wives, fathers and mothers and children'.[77] The home, it seems, had become once again the site of all that was most positive and unproblematic about human relations.

Implicitly, the Guild's general orientation to the woman question in the 1930s was commensurate with the judgement of liberal feminists that equality of opportunity was now a reality. In Ray Strachey's words: 'the main fight is over, and the main victory is won. With education, enfranchisement, and legal equality all conceded, the future of women lies in their own hands.'[78] The establishment of women's formal rights, the thousands of new members joining the Guild every year, the many guildswomen active in co-operative and municipal affairs, and the national and local reputation of the organisation, could all be taken as evidence that guildswomen were now in a position to work alongside men for a better future. As Eleanor Barton wrote in 1928, the year that women received the franchise on equal terms with men:

> Women can still claim today that they are not responsible for the distress and injustice that is rife in the country, but after the coming General Election they will not be able to make such a claim. Then they will have to take the credit or the blame for the Government that is returned, and women Co-operators have a wonderful opportunity now that they all have the vote of seeing that their Co-operative principles are put into practice nationally.[79]

This discourse of equal citizenship also permeated the Guild's pacifist work, which consumed an increasing proportion of its time and energy during the 1930s. Despite attempts to enrol the WCG, as the 'Mother's International', into the illustrious lineage of feminist pacifism,[80] its pacifist arguments tended not to rely upon claims about women's innate aversion to war, as against men's inherent culpability in the matter. Guild leaders identified 'profit making' as 'the main incentive in this terrible business',[81] and pacifism – an individual act of conscience – as the basis for mass opposition to war. Initially, in the Guild's view, a stand for peace would be made through the ballot box: 'We in England have the responsibility of electing our statesmen, so that it comes back to individual responsibility, and those who want Peace must prepare for it.'[82] If that failed, however, all men and women should refuse to take part in war by means of a pledge, 'a consecration by those whose pacifist views are not just a matter of policy and good sense, but of an inmost conviction. Such people know that they can never fight ... These are the people who in the final resort, when there are sufficient of them are bound to bring war to an end.'[83]

By the late 1930s this ethical or moral pacifism dominated the Guild, foreclosing any serious political analysis of the international situation. Despite opposition from members who supported armed intervention against fascism, and maintained that the Guild should be free to play an active role on behalf of co-operative women in the national emergency, the official policy remained one of non-participation in the war effort. The gap that now existed between the leadership and sections of the rank and file was revealed in 1942 when the General Secretary, Cecily Cook, stated that if it was the case that nearly 40 per cent of the membership had left since the outbreak of war because of the peace policy, then 'it is well that the organisation should have purged itself of dead wood'.[84]

The ideal guildswoman was by now presented as first and foremost an ardent pacifist, and in all other matters a loyal supporter of the Co-operative (and Labour) Party; she was no longer, however, an agent of her own emancipation. The supposed equality or freedom of action for women in the public sphere that now informed the Guild's discourse about working women was buttressed by a gender-blindness in regard to the private sphere which not only limited its scope for representing the interests of married women but led it to affirm, in a modified form, their traditional role as wives and mothers. For the greater part, women were once again firmly located in the centre of the domestic sphere, their needs collapsed into a broader and more anodyne concern with the welfare of the working-class family. Like the dog that did not bark, what is absent from the WCG by the time of the Second World War is the consciousness of women's sexual oppression which made its earlier campaigns so remarkable, and which enabled it to produce such radical re-presentations of working-class femininity.

## Notes

1 M. Llewelyn Davies, *The Women's Co-operative Guild* (Kirkby Lonsdale, WCG, 1904), p. 61.

2 C. Hall, 'The Early Formation of Victorian Domestic Ideology', in S. Burman, *Fit Work for Women* (London, Croom Helm, 1979).

3 For a discussion of such working-class norms, see G. Stedman Jones, 'Working-Class Culture and Working-Class Politics in London, 1870–1900: Notes on the Remaking of a Working Class', in his *Languages of Class, Studies in English Working Class History 1832–1982* (Cambridge, Cambridge University Press, 1983).

4 See S. Kingsley Kent, *Sex and Suffrage in Britain 1860–1914* (London, Routledge, 1987), p. 16.

5 For a more detailed account of the WCG, and of the arguments set out here, see G. Scott, *Feminism and the Politics of Working Women: The WCG 1883 to the Second World War* (London, UCL Press, 1998).

6 G. D. H. Cole, *A Century of Co-operation* (Manchester, George Allen & Unwin for the Co-operative Union, 1944), p. 216.

7 M. Llewelyn Davies, 'Preface', in C. Webb, *The Woman with the Basket: The Story of the Women's Co-operative Guild 1883–1927* (Manchester, Co-operative Union Ltd, 1927).

8 M. Llewelyn Davies, 'Co-operation at the Fountainhead', typed MS article for *Life and Labour*, Chicago, K:7 (Sept. 1920), pp. 199–202: 'Material illustrating the work of the guild and kindred interests, manuscript, typed and printed papers, photographs, erstwhile property of Margaret Llewelyn Davies presented to the LSE after her death by L. Harris (1890–?1944)', 11 vols, British Library of Political and Economic Science, vol. 1, item 25.

9 'Meeting of the WCG', Co-operative Union, *Co-operative Congress Report (CCR)*, 1885, pp. 71–2.

10 *Co-operative News*, 27 June 1885, p. 621

11 WCG, *Annual Report*, 1914–15.

12 *Manchester Guardian*, 24 June 1914, Gertrude Tuckwell Collection, TUC Library.

13 *Co-operative News*, 20 June 1914, p. 808.

14 *Ibid.*, 20 Feb. 1897, p. 186.

15 Davies, *The WCG*, p. 151.

16 C. Webb, 'Co-operation as Applied to Domestic Work', Annual Meeting, Leicester, June 1893: 'Material illustrating the work of the guild', vol. 1, item 7.

17 9th Annual Guild Meeting, *CCR*, 1891, p. 113.

18 Davies, *The WCG*, p. 151.

19 *Ibid.*, p. 154.

20 *Ibid.*, pp. 153–5.

21 'Report of Women's Guild', *CCR*, 1892, p. 56.

22 WCG, *Winter Circulars*, Sept. 1894, Aug. 1894: 'Material illustrating the work of the guild', vol. 1, items 9, 10.

23 For example, 'Public Speaking, Some Hints for Guild Members (By One of Themselves)', in three parts, *Co-operative News*, 21, 28 Aug. 1897, pp. 927, 950; 4 Sept. 1897, p. 984.

24 *Ibid.*, 10 Apr. 1897, p. 387.

25 WCG, *Outline of Work with Model Branch Rules* (Manchester, Co-operative Union, 1891); WCG, *How to Start and Work a Branch* (Kirkby Lonsdale, WCG, 1897).
26 *Co-operative News*, 18 Feb. 1899, p. 162.
27 *Ibid.*, 4 Feb. 1899, p. 114.
28 'Education and the Women's Guild', report of joint meeting, *CCR*, 1894, p. 139.
29 Davies, *The WCG*, p. 156.
30 M. Llewelyn Davies, 'Special Education, Divorce and Independence', MS article for German publication (?1933): 'Material illustrating the work of the guild', vol. 1, item 42.
31 *Co-operative News*, 4 Feb. 1899, p. 114.
32 Davies, *The WCG*, p. 156.
33 *Ibid.*, p. 46.
34 Davies, 'Preface', in Webb, *Woman with the Basket*.
35 'Organiser's Report, Report of Women's Guild', *CCR*, 1894, p. 58.
36 M. Llewelyn Davies, *Why Working Women Need the Vote*, paper read at the Southern Sectional Conference, London, 15 Mar. 1897 (Manchester, Co-operative Printing Society, 1897), p. 8.
37 *Ibid.*, pp. 9–10.
38 *Co-operative News*, 13 Feb. 1897, p. 163.
39 *Ibid.*, 20 Feb. 1897, p. 186.
40 *Ibid.*, 20 Mar. 1897, p. 311.
41 *Ibid.*, 29 Oct. 1904, p. 1338.
42 *Ibid.*, 20 Mar. 1897, p. 311.
43 *Ibid.*, 23 July 1904, p. 917.
44 WCG, *The Education of Guildswomen* (London, Co-operative Printing Society, 1913), p. 2.
45 *Ibid.*, p. 4.
46 WCG, *WCG 1895–1916: A Review of Twenty One Years' Work*, Annual Congress Handbook (London, 1916), pp. 10–11.
47 *Co-operative News*, 27 May 1911, p. 667.
48 M. Llewelyn Davies, MS article for Norges Kvinder (1931): 'Material illustrating the work of the guild', vol. 1, item 39.
49 *Co-operative News*, 4 Feb. 1899, p. 114.
50 Miss M. Llewelyn Davies, *Minutes of Evidence taken before the Royal Commission on Divorce and Matrimonial Causes, Minutes of Evidence* (1912), vol. 3 (Cd. 6481), PP 1912–13, XX; M. Llewelyn Davies (ed.), *Maternity: Letters from Working Women* (London, Virago [1915] 1978).
51 WCG, *Divorce Law Reform: The Majority Report of the Divorce Commission*, Spring Sectional Conferences, 1913 (London, WCG, 1913), p. 12.
52 See Davies, *Maternity*, pp. 74, 58, 29, 27.
53 H. Samuel, 'Preface', in *ibid.*
54 *Common Cause*, 11:91, 5 Jan. 1911, p. 637 (thanks to Sybil Oldfield for this reference).
55 *Co-operative News*, 11 Mar. 1911, p. 299.
56 *Ibid.*, 18 Mar. 1911, p. 366.
57 Davies, *Maternity*, pp. 8–9.
58 *Co-operative News*, 13 May 1911, p. 600.

**59** *Ibid.*, 24 June 1911, p. 809.

**60** WCG, Annual Congress, 1915, *The Self Government of the Guild* (London, Co-operative Printing Society, 1915), p. 3.

**61** M. Llewelyn Davies to L. Woolf, n.d., Monks House Papers, University of Sussex. The dispute continued until 1918 when a settlement was reached which did not restrict the scope of the Guild's work.

**62** WCG, *Education of Guildwomen*, p. 4.

**63** *Co-operative News*, 5 Jan. 1929, p. 3.

**64** *Ibid.*, 14 Jan. 1933, p. 12.

**65** *The Labour Woman*, 12:2, 1 Mar. 1924, p. 34. For a full discussion of the 'gender struggles' in the Labour Party, see P. Graves, *Labour Women in British Working-Class Politics 1918–1939* (Cambridge, Cambridge University Press, 1994), ch. 3.

**66** WCG, Central Committee Minutes, 16 July 1923; 19 and 20 Sept. 1923.

**67** *The Labour Woman*, 12:6, 1 June 1924, p. 85.

**68** Scott, *Feminism and the Politics of Working Women*, ch. 6.

**69** See J. Macnicol, *The Movement for Family Allowances, 1918–45* (London, Heinemann, 1980), pp. 141–9.

**70** *Co-operative News*, 31 Jan. 1931, p. 12.

**71** *Ibid.*, 12 June 1937, p. 14.

**72** *Ibid.*, 23 Aug. 1913, p. 1084.

**73** See E. Rathbone, *The Disinherited Family*, introduction by Suzy Fleming, 'Eleanor Rathbone: Spokeswoman for a Movement' (Bristol, Falling Wall Press, [1924] 1986).

**74** E. Barton, *The National Care of Motherhood* (London, WCG, 1928).

**75** E. Barton JP, *Woman – in the Home, the Store and the State* (Manchester, Co-operative Union, 1929), pp. 6–7.

**76** *Ibid.*, pp. 2–3.

**77** *Report of the 27th Labour Party Conference* (1927), p. 192.

**78** R. Strachey, *The Cause* (London, Virago [1928] 1978), p. 384.

**79** Barton, *Woman*, p. 6.

**80** N. Black, 'The Mothers' International: The Women's Co-operative Guild and Feminist Pacifism', *Women's Studies International Forum*, 7:6 (1984), pp. 467–76.

**81** Eleanor Barton, *A New Way of Life* (London, Co-operative Printing Society, 1936), p. 5.

**82** *Ibid.*, p. 4.

**83** *Co-operative News*, 1 Aug. 1936, p. 12.

**84** *Ibid.*, 14 Feb. 1942, p. 8. Membership dropped from 87,246 in 1939 to 49,222 in 1941, rising again to 51,392 in 1945. For the Guild's post-war attempts to recover its former size and influence, see J. Gaffin and D. Thoms, *Caring and Sharing: The Centenary History of the Co-operative Women's Guild* (Manchester, Co-operative Union, 1983).

# INDEX

Note: 'n' after a page reference indicates a note number.